The Weekly Edition

Jean Morken

Andrew Benzie Books
Martinez, California

Published by Andrew Benzie Books
www.andrewbenziebooks.com

Copyright © 2025 Jean Morken

This is a work of fiction. All names, characters, businesses, places, and incidents portrayed in this book are products of the author's imagination or are used fictitiously and are not to be construed as real. Any resemblance to actual events, organizations, places, or persons, living or dead, is entirely coincidental.

All rights reserved. Except as permitted under the U.S. Copyright Act of 1976, no part of this publication may be reproduced, distributed or transmitted in any form or by any means, or stored in a database or retrieval system without prior written permission of the author.

Printed in the United States of America
First Edition: January 2025

10 9 8 7 6 5 4 3 2 1

Morken, Jean
The Weekly Edition

ISBN: 978-1-950562-68-8

Cover and book design by Andrew Benzie
www.andrewbenziebooks.com

*In memory of Rosie, my mother,
whose Irish spirit remains a guiding light.
Sláinte!*

PART ONE

CHAPTER 1

Snow was falling when I left Omaha and headed across the river toward my old hometown. My hands felt like ice as I gripped the steering wheel and focused steadily on the white line. I kept my speed well under the limit even though I had driven the Iowa roads a million times. I knew if I had waited the drive would have been worse, as heavy snow was predicted for that night and a blizzard was coming the next day.

As I continued along, I replayed Ma's words, "He's gone, Kate. Our Liam is gone." She said she knew it the moment she saw Father Murphy coming up the walkway with an army officer at his side. She knew. Her son, my brother, was gone.

Since the day they bombed Pearl Harbor, Ma knew this day might come. She repeated what the young soldier said as he sat across from her. "Mrs. Hurley, your son has given his life for our country." She said she could barely hear his words over the sound of her heartbeat thrashing in her ears.

The officer didn't have all the details of Liam's death yet, nor did he know exactly when his remains would arrive—

probably in four to six weeks—but he said he would let her know as soon as they had more information.

Liam was my only sibling. We had been close since I was old enough to walk and talk. He was my best friend, my strength in a storm. He was the one I turned to with every hope and every care. I pleaded aloud, "How could you take him, God?"

Finally, home. My tires crunched the snow-covered gravel as I crept down our long drive. The warm light from the kitchen welcomed me, as usual, but behind those walls, nothing would ever be the same.

Ma greeted me with red eyes and a tear-stained face. She was happy to have me home, but I knew she wished that Liam had come through that door. I removed my wet shoes and shook the snow from my coat before I hung it on the hall tree.

Father Murphy—Father Declan to us—had stayed with Ma until I arrived. He was Ma's dearest friend, the only one who could have shared the depth of her pain. She held his hand as she tried to explain what little she knew of the circumstances. Then she turned, accepted Father Declan's sturdy embrace, and sobbed in his arms.

"He's gone, Declan, our Liam is gone. Why?" Through sobs, she repeated, "Why did God have to take him? He had such a future, such big plans, such high hopes." Her entire body trembled. "This ugly, ugly war. It took our son."

Ma was barely five feet tall and never weighed more than one hundred pounds, but what she lacked in stature she made up for with strong Irish grit and fortitude. This day challenged every bit of that strength. It was the saddest day of her life. On that day, I think she gave up being a mother.

After Father Declan left, Ma and I shared memories late into the night. She sat in her chair with her sweater pulled close and lowered her eyes as she struggled to tell stories of Liam as a small boy. She cradled her hands around her face as she continued to talk. "Oh, Kate, I used to worry so much about him. Liam was always ready to take the lead when other boys were afraid. He was quarterback of the football team"—she paused and then looked at me—"and then a captain in the army. Why did he have to be a hero?"

I rubbed my fingers and looked at my hands. "He was my hero, too, Ma. He always wanted to protect me, especially when I wanted to do something by myself." Shaking my head and allowing a little laugh, I continued, "Like the time I wanted to learn to drive the tractor. He told me I was too small... told Da I could never do it. And the way he hovered over us and our cars." I swallowed and bit my lip. It hurt so deeply to realize that my life would never be the same.

"I'm going to miss him so much." Ma's voice broke and her shoulders trembled.

Ma went upstairs while I washed our teacups and put away a few remaining dishes. Then I wandered about, reflecting on this old house. I went into the parlor. It still smelled of lemon oil. The wood bookcases shined from their years of meticulous care. Liam's model ships still sail the top shelves. His trophies, mostly from football and baseball victories, occupy the middle shelves. I earned two from 4-H events and one from the County Spelling Bee. They sit on the bottom shelf, flanked by old family pictures.

I used to count Liam's trophies compared to my small number, and I was often jealous. He had more accomplishments, but he had also been given more opportunities. My parents had always told me I could be whatever I wanted to be when I grew up. Yet, when it came time to make decisions, they pushed me toward something "practical," which meant something useful for a wife and mother. That's how I ended up teaching at the all-girls' school in Omaha. My real interest was journalism, but I chose teaching. So I taught journalism at the high school while Liam became coeditor of the local paper, *The Hawthorne Times*. He used to chide me, calling me "small stuff." I envied his job but not his life in the small hometown.

The photos of our immediate family represent history now that Ma and I are the only ones left. We'd been through Da's passing three years earlier. There was some sense of peace for Da as he had suffered so long with his illness. Now the rituals would be for our beloved Liam, a young man so full of promise with so much life left to live.

As I walked into the living room, I rubbed the leather on Da's old chair that still sat by the fireplace. I could see him as he read every night after dinner until he dozed off. I would sometimes sit on the worn carpet in front of his chair and lean back near his knee. I had kind of forgotten about that spot next to my da, a place where I felt that all would be right with the world. When I was a small child, I would sit in that chair with him while he read to me from one of my library books. Then he would plop me down on the floor and go on with his own reading.

When I graduated from high school, he gave me a gold pendant. It is a Trinity knot with an emerald in the center. It was from Ireland. Da had explained that it symbolized heart, mind, and soul. I remembered his words, "Kate, you can do anything in life if these three things remain together. Don't ever forget that, and don't forget how much I love you." My da rarely expressed such personal feelings. I have treasured his words and worn this symbol every day.

Fingering my pendant, I thought, *Maybe it's time to look within my own heart, mind, and soul as Da had encouraged me to do.* I had the feeling my future was going to change, though I knew not how.

I turned out the lights, except for the small hallway light, and headed upstairs. My old bed was going to feel good tonight.

CHAPTER 2

Ugh! Rosie! That damn bird. For as long as I could remember, she, he... I don't really know which, but my brother and I had decided it was a female and named her Rosie. She had served notice outside my window every morning to tell me the sun had risen. Today's serenade reminded me of the time I thought she was at the window because she was hungry. I don't think Liam agreed with me, but together we researched bird diets. We went to the feed store to get the necessary ingredients. We made our purchases and brought the feast home to our bird. A blue jay crowded her out and devoured our purchase. I cried, and Liam put his arm around me and assured me that Rosie would make it somehow.

With that memory in mind, I pulled my comforter up around my shoulders and wished I could stay in bed. Maybe I could make the reality of Liam's death go away. How I wished it wasn't true. *My brother, my best friend, and now he's gone.*

Father Declan stopped by after morning Mass. He was a typical, dark-haired Irishman with lively, blue eyes and a caring heart, but today, his eyes were red and the muscles around them were drawn. His mouth was turned down.

He gave Ma a long hug. "Bless you, dear Ellie." Then he turned to me and said, "Oh, Kate. Sometimes I don't understand God myself. Why did He have to take Liam?" He slowly shook his head.

Ma had a faraway look in her eyes as she faced her friend. She wasted no time in telling him about her plans for the funeral. "Don't try quoting policy to me, Declan. I want some Irish hymns, bagpipes—if I can get one of our local fellows to play—and shamrocks on the altar."

The pastor nodded and smiled. "I'll do my best, Ellie. The bishop doesn't get out this way much in the winter."

He and Ma had known each other since they were high school students at The Academy. He was a year ahead and played on the football team. They had been sweethearts for part of their high school years. Declan chose to follow his calling to the priesthood, and Ma went off to college. Years later, he was assigned to our local parish.

Ma had returned home after college and married my da. Her parents had emigrated from County Cork. She was the oldest with two brothers. Joe lived in a nearby town and would be by later today. Patrick had moved to Ireland and had called twice already but could not come home to console his sister.

As word spread around town, several friends and neighbors stopped by to share condolences, memories, and, of course, casseroles. I recognized almost every face that came through the door and everyone remembered me, though Liam was better known now. After all, he was a man about town having acquired part ownership of the newspaper.

I was two years younger than my brother and the quiet one in the family. Liam had the dark hair and blue eyes. I had auburn hair, like my da, and hazel eyes. I held my own at home but sometimes rode on Liam's coattails in our school and social activities.

The wait for Liam's arrival, which turned out to be only four weeks, seemed endless. During that time, Uncle Joe and Aunt Nell stayed with Ma and helped plan for members of the American Legion post to meet the train and to provide the military salute at the cemetery. Joe and Nell assisted her in selecting a headstone and asked the women's auxiliary to lend a hand with the reception after the funeral. For me, it would be a return to Omaha and a week of planning and decisions.

CHAPTER 3

Sister Edward Joan, the school principal, had found a substitute who could cover most of my classes, but my main concern was the school newspaper. I spent as much time as possible with *The Champion* students, making sure they understood all the details. We had recently applied for the National Student Journalism Award. The students, the other faculty, and I all thought we had a good chance of winning it.

With everything covered, I was ready to meet with Sister Edward Joan. She was at least twenty years my senior and reminded me of my aunt Nell. She was kind and caring but also a strong, independent woman. I accepted her condolences and explained my plan.

She skimmed my outline and peered at me, nodding. "Looks like you've thought of everything as usual, Kate. I'm sure we'll get by. You stay with your ma as long as she needs you." She paused. "We'll miss you. *I* will miss you. You know, Kate, you're one of my brightest teachers. You've got drive and you're smart. The students love you. I would like to see you come back but... well, things sometimes change. You will do well no matter what you do or where you are."

She paused again and looked at me. "Can I offer you a piece of advice?"

"Of course, Sister." She was a thoughtful, perceptive person, and I always treasured her wisdom.

"Stand up for yourself. You're sometimes too ready to put others first. I have seen you do that with faculty. Stay focused on your own goals. Don't take a back seat to anyone. Remember, dear, don't hide your light under the bushel basket." She took both of my hands and smiled. "You have too much to offer. Live your own life."

I rather enjoyed the drive back home now that the roads were clear and dry. The skies were bright blue, though the air was icy. Sister Edward Joan's words flowed through my mind as I navigated the familiar route. I smiled to myself as I remembered how, over the years, she had taught me that if you stick to your guns, life has so much to offer regardless, perhaps due to one's circumstances, position, or gender.

The sky was fading to a deeper blue as I pulled into Ma's driveway and gazed at the old house. Now it's just me and Ma, the Hurley women, to take care of our home, Liam's share of *The Hawthorne Times*... everything.

I nodded to myself as I uttered Sister Edward Joan's words, "Stand up for yourself and live your own life."

I guess that all my life I felt like second fiddle to my older brother. I loved and admired him, but I was envious, too. My parents always talked about his bright future while they, Ma especially, patted me on the back and involved me in domestic chores. They supported my plan to go to college but steered me toward options they thought would be useful for a female. Now I was on my own. I didn't know what might lie ahead for me, but I knew it would be my chance to follow my dream. Was I up to the challenge?

CHAPTER 4

Three days later, in a biting snowstorm, Uncle Joe, Aunt Nell, Ma, and I went to the train depot to accept Liam's remains. There we met Father Declan and members of the American Legion post. Given that Liam was a captain, his body was accompanied by a major from the army who greeted me and Ma and presented us with a neatly folded American flag. The American Legion members stood in a salute while Father Declan and I were positioned on either side of Ma. He put his arm around her as she accepted the flag with her trembling hands. I wiped my tears and stifled a sob.

After offering his condolences and praise for Liam's service, the major got back on the train and the hearse received the body. I took Ma's hand as we returned home to face the next few days.

The morning of the funeral finally arrived. Ma and I entered the church, a large church for our small town. This stately, old building was the place of my baptism, the place where Liam and I received the other sacraments of our faith. It's also the altar where my parents recited their wedding vows. It was the dwelling house where we said our final goodbyes to Da. These memories spawned an awareness of the new emptiness in my heart. Now we were here to say farewell to Liam... in this hallowed place where we worship the God who took my brother away from us.

Ma stood frozen at the back of the church as she looked across the crowd gathered in front of us. She is usually so strong and brave, but I didn't see that in her face today.

"Come, Ma," I coaxed her, and then held her icy hand. She started to stumble as she took her first step. Uncle Joe quickly moved to her side, and we proceeded down the aisle. We followed behind the casket, accompanied by the pallbearers—two cousins and four of Liam's best friends. A lone bagpipe led the way.

When we reached the front of the church, Father Declan came down from the altar, blessed the casket, and greeted us. I had never seen him with tears in his eyes. In his eulogy, he said things I'd never heard about Liam as he told stories about my family. He seemed to have known them better than I did. Ma was fortunate to have such a supportive friend as her pastor. I knew he would help her—help us—through this.

The descension of visitors at the house was like a repeat of the previous weeks. Roger Ferguson, Liam's partner at *The Times*, was one of the first to arrive. His brief visit was formal and obligatory. He cocked his head as his greasy, dark hair fell over his eye. "I'm so sorry, ladies. Liam was a good man, and we will miss him." Then, looking over Ma's shoulder, he said, "Let me know if there's anything I can do. I have to run now. I need to get back to the paper." I breathed slowly and cringed, remembering Ma's comments that he did not welcome her presence in the office. I knew she had a tough road ahead of her.

At the end of the day, after everyone had left, Ma and I sat down with a cup of tea, this time with a splash of brandy. I put my head back on the divan. Ma took off her shoes. Now we could endure our pain in private before we had to begin our new life without Liam.

"I'm glad it's over, Kate. I know everyone means well, but I can't handle any more visitors. Just like after your da passed, I have to move forward. Right now. I don't like the idea, but I have to face it, especially *The Times*. That paper was your brother's dream, and I'm not going to let Roger Ferguson destroy it. Liam's dream won't die with him."

Not sure where I fit in with her plan, I nodded. "I'll help you all I can."

The next morning, Ma came downstairs as I was finishing my first cup of coffee. I started the bacon as we discussed our plans for the day and the week ahead. We decided to get things done around the house, return a couple casserole dishes to some friends out in Woodland, and take the altar cloths to the church. Ma brought them home every Friday, washed and ironed them, and gave them back to Father Declan every Monday. She'd done this every week for as long as I could remember.

Our errands filled most of the morning. Returning the altar cloths to the church concluded our list. Father Declan was busy in his office but always hospitable. He invited us to stay for a cup of tea, a welcome suggestion after our day of chores.

When we arrived home, there was a stack of cards in the mail. Mixed among the cards was a letter from Liam dated December 12, 1944.

Ma's hands shook. She bit her bottom lip, held the letter close to her chest, and sat down at the table. She wiped the tears from her eyes and forced herself to read.

Dear Ma,

The weather has turned chilly over here, a little cooler than home right now. My outfit has seen some heavy front-line action, and we have been teaching the soldiers how to use antitank arms in preparation for more events. We don't know day to day what might happen. I must say that the fighting caliber of the men in my outfit is the highest I have seen since I've been over here. The men are ready to go when called.

We have lost two men, and it is really sad. We lost a young lad last week. I swear he was only a boy, Ma. I prayed with him when he was dying. And then I cried. At times like that, I long to hear Father Declan's comforting words. We could sure use more chaplains over here.

There is nothing good about war, but it brings out the best in some men. I have seen heroes, men of compassion and grace, and many men of goodness. I doubt I will ever see them again once I return home, but I will never forget any of them.

I didn't get a chance to tell you before I left home, but I have a girl back there. I met her at a dance at The Grange. I had been seeing her for a while. I wanted you to meet her, but she wanted me to meet her parents first, and they are not in good health, especially her mom. I can't wait to get home and introduce you. She's special, Ma. I think she's the one.

I hope and pray that all is well at home. Give my love to Kate and to Father Declan. Please ask him to pray for all of us over here.
Love,
Your son, Liam

Ma folded the letter, returned it to its envelope, and again held it close to her heart. In her usual strong way, she had endured all the events surrounding Liam's death, distracted by everything she had to do. This moment let her acknowledge the depth of pain in her heart. She broke down and allowed herself a good, long cry. I put my arm on her shoulder and cried silently with her. Somehow, I knew that together we would find the strength to take on our new challenges. She was determined to see Liam's dream come to fruition.

CHAPTER 5

Ma seemed to be in a fog the next couple days, but on Thursday evening, we sat at the kitchen table until almost midnight. She leaned forward, her blue eyes intense and clear. "I've been stopping by *The Times* once a week since Liam left for the war, but I don't think that will be enough now that he's not coming back to do his job." She paused, looking thoughtful. "It's time for Roger Ferguson to realize I'm a permanent fixture in that office, and I won't be going away. He has the final say until the end of the year, but I'll be in on every decision."

Roger Ferguson was ten years Ma's senior and one of the "good ol' boys" in town. He had run *The Times* for almost twenty-five years. He was known for his business expertise but also for some shady practices. He managed to keep the bad news hidden and the paper looking good. It helped that he was good buddies with the Hawthorne sheriff.

Liam was the exact opposite and hoped to repair the paper's reputation after Roger retired next year.

Ma's voice didn't break one bit that evening as she spoke in a steady, low-pitched tone that I'd not heard before. "I am going to stop in tomorrow. Liam has an office there, and it will be mine from now on. I need to be there to know what's going on."

I brought us more tea and put a hand on Ma's shoulder. "I know you have the will and a plan to do this, but I would be happy to help. I've been running my school's paper for three years, and I've learned a little along the way." I knew Ma wasn't asking for my opinion. She had thought about this and made up her mind. "I know you can handle whatever comes your way, but I'd really like to help."

She cradled the warm cup in her hands. "No. No, I want to handle this myself."

Ma came down for breakfast wearing her gray suit, a green, silk blouse, and a determined look in her eyes. She ate very little, took a few sips of coffee, and headed to the office.

The minute she arrived, she was taken aback. The assistant editor, John Powers, was in the process of moving into Liam's old office. She halted at Liam's door. Her heart pounded in her chest, and her eyes began to blur. She turned and marched down the hall to Roger's office.

"Hell's bells! What do you think you're doing?" she yelled as she pointed toward Liam's office.

Roger looked up, brushing the dark hair from his forehead. "Ellie... I'm sorry, dear. I know you're having a difficult time. I didn't mean to upset you, but it just made sense to give John more room."

"Not in Liam's office. That's my office now. You can just tell him to quit unpacking and find another spot."

Roger's jaw dropped and his eyes narrowed. "You won't need an office that big, Ellie."

"I plan to be here every day starting Monday, and I'll be using *my* office." She turned and marched out before Roger could see the tears forming in her eyes. Keeping Liam's spirit alive was going to be painful, but this was her right, her duty to her son, and she wasn't backing down.

On the way home, she stopped by the church to pick up the altar cloths to be washed over the weekend. Father Declan was in his office. He set his papers aside, stood up from his desk, and invited her to stay for a visit.

Ma's lower lip quivered as she readily accepted his hospitality and a warm hug. "Oh, Declan, I'm not as strong as I thought. It's so soon but… but I have to do this now, or I'll really have trouble with Roger Ferguson. I don't trust that man for one minute."

Father Declan kissed the top of her head and held her close for longer than he'd want anyone to see. "I know, Ellie. It's hard for me, too. It will just take time."

Ma returned home with the altar cloths. Over the weekend, in addition to doing the church laundry, we spent a little time in Liam's room. We didn't plan to clean things out, but she wanted some mementos of Liam to put in her new office. Together, we selected a picture of his Academy football team and one of him in his army uniform. "Look at this one, Kate. He was so handsome."

I took the picture, sat back, and smiled. "He was a good-looking chap. Guess I never noticed, but some of my girlfriends used to tell me so."

From the parlor, she selected a family picture that included Da. To my pleasure, she asked if she could bring in the award I had received for making the Dean's List in my first year of college.

After supper, we sat at the table. Ma looked at me with a sparkle in her eye. "I have some ideas about what I might do at *The Times*, but I guess I could use your help." Her voice had softened but didn't crack. "You know I've written for the church bulletin. I wrote proposals and things for your da, but I haven't done much else." She paused and put her hand on mine. "I know there's no room for you at the office, but could you help me from home, at least for a while?"

"I'd love to help." I pulled my chair closer. This would be a chance to get involved with real journalism. "Real" was the term Liam used when comparing his work to mine. He always chided me with a smile, but he often made me wish I had his opportunities.

Ma's wheels were turning as she got up to get a pencil and paper. It was the strongest I'd seen her since before she received the news about Liam. She walked around the table, tapped the pencil on her lip, and spoke to no one in particular.

"I think I should approach Roger with a plan. I can take

over some things that used to be Liam's responsibilities and leave the politics to Roger. It's his favorite topic. And... I have an idea"—she paused and looked at me with renewed strength in her eyes—"a way for me to get some stories and to let everyone know I am part of *The Times*. How about 'Coffee with the Editor.' I could get a table down at Emily's Café. Em would probably like some extra business on Mondays. Roger doesn't go to her place much, so he wouldn't be in my hair."

Emily was a fixture in our town, and her café, which had been around for over twenty years, was a gathering place for everyone with a story to tell or news to share.

I agreed with her idea. Ma knew almost everyone in town, either through church, school functions, local politics, or her work helping Da at the bank. People trusted her.

"You and I could go over the ideas together, and I will let Roger know at our Tuesday meetings. These meetings are something new for his schedule, and I don't think he likes them much." She had a devilish twinkle in her eye. "I can tell him what stories I will be submitting each week, then we can get them ready by Thursday for the Friday edition. John Powers will still be covering lots of Liam's features, but I can do some of that, too. John's a hard worker, and Roger puts a lot on him. I think Roger may have big plans for him. I like John, but we'll have to see about those plans."

Ma spent the rest of the week doing her usual errands but included a stop to see Emily. The café was busy on Saturdays, but Emily took a break and sat with Ma over a cup of coffee. She was about Ma's age, but she had gone to the public school in Woodland. She had beautiful, salt-and-pepper gray hair gathered into a bun. She was taller and heavier than Ma but appeared trim, probably due to being in constant motion as she created meals and desserts relished by a large following of regular customers.

"I will help you any way I can, Ellie. Mondays are perfect, especially in the afternoon. It's usually slow in here at that time. You could stay as long as you want."

"That's great, Em. Let's give it a try. Now I need to publicize it so that I get some folks to come. How about a notice in your window?"

"Sure. The sooner the better."

By the following Monday morning, Ma had a carton of things ready for her office. We decided that she would meet with Roger on her own, and I wished her well. She lugged the box in and was pleased to find Liam's office waiting. She pushed her collection into a corner before their meeting. Roger offered tea, but he didn't move toward getting it.

"Not necessary, Roger," she said with a forced smile. "I'd like to review my plans with you. I'm sure you're busy and"—she nodded toward John's office—"thanks for taking care of the space. Now I'd like to go over Liam's usual workload and tell you about my plan to bring in some community stories."

"Sure, Ellie." Roger inhaled slowly. In support of her plan, he agreed to put an article in Friday's edition about her role with the paper and let people know about the "Coffee with the Editor" plan. Two steps ahead of him, Ellie handed Roger the article I had written over the weekend. Roger's jaw dropped as he nodded and looked at his new partner.

When Ma arrived home, I was waiting at the door. The spring in her step and the gleam in her eye told me things had gone her way. I couldn't wait to hear the details. Ma put her notebook on the table and removed her coat.

"I think it's time to celebrate our new adventure. Shall we have a little brandy before supper?"

One of Liam's friends, Paul Kelly, had brought a bottle over after the funeral in case we needed it for *medicinal* purposes. Ma poured a small goblet for each of us. Quoting Da, we raised our glasses, toasting our new beginning, "Sláinte!"

Ma filled me in on the details. She'd have to let Emily know to reserve a table by the window for the next Monday afternoon.

CHAPTER 6

The following Monday, dressed in her navy skirt and her favorite gray, nubby wool cardigan, Ma set out on her usual errands, including a stop at the church to drop off the clean and expertly ironed altar cloths.

"Good luck today, dear Ellie."

"Thank you, Father. And thank you for the notice in the bulletin. Better than Roger putting it on the fourth page of *The Times*." She rolled her eyes.

"Ah, Ellie, you'll set him straight, I'm sure." He put his hand on her shoulder as he saw her to the door.

"Yes, you can bet that will change." The note in *The Times* was smaller than she'd planned, and it was on the fourth page, right next to the notice about a bake sale at the Methodist Church.

After lunch, she went down to Emily's. Em had set a table for six, decorated with fresh flowers and navy-blue napkins, right by the front window. A fresh pot was brewing in the kitchen, and a tray of her popular blueberry scones sat atop the counter.

"Emily, it looks lovely. Thank you!"

Emily gave her a hug. "You'll do great no matter what I serve, but it won't hurt to put out my best. You mind your ladies. I'll keep the coffee coming." Emily was a fixture in Hawthorne. Everyone knew her. She provided support to her customers and knew when they needed quiet and when they wanted to share a few words. Most of all, she kept the gossip to herself.

The café was located in the center of town. Its walls were lined with windows, topped by blue-and-green-plaid curtains. There were only eight tables, but people didn't mind standing when there was news to share. Emily's cooking was the highlight of the place, morning, noon, and evening.

At one o'clock on the dot, three ladies came through the front door and headed toward Ma as she was arranging her pencil and notepad on the table. Two were from her church, and the other was someone she recognized, but she didn't remember her name. Each of the ladies took one of Emily's scones and sat down with a cup of coffee.

"Ellie Hurley, it's about time we got someone who will listen to us." It was Mary Conlon, who had lost her son almost a year ago. Mary proceeded to tell her a story about her son's heroic deeds in the war. She wished that there was a way to share it with people in Hawthorne, especially other parents whose sons had gone to war.

Maggie Higgins wanted to tell people about her niece who'd made the Dean's List at the prestigious women's college in Omaha. "People should know how well our Hawthorne kids are doing. It speaks highly of our schools."

The third lady—the one whose name she couldn't remember—introduced herself as Karen Acton. She lived on the west side of town and had four children, the youngest of whom had diabetes. Karen's eyes were drawn tight. She wrung her hands in her lap. "I'm worried that people don't know how to handle diabetic emergencies. Do you think you could get some advice into the paper?"

Ma left Emily's, satisfied that she had some ideas and a lot of work to do. We worked together that evening, outlining some articles based on the ladies' input.

The next morning, armed with a full agenda and a plan for three columns, she arrived in her office an hour before Roger came through the door.

"Good morning, Roger. The Coffee went well yesterday. I'll tell you about it when we get together at nine."

"Nine? Oh, of course." He sighed. "Nine, sure." His shoulders sagged as he started down the hall.

"Will John be joining us?" she called after him. "I'd like to know what he's got this week."

Roger paused and gritted his teeth. "I'll let him know."

Promptly at nine, the editor sat behind his desk. Ma and John were seated opposite him, John looking pale and tired. Both men appeared surprised at the articles that originated from Ma's meeting. She assured them she'd have them written up by Wednesday afternoon and offered to help with some of John's workload.

John had checked on a Sunday afternoon accident on Highway 17 that put two people in the hospital. He was also following up on a story about two Woodland youths who were caught "borrowing" a car from a neighbor. Supposedly, the boys just wanted to try it out, but unfortunately, their inexperienced driving did some damage to the gears and the neighbor reported it to the police.

John glanced at Roger. "Thanks, Ellie, but I can get it all done by deadline."

Ma and I worked all evening on her stories. A call to Doctor Leary about the diabetes article provided some very practical information. He agreed to let Ma quote him. Doctor Leary was a fixture in our town, having delivered most of the babies born over the last thirty years. He was getting up there in years but was nowhere near retiring.

"Good luck, Ellie. I think it's good for you to be doing this."

Ma firmly instructed Roger, "Put the diabetes article on the front page." She confirmed that the notice about the Coffees was larger and in a more prominent location. Neither of the men was very enthusiastic, but they agreed to give it a try. Roger's new partner was going to get her way.

When she arrived at Emily's on the following Monday, three ladies and one gentleman were seated at her table enjoying Emily's devil's food cake. Two of the visitors presented similar stories, so Ellie decided to combine them. At the end of the day, she departed for home with material she thought would appeal to the people of Hawthorne and to subscribers in the surrounding areas.

At nine the next morning, her colleagues were waiting for her in Roger's office. "Well, what do you have for us today?" Roger smirked.

John looked from Roger to Ellie. "My wife heard some good comments from the ladies on the school board, especially about the article on diabetes."

Later that day at home, Ma and I worked together and had some new articles ready for print by noon on Wednesday. I was getting as much pleasure as Ma since I missed my involvement with *The Champion*. I thought, *If Liam could only see us now, he'd be cheering us on.* Whenever Ma walked into her office, she looked at Liam's picture. I think she felt him peering over her shoulder. Perhaps taking over Liam's role was keeping her heart strong. The challenge was helping her cope with her pain.

I planned to go to the office with Ma on Wednesday just to see how things were going. Ma's articles were human interest stories, as opposed to the factual reporting stories that the good ol' boys were accustomed to putting in the paper. Though I don't think he would admit it, Roger was noticing that Ellie's contributions might be appealing to the readership.

We were having breakfast when the phone rang. It was Roger, sounding rather urgent. "Ellie, we have a problem. John had a heart attack last evening and is in the hospital.

The doctor says only time will tell how he will recover, but in the meantime, we'll need a little help down here. Do you suppose you could put in more hours this week and perhaps next week? I don't know how long he will be out."

"Sure, Roger. I do hope John is going to be okay. Perhaps Kate could help us a bit, too."

"Whatever you ladies can do."

Our small-town paper served many purposes. It not only conveyed the national news, but it also reported local happenings, correcting the gossip and mandating accountability. Ma and I talked about these responsibilities as we went into the office together.

Roger was sitting at his desk with a cup of cold coffee in front of him. He rubbed his brow as he glanced up and greeted us. "Let's get together and talk about John's assignments." He and John had worked together a long time, and I don't know if his concern was more for John or for the paper.

At nine o'clock, Roger and Ma reviewed the stories John had submitted on Tuesday afternoon, noting some things that needed more follow up before the final publication. Roger phoned the print room to see if they could delay the deadline until five o'clock on Thursday.

Ma agreed to check on the status of the people injured in the Sunday afternoon wreck. I volunteered to follow up on the police report regarding the two Woodland boys.

*   *   *

Having been to the community hospital many times, Ma headed down to the ward to see what she could learn about the accident. The clerk at the nurse's station wasn't very helpful, giving Ma just a general statement about the conditions of the two victims. Knowing she could find a better answer, Ma walked down another hall until she ran into a nurse she knew from when Da was in the hospital. Ma greeted her warmly.

"I'm so sorry about Liam, Mrs. Hurley." She knew him from school and was so saddened by his passing. "He was such a great guy."

Ma accepted her kind words and then inquired about the accident victims. "I heard there was a bad wreck Sunday afternoon."

"Yes. Both victims were from Hawthorne. One is recovering quickly, but the other is still in pretty bad shape. He might have to be transferred to Minnesota."

"Serious, huh?"

"Yes," replied the nurse. "You know, the car came right up over the hill and ran into the back of the thrasher. I hear the farm equipment was being driven by a sixteen-year-old. It's a shame. I guess the boy was pretty upset, but he didn't really do anything wrong. It's just that he wasn't licensed."

"Oh, so sad. I hope both people recover quickly." Ma marched back down the hall and headed home.

* * *

Meanwhile, dressed in my trench coat with a pencil tucked in the band of my hat, I went over to the police station in Woodland. It's not really a "station." It's just a small room behind the post office.

"Excuse me, I'm from *The Hawthorne Times*. I am investigating the police report about the boys who stole the neighbor's car last weekend."

The officer at the desk peered over his glasses at me. "Why do you want to know? Boys will be boys. No reason to put anything in the paper."

"The people of the county always want to know when there is a theft in the area, whether it is something for others to worry about."

"No worry, miss. It's all taken care of."

Puzzled at the lack of response, I left the station, wondering how else to get the news.

On the way home, I stopped in Emily's for coffee and eyed the last piece of the day's apple pie." Just as I was about to ask for it, in walked one of the Cunningham boys from Woodland.

"Any pie left, Emily?" he asked over my shoulder.

I turned and smiled at him. "I think I remember you. Aren't you Peter's brother?"

"Yes, I am. I'm Michael, and I believe I remember you, too. Aren't you Kate Hurley?"

"Yes. Can I join you for a minute, Mike? It's nice to see a familiar face." I turned to Emily and asked for a slice of banana bread.

As he sat down with his slice of apple pie, Mike shared the family news. The Cunninghams had been a fixture in Hawthorne for many years. The law practice had been started by Mike's grandfather and was widely respected for its integrity.

"Pete plans to move back home as soon as his bar exam is over," Mike told me. "I have no doubts that he will pass the exam. He'll join my dad's practice."

Mike had started in law but decided his strengths were more along the lines of business and advertising. He worked for the bank in Woodland and for some of the small businesses, handling their publicity.

After we caught up on the family news, I asked about the incident in Woodland when two boys "borrowed" a neighbor's car.

Mike laughed. "I suppose that's what most people heard. The boys—one was Richie Richardson, the sheriff's son—were drinking and decided to take the car for a joyride. Neither of them knew how to drive, especially not when they were half drunk. It's lucky they only did some damage to the gear shaft. If they'd driven very far, they might have wrecked the car, or worse. When the neighbor learned that one of the boys was the sheriff's son, he agreed not to press charges, but I'm sure the sheriff will have to pay for the repairs.

Hopefully, the kid will learn something. He's been in trouble before."

*   *   *

When I arrived at the office, Ma was already on the phone confirming the story about the boy driving the thrasher. I slid my notes over to her, and she was able to authenticate my information as well. It's public information if you know how to get it, and Ma had lots of connections.

By five that evening, Ma and I handed our finished articles over to Roger. He looked over his glasses at us and said, "Nice work, ladies."

We headed out the door, tired and famished. It had been a long day, and we were going to recuperate with a sip of brandy before eating our leftover stew.

CHAPTER 7

Excited to see our work in print, Ma and I rose early, had a quick bite of toast, and headed to the office. Roger wasn't in when we arrived, but there were several copies of the latest edition on his desk. We helped ourselves to a couple copies and carried them to our desks. I looked through the paper front to back, then back to front.

Ma yelled out just as I started to get up from my desk, "Hell's bells, Kate! There's not a single word from either of us in this rag! What's this article about the town council's June meeting?"

My head pounded as I stomped down the hall, shouting, "What the bloody hell happened?"

Ma's face burned red and her jaw tightened. "Roger Ferguson has a few things to learn. He is not the sole owner of this paper, and he can't get away with this. Liam would never have let him operate this way, and neither will I."

We neatly refolded the papers, laid them back on Roger's desk, and left the office.

Emily's was crowded on this chilly morning. The regulars were talking about the daily news in their usual ho-hum manner. Everyone who came through the door recognized Ma.

"Good morning, Ellie."

"I like your articles, Ellie."

"Nothing too exciting ever happens, but you're sleuthing out some good stories."

We sought out the corner table a little out of earshot from the others. We ordered coffee and breakfast. Ma's jaws were still tight as she moved the food around her plate. "Do you think there is more to this than Roger's fat ego and mulishness?" she asked in a low voice. "You'd think he wants the paper to succeed as much as we do, but he's so arrogant. If he didn't like my article, he could have told me." She paused and picked up a forkful of egg. "I could wring his neck."

Emily poured us each a second cup.

"You know, Mike said that the sheriff's son had been in trouble before," I offered, "yet there has never been anything in the paper about him. I'm thinking there must be more to this than either of us knows. Maybe I can talk to Mike before Monday."

"Hmm." Ma nodded. "But today, let's just ask Roger up front what happened to your article. He can't say there wasn't room since he put in that article about the town council issue that doesn't come up until June! And I'm not taking his poppycock for an answer."

I knew Roger was in for an earful.

Roger's car was parked in front of the office just behind another car that, I was pretty sure, belonged to Sheriff Richardson. As we entered the front door, we heard the sheriff about to leave. "Thanks, Roger, good work. You saved me again. Those gals are in over their head. Some women…" We almost ran into the lawman as he came out of Roger's office. "H-h-hello, ladies. Uh… nice morning, huh?"

Ma inhaled and bit her lip. Her eyes narrowed as she glanced at me. "It's a little cool out there, Sheriff. Don't leave on account of us," replied Ma.

Roger didn't look up as we entered his office. "Good morning," he mumbled without glancing at us.

"Have you examined the paper yet, Roger?" Ma asked through gritted teeth.

Still focused on his desk, he replied, "Sure have. I always see it first thing."

"So what happened to the article about the car theft over in Woodland?"

"Ellie, Ellie." He peered up, shaking his head. "It wasn't a theft. Just juvenile mischief. The boys were *borrowing* the car."

"Roger, you know it was more than that, and you didn't answer my question. Kate did her research on that article and just put the truth out there."

"Kate, Ellie. You have to be careful when things involve a prominent person."

"That's news to me, Roger. Our citizens expect more

from their paper. We did our research. We confirmed our information with the police record. So enlighten me. How did the article get left out?"

Roger scowled. "The town council issue needed to be publicized early so that people could... could plan to attend the meetings."

Ma stood tall, arms akimbo. "You need to remember, Roger, that I own 50 percent of *The Hawthorne Times*, and you have to consult me if you want to leave out something I wrote. Things are changing here, Roger Ferguson, and you'd better get used to it. I don't know what you're up to, but Liam would not have put up with this malarkey, and neither will I."

Ma stomped back to her office. Shaking her head, she looked at Liam's picture. "How did you put up with him, son?"

The following Monday, when Ma walked into Emily's for her "Coffee with the Editor," four ladies were perched at her table enjoying Emily's lemon pound cake.

"Thanks, Em. Your pound cake looks perfect."

"My pleasure, Ellie. Thank you for the afternoon business."

One of the ladies, a familiar face from Woodland, was leaning forward with her hands folded on the table, her pound cake untouched. She waited for the other three to finish their stories. Two of the ladies shared information about their sons who were overseas. The other sought to get publicity for the school play, which was coming up in April.

The lady from Woodland listened quietly and smiled at the first three. "I enjoyed listening to your stories, but you don't need to stay around. You must have things to get done before supper."

The three said their goodbyes, got up, and left.

Ma turned to her informant. "You look familiar. I'm sure we've met."

"I'm Maggie Cunningham. My boys, Peter and Mike, knew Liam and Kate at The Academy."

"Oh yes, nice to see you again. Kate has seen your son Mike recently, too. And I hear that Peter is coming back home to go into business with his da. So wonderful for you."

Maggie Cunningham looked around the café and lowered her voice. She was a petite lady with a kind face and a lively smile. Her voice was quiet, but she stared Ma firmly in the eye. "You know, there have been a few incidents involving the sheriff's son in Woodland, and he always seems to get out of them unscathed. I'm surprised nothing has ever been in the paper about his shenanigans. Maybe he has never broken the law, but he has destroyed property and offended a lot of people. Yet he walks with his head held high, like he's so innocent and important. I think his dad is the one who gets him out of his jams. Then he goes and does something else. I don't really have a new story. I just wanted to put a bug in your ear so when something else comes up, you might be aware of his history."

Ma smiled and replied, "Thank you for the tip. And thanks for stopping by. I'll keep your comments in mind. Say hello to your family for me."

That evening, Ma reviewed her meeting with me. "Not much news, but Maggie Cunningham shared some interesting comments."

"Good contact, Ma. She knows what's going on around town. Her husband and boys do, too. Let's keep in touch with that family."

We agreed that we wouldn't do anything more about the Woodland car theft, following Ma's principle, *Give him enough rope, and he'll hang himself.*

We had our meeting with Roger on Tuesday and followed up with ongoing stories. Ma visited the hospital and finagled an update on last week's car accident. There was no new evidence about the car theft in Woodland.

Wednesday arrived in full bloom. It was St. Patrick's Day. Every Hawthorne resident was dressed in green. The Grange in Woodland had been converted to an Irish pub with green and white streamers strung over the bar. All the young fellows—Irish or those pretending to be—were drinking green beer. Among the many familiar faces, I saw the Cunningham brothers.

Father Declan was there wearing his obligatory Roman collar, a shamrock in his lapel. "Sláinte, ladies. I thought I might see you here. Happy St. Paddy's Day!"

"I wouldn't miss it, Father Declan," said Ma, trying to spout an Irish brogue.

"Nor would I, Father Declan. Something about corned beef and cabbage being required once a year." It isn't my favorite dish, but on March 17, it was an Irish obligation to enjoy it.

It was an evening of laughter, cheers, and singing. Ma's eyes watered when the band played "When Irish Eyes Are Smiling," but they cleared up with her first bite of the corned beef. This was one of Liam's favorite celebrations. Despite her broken heart, Ma would never miss it.

After the boisterous celebration, a rowdy group started fighting in the parking lot until the manager of The Grange had to summon the sheriff to break up the brawl. When the sheriff arrived, he arrested four of the scufflers, including his own son. No one was hurt in the disturbance, but a rock flew up, landing on the window of the manager's car.

The next morning, Emily's was abuzz with the news of the fracas and the arrests by the sheriff. Everyone had heard that he had to cuff his own son. Sometimes things get around more quickly via the grapevine than they do through the newspaper. Per the morning gossip, the boys were arrested last evening, stayed overnight in the jail, and were released this morning after they had sobered up. No one pressed charges.

Ma and I listened closely to all the conversations and decided to investigate. Before I headed out to The Grange, I pulled up to drop Ma off at the office, and there it was again—the sheriff's car. Ma shrugged and shook her head. "Here we go again. Let's both go in."

The sheriff was in Roger's office, leaning back in the big, black, leather easy chair, shaking his head, mumbling something I couldn't understand. As Roger looked up and saw us, his head jerked slightly. He said, "Good morning" in a loud voice, and the sheriff sat forward in his chair.

"You missed a good party at The Grange last evening, Roger, but I hear you got in on the action afterward, Sheriff," Ma said.

Roger folded his arms, closed his eyes, and clenched his teeth.

The sheriff responded, "Yes, it was quite a rumble, Ellie… a little too much celebrating for the boys."

Ma replied, "I guess a night in jail sobered them up, but it didn't fix the manager's car window." She paused. "It must be difficult to cuff your own son."

"Yes, Ellie, it's something any father would hate to do, but it's my job," the sheriff said. "Thankfully, no one committed a crime, and they all went home this morning. They'll be paying for the car window. Boys learn some things the hard way."

"Kate is going to check some of the details," Ma advised as she nodded her head toward me.

The sheriff, turning red and narrowing his eyes, glared at Roger. "Ladies, I think I can answer any questions you might have. It was a little too much firewater for boys just learning to drink. The fight started over a minor disagreement, and no one was hurt. They'll pay for the window. What more do you want to know?"

"It's not me who needs to know, Sheriff. This is not the kind of thing that would make the big-city papers, but it's news in a small town. Folks like to know what's going on. Publishing the news keeps people accountable." Ma knew that a brief article about the brawl might put the sheriff on alert to address his son's problems.

Ma and I walked to her office and closed the door. We agreed not to do anything more about it but maintain our "wait and see" approach. This will catch up with them in the end.

CHAPTER 8

Although I was missing the liveliness of the city, I was beginning to get comfortable back in my hometown. Ma decided that a tea was in order, and she invited several of her friends and the few remaining classmates from my days at The Academy.

Once everyone arrived, I guided them to the nourishments and encouraged them to sit in the living room near the warm fire. I circulated around the room and poured tea or coffee as each desired, eavesdropping along the way. I heard about their husbands' work, their children, and their garden club activities. I didn't get any newsworthy stories.

After all our guests left, Ma and I cleaned up the living room, stored the leftovers, and did the dishes.

Ma leaned back on the kitchen sink and dried her hands. "I heard some of the girls asking if you considered moving back to Hawthorne. Have you thought about that at all?"

"You and I have been so busy that I hadn't really, until today when they were asking me. These were my closest friends growing up here in Hawthorne, but our lives have taken different paths. Listening to their gossip made me wonder if I would fit in here in Hawthorne." I glanced at Ma. She just nodded. I continued, "I really like my work at Saint Anne's, and I'm not really searching for a mate right now… or right here." I laughed. "What are you thinking?"

Ma took my hands in hers and looked me in the eye. "I couldn't have survived these past weeks without you, and I have lots of room in this old house. But if Hawthorne doesn't seem like the place for you, I'll make it on my own. I have lots of friends here and plenty to keep me busy."

I gave Ma a hug and stepped back to look at her. "We both have a lot to think about."

Just as we finished the dishes, the phone rang.

"Congratulations, Kate! You did it. *The Champion* won the NSJ Award!"

"Edith, really? That's great news. When did you hear? Do the students know yet?"

"Sister Edward Joan and I thought you might like to be here when she announces it. Any chance you could come in for the Friday assembly?"

"I wouldn't miss it for the world."

I got off the phone and told Ma the good news.

"Glory be, Kate! That's wonderful." She had a broad smile and gave me a hug. "I know you worked hard for that. I'm so happy for you."

I left Hawthorne Thursday morning, a beautiful, sunny, dry morning, making it an easy trip. It was great to see the teachers and catch up on the news from Omaha and school.

The end-of-year activities had begun. Senior prom was coming up, and the kids were all abuzz with finding dates and dresses and decorating the Park Ballroom.

When Friday afternoon came, I donned my maroon dress and arrived at school an hour before assembly to meet with Edith and Sister Edward Joan.

Several of the girls greeted me in the hall. "Miss Hurley! Miss Hurley! We've missed you. You're back?"

They didn't know about the award yet, so I chose my words carefully. "Not yet, but I plan to come back next fall. You seniors won't be here, so I thought I'd stop in to see what you're up to without me."

They shared their plans for the next year. These girls were talented students who genuinely wanted to pursue their education.

I arrived at the principal's office to see Edith and two of the other teachers waiting. As I entered, they all stood at once and exclaimed, "Congratulations, Kate!"

As sincere compliments came from each in turn, I was speechless. I had goose bumps, and tears came to my eyes.

Everyone asked about Ma and how things were going in Hawthorne. I described my work at *The Times*. I realized it had become a replacement for my work with *The Champion*, minus the student involvement. My new coworkers, connivers that they were, were more difficult than students.

The bell rang for the assembly, heralding us to the auditorium. We were anxious to share the good news with the students. Saint Anne's was larger than The Academy where I went to school, but the student body was small enough that I knew most of them, especially the seniors.

I took a seat next to Edith in the front row, while Sister Edward Joan drew near the podium. After several announcements, our principal approached the plaque, hiding the award until she'd finished her sentence. She pulled off the cover with a flourish. "Students, faculty, and all staff who helped us to accomplish this milestone, I present to you and to Miss Kate Hurley the National Student Journalism Award for *The Champion*." She revealed the plaque with its gold-embossed lettering.

> *The National Student Journalism Award for Excellence*
>
> *St. Anne High School*
>
> *Omaha, Nebraska*
>
> *The Champion Newspaper*
>
> *1944–1945*

"My congratulations to all!" The students leaped from their seats with loud applause and cheers. Tears ran down my face... tears of joy blended with tears of sadness, secretly reflecting on my uncertainties about next year.

We celebrated with cake and fruit punch after the assembly. Many of the seniors had plans to attend college in the fall. Some saw futures as writers or journalists. My heart swelled with pride as I knew I had helped steer them in that direction.

Before I left, I met with Sister Edward Joan. "I think of your words often, Sister. I'm helping Ma with our hometown paper, but it will be a while before I might have an independent role. *The Times* could be a good opportunity for me to do what I have always wanted"—I paused and looked at my mentor—"but I'm not so sure how I will fit back into the small community. I have a lot to think about over the next few weeks."

"Do what you think is best. We would miss you here, but you need to be where you can use your talents. Don't hide that light!"

CHAPTER 9

It was dark when I arrived back home. There was a light on in the kitchen but no sign of Ma. This was her Altar Society meeting night. I took advantage of the quiet time to soak in a warm bath and dwell on the decisions in my future. I rubbed the Irish knot that hung around my neck.

I went downstairs just as Ma entered through the back door. She hung up her coat and gave me a warm hug. "How was Omaha and the award ceremony?"

"Terrific." I smiled as I thought of all the girls. "It was great to see everyone, and as for the award, I had goose bumps the whole time I was there. Everyone was so excited, and I was so proud... excited for myself, honored for the girls. They didn't know until Sister Edward Joan uncovered the plaque."

"I told Father Declan. He is so proud of you, too. You would think he was your da." She smiled and laughed.

"Anything new here?" I asked.

Ma updated me on the latest news and discussed her plans for the next day.

"Sounds like you will have a busy morning. Let me know if there is anything I can do to help."

I gladly accepted the opportunity to go to the office in the morning and assist with the weekly stats. The weekly statistics—notices of births, deaths, and marriages—weren't very exciting in Hawthorne, but it gave me some involvement with the paper.

I entered *The Times* through the front door, walking past Ma's office where she was on the phone with Doctor Leary. The door to Roger's office was closed, so I went directly to John Powers's desk to work on whatever might be on the schedule. Finding a note from Roger about the garden society meeting and one about a wedding in Woodland, I gritted my teeth but went to work on them. I guess the society items would be my role for a while, but if Ma was doing something she liked, I could tolerate this until I knew a little more about my future.

After supper that evening, I received a call from Paul Kelly, inviting me to see the Gregory Peck movie at the Hawthorne Cinema. Feeling it was time to get out in our small town, I accepted.

Ma smiled and raised an eyebrow. "Sounds like fun, Kate. I'm sure you'll have a good time."

"It will be great to have some fun in this town."

Reverting back to shoptalk, Ma reported, "I got an

interesting lead from Maggie Cunningham at my Coffee today. There's been a trial taking place in the Woodland County Courtroom. Maggie heard that the judge reprimanded one of the attorneys by putting him in handcuffs!" Ma shook her head. "I find it a little hard to believe. She said it was because he wouldn't comply with the judge's order to take a recess."

"That sounds preposterous. How can you find out for sure?"

"Well, I know a couple lawyers—they were friends of your da—who might know more about it, and I believe I can look up the court records." She smirked. "You think the judge might have overstepped his bounds?"

"Sounds like a noble story!" I rolled my eyes. "Ha! Better than mine will be about the Woodland wedding and the garden society."

"Argh! That Roger. We'll have to work on him. I guess he sees you as short term. John returns next week, and he'll move back into his office. Roger will probably transfer some of the society stories back to me." Nodding her head, Ma continued, "I'll find my own news, like this county trial." She paused, looking at me. "Do you mind working from home? You've been a great support."

I bit my lip. "It's okay for now, but we need to talk. Do you see a bigger role for me at some point? I enjoy my work in Omaha. Getting the NSJ Award meant a lot to me, but there's not much more to do there. I love journalism. If I could see a future with *The Times*, I just might find a place back here."

Ma glanced down at the floor. "I know, I know. I've seen it these past few months. I've observed your talent and your love of journalism. It makes me realize I shouldn't have discouraged you when you wanted to study it in college. You really have a knack for it, my girl."

The next morning Ma turned in her Coffee stories, while I continued working on the society news. "For now, we'll make it work, Ma, but I have to think about my future."

The next morning, Ma turned in her article about diabetes and another brief Coffee story, while I continued working on the society news. Ma then headed over to the county courthouse to see what she could glean about the cuffing incident.

She returned home, laughing and shaking her head. "Some men never grow up. It's hard to believe, but it's true. And guess who the lawyer was… and the judge? They are both well known in the county. The lawyer was none other than the sheriff's cousin. I wonder if Roger will try to squash this one."

We worked on the story together and had it ready for print on Wednesday morning. We drove to the office together. Roger accepted my stories without much reaction, but his eyebrows went up as he read Ma's story.

"Ha! How did you get wind of this one?"

"I've been in this town a long time, Roger."

* * *

By the end of the week, I was ready for a little distraction, and I looked forward to an evening at the cinema and refreshing an old friendship. I could see why he and Liam were such close chums. Paul had an honest face and a sincere smile. He looked you in the eye when he spoke. His red hair and muted freckles gave him a boyish appearance.

The movie was excellent. Gregory Peck was dashing, and I enjoyed every minute. After the movie, we strolled down the street to Hawthorne's only late-night café.

Paul leaned forward onto the table with a faraway look in his eye. "There's something I want to tell you. It's not a happy chapter in my life," he said, glancing down at his hands. "I married a girl shortly after college. We eloped because my parents didn't like her, but the marriage was annulled six months later. I found out that my new bride had been married before."

His soft-blue eyes were moist. "It took me a while to start dating again. I told Liam… swore him to secrecy. No one in Hawthorne, except my parents, are aware. I thought you should know." He looked back down at his hands. "It's hard to talk about."

I hesitated but leaned toward him and finally managed to respond. "I'm sorry, Paul. That's heartbreaking. Thank you for trusting me with your story."

We were silent for a while, then I spoke. "Paul, I'm not

sure about anything in my life right now, and I don't want to give you the wrong idea. I like your company and your friendship."

We left the tavern and Paul took me home, giving me a light peck on the cheek as he said, "Good night, Kate. It's been a nice evening."

"Thank you, Paul. I enjoyed it."

CHAPTER 10

The phone was ringing when Ma entered the office on Monday morning.

"*Hawthorne Times*," she answered.

Judge Monahan roared back at her. "Where did you get this story? The whole town is talking." The judge demanded to meet with her, wanting to know the source of her information and whether she planned to provide further explanation or detail.

The lawyer, who was indeed the sheriff's cousin, rang shortly after with similar questions, though his interest was from a different point of view.

Meanwhile, Roger sat at his desk, working on the item for the town council agenda, occasionally looking up toward Ma's office.

Ma called me at home. "Kate, could you take my Coffee meeting this afternoon? My phone is ringing off the hook."

I did as she asked and went to Emily's at one o'clock. Emily had my favorite lemon pound cake ready. I took my place at the table she had set up by the window.

My first visitor, a woman from Woodland, was beaming. "My daughter just had twins. If it weren't for the expertise of the ambulance drivers, she might not have made it in time. They were so fast and skillful. They really know what they're doing. I don't think people appreciate them enough. We need to make sure the town and the county support them with adequate funds."

I smiled at her. "You have a sincere issue here. I'll see what I can do. And congratulations on the twins."

Next in line was Mrs. Cunningham, now a regular at Ma's Coffees, this time with exciting news about her son. "Peter passed the state bar exam, and he'll be returning home to practice law with his da. The firm will now be called Cunningham, Foley, and Cunningham."

I put my hand over hers and promised to get something in the paper. I was relieved that she wasn't sharing any gossip today. Her stories often meant chasing old news or unfounded rumors.

After dinner that evening, Ma and I laid out our plans for the rest of the week. She had agreed to meet with the judge and lawyer separately. It was a little hard to take their concerns seriously, except that some poor client was caught in the middle.

"Maybe you could join me. It might be good to have a witness to their comments. Help me keep the stories straight. These guys are smart and clever. They can both be finaglers."

"It's going to be a busy day. John will be back at work, but he won't be able to handle his full workload. Roger is working on the town council agenda. Ha," she added with a devilish smile. "I wonder where he's at with that urgent topic."

Promptly at nine the next morning, Ma welcomed John Powers back to the office. He was ten years older than Ma, medium height, and thin. Today, he looked pale and worn but expressed enthusiasm about getting back to work and hearing about the goings-on around town.

John tilted his head and looked at Ma. "Being out of the office gave me time to get in touch with the people who read our paper. *The Times* is of major importance to our folks, and they expect the truth. You know this, Ellie, I know you do. Our diligence means a great deal to both them and us. It's our reputation, our livelihood. You know, Ellie, I'm glad you're with us."

Ma always liked John and wondered how Roger and the paper would have made it without him. He had lived in Hawthorne all his life. Like Roger, he was a member of the Lutheran Church. Unlike Roger, John was a humble man, even a little timid—perhaps too timid—which made it hard for him to do his best under Roger's thumb.

Roger wanted Ma to give John some of her stories. She wouldn't let go of either her diabetes article or the cuffing story. Out of loyalty to me, she wouldn't give him my ambulance story. Roger would have to find some other items for John.

To start, he followed up on some of the town's weekly minutiae—the obituaries, birth announcements, and wedding notices. He'd get back into his usual role next week, allowing him to work just half days until his health was steady.

Judge Monahan came to Ma's office Tuesday afternoon, entering through the back door. He closed Ma's door behind him and pulled himself up to his tallest height, which wasn't much taller than me. His dark-brown eyes darted around the room, looking for a place to settle. I had brought in an extra chair.

"Nice to see you, Ellie. You, too, Katie. It looks like you're up for a new hobby in your lives. Do you know what you're getting into?"

"Of course I do, Judge," said Ma, "and it's nice to see you, too. It's been a long time."

"Yes, my Carrie said to tell you hello. You should get together with her sometime. She plays cards every Monday afternoon. I'm sure she and the girls would welcome you. You might like to join them too, Katie."

Ma ignored the invitation. "Let's get to the point, Judge. What really happened in that courtroom? I can't say I've ever heard of a judge cuffing a lawyer."

"Well, Ellie, you wouldn't understand."

"I'm not sure anyone would, Judge." Ma didn't crack a smile. "It doesn't sound like the usual procedure… maybe for a criminal on trial, but not for a lawyer, a colleague at that."

The judge sniggered and glanced down at his lap. "Well,"

he said in a firm voice, "I denied what I thought was an unreasonable request and told him to return to his seat. He approached me in an almost threatening manner, raising his voice."

Ma suddenly recalled that Vince Harbin and Judge Monahan were friends, but their sons were rivals for the quarterback role on the Woodland High football team. Leaning forward and biting her lower lip, Ma said, "Kind of like a football maneuver, right, Judge?"

The judge sat erect. "Now, Ellie, it wasn't like that at all. Vince was out of line. He disrupted the usual proceedings. I had to take charge, let him know who was in control. It's my duty to maintain order in my courtroom." He rose and nodded at me and Ma. "Good day, ladies."

As Judge Monahan stomped out the back door, Vince Harbin came in through the front, walking past Roger's office with a wave to the editor, who was leaning over his paperwork. Vince stood six feet tall and had dark hair and eyes. His features were sharp and defined, but he had a ready smile.

"How are you doing, Ellie? And, Kate, how are you? I haven't seen you since the funeral," he said, shaking his head and sobering his smile. "Again, I offer my condolences. Such a loss."

"Just fine, Vince. *The Times* is keeping me busy, and Kate is home for the semester."

"Well, you're sure getting wind of the latest tales of

Hawthorne. How did you hear about my being taken hostage?"

"You know I've been around here a long time, Vince. Not much happens that I don't hear about. If I don't hear it, Kate will. She's in touch with a lot of old friends." Ma gestured toward the still-warm chair. "Do you want to tell me your side of the story?"

"Not much to tell, really. Judge Monahan wouldn't listen to all my details. I think he'd already had his mind made up and wasn't going to hear the whole story. You know a judge is not supposed to be biased. He just wanted me to lose the case. He wasn't being fair, and I wasn't going to let him get away with it. My client deserves justice."

Ma shook her head. "It sounds like a competition between schoolboys that got out of hand, and your poor client is suffering in the process."

Their conversation was brief. Vince Harbin left. Ma swiveled in her chair and looked at the picture on her bookcase. I could read the question in her mind. *How would Liam have handled this one?*

CHAPTER 11

The following Monday morning, I headed to Ma's office while she took the altar cloths to the church. I let myself in the back door and headed down the hall. As I neared John's door, I heard some gasping sounds. Through the open door, I saw John lying on his floor, moaning and gasping.

"John, John! Holy Mother of God, John!" I knelt down beside him as he gave another loud gasp. My heart pounded as I got up, ran to the phone, and called the operator to get an ambulance.

I returned to John's office.

"Help me, help me," he moaned, clutching his chest. He was pale and sweaty.

I took his hand and tried to steady my voice. "You'll be okay, John. An ambulance is on the way. Please just relax and keep breathing, please." My heart pounded as I tried to remember my first-aid training. My training was directed at school emergencies—choking, seizures, fevers, but not heart attacks. "Please, Lord, let the ambulance get here soon," I prayed, "and where is Ma or Roger?"

John's breathing was more relaxed but slower. His eyes

opened and closed, and he slurred his words as he tried to speak. "Call Marilyn. Be sure to tell her and the kids that I have always loved them. I think this is it, Kate."

"I know we're of different faiths, John, but we believe in the same God. Let's pray together. Our Father who art in heaven…" I squeezed his hand as his breathing continued. His eyes closed, and his head rolled to the side.

As soon as I heard someone trying to get in the front door, I ran and opened it to greet the ambulance attendants. While they tended to John, I went to the phone, called his wife, and directed her to the hospital.

After the ambulance left, still trembling, I sank down into Ma's chair, just as she and Roger were entering through the back door.

Ma ran to her office. "What happened? What happened? We saw the ambulance. Was it John? Oh, dear God. I knew he came back too soon."

Roger's face was pale. "Is he going to be okay? Did you call his wife?"

I explained how I found him writhing on the floor, holding his chest, and that he appeared to lose consciousness just before the ambulance arrived. "And yes, I had called his wife, and she's going to meet him at the hospital. I hope she gets there in time."

Roger left to go to the hospital as Ma put her hand on my shoulder. I knew I had done all I could, but I explained every step to Ma. "I tried, Ma, I tried, but I don't think he's going to make it."

"It's good that you found him when you did. His family will be glad to know he wasn't alone. I think he has two sons and a daughter, but they don't live around here. His wife has a sister in Woodland. I'll try to call her."

The operator was able to reach John's sister-in-law, but Ma was unable to speak. She gave me the phone. I gave the woman a brief explanation of what I knew and told her that John and his wife would be at the hospital.

I helped Ma to her chair and suggested we just stay in the office and wait for more information. It wasn't long before Roger called. He told us John died shortly after he'd arrived at the hospital but was able to share a few words with his wife. His wife's sister was with her.

I asked Roger if there was anything that either Ma or I could do.

"Just stay there in the office, I guess. I'm glad that you were with John. If it weren't for you, his wife wouldn't have had a chance to say a final goodbye. I'll be back at the office as soon as possible. Please handle the calls until then. Thanks."

It's the first time I heard Roger sound so sincere and appreciative of my and Ma's help. It's the first time I had ever heard him say "thanks."

Neither Ma nor I had been in a Lutheran church before. I was struck by the bareness that I sensed not seeing a crucifix over the altar. Other than that, it looked like any other church. The minister was warm and devout. He delivered a beautiful eulogy, revealing his closeness to John and his family.

John's three children and four grandchildren sat with Marilyn, the new widow. She wore a black dress over her thin frame, and a simple strand of pearls circled her neck. Her black veil hid her face so I could not see her eyes, but those of her three children were rimmed with red. How painful it must be for them, and I remembered my pain when we lost Liam and Da. There are some things in life, all in God's plan, that are bound to happen but for which we are never prepared.

We followed the procession of cars to the cemetery and then stood around the new grave. Something about the warm, spring morning seemed to ease the sorrow. I enjoyed the sun on my back as I listened to the minister give the final blessing and watched them lower John's casket.

After the burial, we stopped by the Powers' home. "Mrs. Powers, I am Kate Hurley, and this is my mother, Ellie. We both worked with John. He was so talented and committed to doing the best for our community. We'll miss him at *The Times*. He's a loss to all of us."

Roger was at his desk when we returned to the office. He looked up and said, "I started an article about John. He was with *The Times* for twenty-eight years and devoted a lot of time to our community." He asked if there was anything special either of us wanted to contribute.

We shared what little we knew and then went together to Ma's office.

After a while, Roger brought his finished product to me and Ma and asked us if we would read it—a first for him to ask an opinion from either of us. It was the nicest thing I had seen written by Roger, and I think it truly came from his heart. Perhaps there was a decent man inside that crusty shell.

At the end of the day, Ma asked me to join her in Roger's office.

"Kate," he started, "we could sure use your talent here, if you're interested." Roger's face was relaxed, but his eyes were tense as he called me by my first name, something I didn't often hear from him.

Ma glanced at me with a slight smile. "That would be great, Kate. What do you think?"

In my heart, I knew the answer, but I couldn't get the words out. This is where I wanted to be, where I knew I belonged. I looked from Ma to Roger. Then I smiled, nodded my head, and said, "Yes, I'll do it." It was an instant decision, but I knew it was the right one. A need and an opportunity came wrapped together, and I wanted to be the one to fill both.

Ma and I celebrated at home, and the next day, I called Sister Edward Joan.

"Glory be, Kate. I'm not surprised. We'll miss you. Remember, dear, don't hide that light!"

A warm sensation came over me as I smiled into the

phone. There would be lots to think about before the end of the year. It didn't happen the way that I'd planned, but I finally began my career in journalism.

PART TWO

CHAPTER 12

Ma and I attended "Coffee with the Editor" together the following Monday. We needed a larger table as several women from town wanted to congratulate me on my new position and welcome me home to Hawthorne. Their sentiments—some spoken, some communicated silently—were all the same.

"This means a new future for our newspaper and for our town."

"It will be good to have you women involved and representing all of us."

"Thank you for your courage!"

Throughout dinner that evening, and long after, Ma and I talked about the possibilities this opportunity presented. Ma was always a strong, independent woman. Until Liam died, she saw her role as that of a wife and mother. Things would be different from here on as she got back to being the independent person she used to be. She had earned a college degree, an accomplishment not common among women of her generation. She had been active in social and political causes, both in college and in her younger years in

Hawthorne. Now she had the opportunity to get back to those interests.

For now, I agreed to follow current events and get to the root of community rumors, and I knew there were bigger opportunities ahead.

Ma decided to add an editorial approach, developing a column called "A word from Eleanor." We would present our ideas to Roger. With two Hurleys on board, he would not be able to overrule, but we wanted his support.

The next morning, after a cup of coffee in Ma's office, we approached him together and presented our plan. To our surprise, he was supportive, citing the increase in subscriptions after some of Ma's initial articles and her success with the Coffees. We talked about some of the logistics and decided that writing a column once a month might be a good way to ease into the new format. That way, Ma could still help with the usual reporting responsibilities and continue the follow-up on other current stories.

We also discussed the year ahead. Roger was scheduled to step down as Liam was to take on the senior role January 1st. Now Ma was in Liam's place. I knew she had some concerns about losing the expertise provided by John's and Roger's years of experience. We would need some link to the paper's history.

Ma quickly rose to the challenge of her plan. "A word from Eleanor" appeared on the first page of *The Times.*

Welcome to a new point of view from your local publication. For those of you who don't know, there's been a change in staff at The

Hawthorne Times. *Sadly, we lost John Powers to a heart attack two weeks ago. John was a man of integrity, dedication, and fervent ambition, and he is irreplaceable. Like all of you, we will miss him greatly. Although it will be a challenge to fill his shoes, my daughter, Miss Kate Hurley, has agreed to step in as our new assistant editor. She will combine her years of experience in journalism with her knowledge and love of our community. It will be a privilege and a pleasure to have her at my side.*

The recent change to a female majority on The Times *staff is new for Hawthorne, but it's not at all new for the publishing industry. As far back as the 1600s, women played integral roles in the publishing industry.*

The first printing business was founded by a woman, Elizabeth Glover, who emigrated from England to Massachusetts. Her husband died during the journey to America, and she took over his business in 1638. She was the first of many successful women in the publishing industry over the next two hundred years.

In fact, Ben Franklin had a female partner, Elizabeth Timothy, who was the first female publisher and editor in America. Together, they operated the South Carolina Gazette.

Female journalists were among the first to report on the Revolutionary War, including Anna Zenger, who received instructions from her husband, who was imprisoned for libel. His case, along with other events, prompted our founders to incorporate freedom of the press into The First Amendment.

Today, our First Lady has her own regular column and has written for numerous publications.

Many of the brave women before us were not recognized because they were forced to work under the cover of a male family member's name or assume a male pen name to allow their work to be published.

Fortunately, Kate and I do not have to fight such obstacles. We promise to honor the heroic efforts of these women and all in the profession of journalism. We Hurley women will contribute to the pages of The Hawthorne Times *independent of outside influences. We promise to relay the news to you in a thorough, fair, and unbiased manner. It is a new day for Hawthorne, and we are proud to be part of its future.*

Ma and I discussed her first column, realizing there was so much more to say.

"There will be many opportunities ahead of us," she said as we shared a hug.

We agreed that it was a good introduction—so good, in fact, that it didn't require Roger Ferguson's approval. It went into Thursday's edition, left column, front page.

I continued to report on the daily stats, but my role quickly expanded, facilitated by the national news that made headlines all over the country. On April 12, 1945, President Roosevelt, our beloved FDR, our thirty-second president elected four times, died.

That news comprised a special edition of *The Times*. Roger's contribution to the report touted Roosevelt's accomplishments, especially the development of the New Deal, Social Security, and his work in bringing together unions, big-city organizations, varying ethnic groups, and other entities in support of the Democratic Party.

My focus was on Mr. Roosevelt's valiant battle with polio

and his establishment of the treatment center for polio in Warm Springs, Georgia.

Ma zealously seized the opportunity to describe FDR's widow, a woman who was an American politician in her own right and one of Ma's heroines. Having served as First Lady for twelve years, she had many accomplishments, and as Ma pointed out, she did it while raising six children. Eleanor's personal life was challenged by the deaths of both of her parents before she turned fifteen, by living alongside an overbearing, interfering mother-in-law, and by her husband's personal and public affairs.

After FDR was stricken with polio, Eleanor gave speeches and appeared at campaign events in his place. She was a controversial First Lady who sometimes openly disagreed with her husband. With a mind of her own, she reshaped and redefined the role of First Lady, and she advocated for the increased roles and rights for all females. She would make her own place in history, even after the death of her husband, and as a role model for all women, including journalists, who wanted to take a meaningful place in society. Ma and I would talk about her often.

CHAPTER 13

I went into *The Times* over the weekend to organize my office. I brought a few treasured books and propped them up on the side table. I supported the books with the bronze bookends that Da had given me. One of the bookends was an Irish harp, the other a Celtic knot. On the opposite end of the table, I set a photo of our family and another of me and Da. I also brought in a picture of my *Champion* students at Saint Anne's. It was one of them holding the NSJ Award. Next to it, I placed a small, wooden plaque, a gift from Sister Edward Joan. It was a phrase I would read every morning, "Don't hide your light under a bushel basket."

A sensation of warmth came over me as I surveyed my new—*my own*—space. I ran my hand over the polished, honey-oak surface of the desk and added supplies to its single drawer. I fixed a cup of Earl Grey and began to review my calendar. I swiveled in my chair, thinking that this is what I had wanted for so long. Soon my euphoria was struck by reality as I saw John's file cabinet, its drawers stuffed to overflowing.

I waited until the next weekend to come in and tackle his

files. I discarded anything more than a year old. The rest I sorted according to topic—society stuff in one pile, local news stories in another, and national news or politics in a third.

There was a file in the back of the bottom drawer labeled *Kill File*. "Hmm." I wondered what I might find here, guessing that it would be full of dead stories that never made the news, so why keep them? These were stories John had written, but for one reason or another, he, or someone else, decided not to publish them. The first few stories were old news that never amounted to anything, but I sat up quickly as an intriguing title caught my eye—"Small-town Brothel with Big-time Clients."

A chill went down my spine as I leaned over my desk and opened the file. The small town was only identified as a "community about thirty miles northeast of Hawthorne." The big-time clients were not identified by name, although John, or someone, had penciled in some initials and question marks here and there. The article had been written three years ago, and as far as I knew, it was never mentioned in any newspaper. It told of an arrest that did not appear to be prosecuted, and there were no reports of other follow-ups.

I silently wondered, *Do I dare find this small town or try to decipher the initials? Is this a way to start my journalism career? Should I even discuss this with Ma?*

I hid that file in the bottom drawer of my desk for inspection at a later date, curious as to how much Roger knew about it. After three years, what's another few days or weeks.

On Monday, Ma and I came to the office together. I did my usual statistical write-ups and then pulled open my bottom drawer. Just as I was reaching for the file, Roger walked by on his way to lunch, accompanied by the sheriff and Frank Peterson, Hawthorne's mayor. I wondered if it was business or pleasure.

"Good morning, boys," I offered. They nodded in unison as Roger looked my way.

I closed my drawer and went to Ma's office to join her for lunch. "Where do Roger and his cronies go for lunch?" I asked. "Have you ever been invited to join them?"

She laughed as she looked at me. "No. Roger always says he's going for a business lunch. It's a wing of his good ol' boys' club, you might say. You can bet we'll never see them at Emily's."

We went home for lunch and returned to the office, then Ma left to host her Editor's Coffee. After she left, I got in my car and headed northeast in search of a "small community." According to the map, three different towns fit the distance and direction of "thirty miles northeast." I proceeded down the road. Spring was in the air, and the scent brought back many memories as I traveled between the fields of sprouting alfalfa and sorghum. The thought of a brothel in this tranquil area was incomprehensible.

The first town was Bickford, a familiar place since I'd

been there with Uncle Joe once when he went to shop for tools and building needs. There wasn't much here—a hardware store, a bank, and a small dry goods–grocery store... the usual necessities for a small town. The homes in this little place were wood frame, two-story structures. All were painted white, beige, or soft gray. I certainly didn't see anything that might serve as a brothel.

Next on the map was Hunter Creek, about seven miles down the road, another little burg that supported only a few businesses. There was a feed store that brought in farmers from all around. Just down the street was a clinic building that housed the doctor, dentist, and a small pharmacy. The central building in town was the Methodist Church. There was also an elementary school whose graduates had to be bused to the high school in Clayton, the next town on my list. A quick drive through Hunter Creek's neighborhood revealed a collection of homes similar to those in Bickford.

I was beginning to think this was a wasted afternoon, but I continued toward Clayton, the largest town on my list, though the population wasn't much more than three hundred. The little "downtown" was two blocks long, the main building being the post office on the corner. The library was situated on the other end. In between were the dry goods store, a meat market, and a small hardware store. I parked the car to stretch my legs and take a stroll. The post office and the businesses were slow, and the library was almost empty. *Hmm... no brothel prospects here.*

Returning to my car, I drove through the area of Clayton

homes. They were much like the Bickford and Hunter Creek neighborhoods. One had a compact sign in the window indicating that beauty services were available. I circled back around and started for home.

As I drove back down the diminutive business street, I saw what looked like Sheriff Richardson's car. I wondered if his jurisdiction extended down this far, or if other interests brought him here... perhaps the hardware store? Trying not to be conspicuous, which was almost impossible in such a small place, I parked around the corner. I didn't have to wait long before I observed the sheriff coming out of the hardware store carrying a large bag. Nothing suspicious, but I made a mental note and started up my car.

As we devoured Ma's meatloaf that evening—it was the best—she told me about her Coffee. She'd heard some heartwarming stories about local boys who were overseas and received more news about the ambulance services, nothing much that would make exciting headlines.

After supper, we had tea and retired to the living room, each with our respective books, mine being that old Victorian novel, *Jane Eyre*. Ma was reading a new best seller, *The Robe*.

I got up twice, setting my book down as I went for more tea. Waiting for the water to boil, I gazed out the window over the sink and pulled my old cardigan tighter around my shoulders. "What stories lie in the darkness?" I asked myself.

The next day, I decided to tell Ma about the brothel story.

I couldn't keep it to myself, and I wanted to know if she had ever heard anything about such businesses in the area.

"Bloody hell, Kate! There were tales about that three or four years ago, but nothing ever came of them. Surely, not in the paper. I think the town was Clayton. And you wouldn't believe the names that were attached to the story. The hottest names in town were being thrown around. Nothing ever came of the story as I guess no one could prove it."

I agreed to bring the file home so we could study it together and perhaps take another drive.

It was a busy week at the office. Roger had to attend a town council meeting and his quarterly meeting with other county editors, a group that met to share information about new publishing tools, printing devices, and news sources. Some of the men shared more than others. All of them wanted to be recognized for having the best paper in the county. Ma will be facing a challenge when she takes over next year and tries to find a way to join their circle.

Meanwhile, she and I worked on our stories in the office in the daytime and probed the brothel file in the evening at home, often staying up until midnight. We reviewed the map showing communities east of Hawthorne, and we guessed at the initials penciled in the margins of the draft article.

"HR... could that be the sheriff?" I asked. We always just called him Sheriff or Sheriff Richardson, and his friends called him Rich.

"I hope these aren't who I am thinking. It could be a

council member who ushers at our church." Ma sighed as she looked at me.

A third set might indicate a publisher from one of the little communities "east of here." And I shuddered to think about it, but some unidentified references might be pointing to Roger and to the Hawthorne mayor.

The look in Ma's eyes faded, and she shook her head. "Kate, this story was probably killed because it might implicate a few well-known men in town." She paused. "But it could devastate the innocent bystanders. There are lots of stories that would make sensational headlines for a day but ruin lives forever." She glanced at me and then continued, "I always ask myself, 'What would Liam do?'" She bit her bottom lip. "I wonder if it's still going on."

"Perhaps there's a resource in Clayton," I offered. "One of the homes that I saw had a sign indicating that it serves as a beauty shop. If it's anything like Hawthorne's beauty shop, it could provide lots of gossip."

Ma knew a couple women who lived in Clayton who might get wind of the latest news, but how would she approach them? "Maybe it's time to take 'Coffee with the Editor' on the road… just for a time or two, never to really depart from Emily's."

Once our articles went to the printer on Thursday, we decided on a little road trip to check out the communities. Ma was welcome wherever she went, and we started at Lori's Beauty Shop. Ma didn't know Lori, but it wasn't uncommon to drop in and ask about her services. She could size up the shop to see if she recognized any of the ladies and check if there might be a corner to fit a table for coffee.

Sure enough, one of the customers recognized her and waved her over, introducing her to Lori and other women in the shop. "Ladies, this is Ellie Hurley, the new coeditor of *The Hawthorne Times*."

"And this is the assistant editor," Ma said as she introduced me. We realized that we were already the subject of local gossip, and the women wanted to know more. Thus, a Coffee in the Corner was a welcome idea. In fact, that would be the name of Ma's Clayton meeting—"Coffee in the Corner."

Friday was a busy day for the beauty salon, so it seemed to be a good choice. The ladies with appointments could come in a little early or stay after their appointments to talk with Ma. Lori offered to provide a small table for the corner and put on a fresh pot of coffee. Ma would bring some little treats from Emily's.

On Monday morning, Ma approached Roger with her plan.

He paled and even twitched at the mention of Clayton. "But Ellie, you seem to be getting plenty of input from Emily's, and that end of the county is well covered by the *Clayton Courier*."

"Really, Roger?" She raised one eyebrow. "This won't take away from my Coffees or the *Courier*. It will give us some good connections to events we might not otherwise see in print."

"That's just it, Ellie. We get enough news right here in town, you know... uh... things our subscribers want to know, things they're interested in. I don't think we need to go out of town."

"You know, Roger, people go out of town for many things, thinking they don't want all of their business known in town."

When Roger grabbed the corner of his desk, Ma realized that she'd hit the nail on the head. She knew Roger was over a barrel, and Roger knew she wouldn't budge. The announcement was in the next edition of *The Times*. Two weeks later, Ma held her first "Coffee in the Corner."

Lori had put a flowered tablecloth on her corner table, and it was far enough from the salon chairs to allow a little privacy. It wasn't much different from the Coffees she held at Emily's—similar stories about the boys away at the war, local social notes, and other information people wanted to see publicized. Several ladies turned out just to chat with Ma. Some came to share condolences about Liam, while others wanted to congratulate her on her role with *The Times*.

"Not much more than local gossip," she told me later. "Not much was going on in the rest of the town, either, especially for a Friday night, but I'll be back."

CHAPTER 14

At her third Coffee in Clayton, Ma received her awaited lead—a rumor about Hawthorne's mayor. She shook her head and swallowed hard as she relayed the gossip to me. "According to my confidante, Mayor Peterson used to visit the brothel and had 'rescued' one of the workers. Supposedly, he is still supporting her and her child."

Ma knew Josie, the mayor's wife. "It makes me sick to think this could be going on. How can a man be so stupid, so selfish? Josie's a lovely woman. They have three children, and Josie is always busy helping at school or church." Ma's voice cracked as she continued, "I hope it's not really him, but I think we've pretty much confirmed the rumor that there's a brothel somewhere."

Ma looked at me, or maybe through me, and in a faraway voice said, "Liam once told me, 'You hear so much about your neighbors and your community, and then you confirm it and filter what is appropriate for publication, beyond what sells newspapers.' You know the golden rules as well as I—confidentiality, judgment, discretion. In a small town like Hawthorne, your integrity, your career, your business... in fact, your livelihood… can be made or destroyed by one bad decision. Liam was ready for this, Kate." She paused, raised her eyebrows, and said, "Are we?"

I knew the rules well. I had taught them to my students. "You have the credibility, Ma. I hope I can earn it. At least we don't have to worry about being one of the 'good ol' boys,' and our closets don't have skeletons."

Ma took a deep breath. "Yes, you're… oh, God, I hope you're right. And I hope that's enough."

Ma did the altar cloths first thing Saturday morning and then left for a walk. She was gone almost two hours and then went to her room upon her return, explaining that she needed time to think. She remained subdued throughout the weekend and seemed to revive a bit when Monday morning came around. I offered to drop off the altar cloths, but she insisted on doing it herself, stating she had some free time on her calendar.

I went to the office around nine. Ma didn't arrive until almost eleven. She made a few phone calls and then headed to her Coffee at Emily's. We didn't hear any more rumors about the brothel, nor did we talk about it any further.

Spring wore on and we moved into summer. The news of the day took precedence. The war was coming to an end. Germany had surrendered in April. The Allies bombed Japan. Hirohito announced Japan's surrender on August 15.

Ma lamented that Roosevelt didn't live to see the end of

this war, but neither did Mussolini or Hitler. World War II was a costly, bloody war with the United States losing more than four hundred thousand men.

The Labor Day picnic was a chance to celebrate and welcome home the survivors. We sat with Roger and his family. At the sound of the microphone tapping, I glanced over at Ma at the other end of the table. We both winced as Mayor Peterson began, "Welcome, ladies and gentlemen of Hawthorne, and welcome to our guests from other areas."

Ma reached for her iced tea and looked back at me, both of us knowing that a greeting from this mayor would never be the same.

CHAPTER 15

The people of Woodland sponsored a fall festival the first weekend in October. It had always been their tradition to put on an *Oktoberfest* to honor the residents' mostly German heritage, but they had canceled their celebration the last several years. With a backdrop of the red and gold leaves and a chill in the air, this year's festivities focused on a cheerful and patriotic theme. The menu included hot dogs and potato salad in place of the old bratwurst and kraut offerings of previous years, and the music was a collection of traditional American pieces to express the festive postwar mood.

As usual, the beer flowed freely and oiled the robust spirits of the younger fellows in attendance, but the bickering and brawls of St. Paddy's Day were not repeated. Some, including young Howard Richardson, overindulged. Richie, as everyone knew him, was now old enough to drive and thought he had the world in his hands, though on this night, he should never have had the wheel in his hands.

As he headed away from The Grange, alone in his car, he swerved across the center line and hit another car head-on, causing major damage to both cars but, thankfully, only minor injuries to himself and the occupants of the other car. Richie was cuffed and taken away by the deputies.

The sheriff was at Roger's desk the next morning when Ma arrived.

"Why, hell's bells! Fancy seeing you here this morning, Sheriff."

"Good morning, Ellie," said Roger and the sheriff in unison. Her business partner looked down at his desk while the sheriff flinched and squirmed in his seat.

Ma wasted no time or words. "I hear Richie had an accident last night. Is he doing all right?"

"Well, thanks for asking, Ellie," said the sheriff, "he'll be fine. That boy has such bad luck."

"Bad luck?" She paused and raised an eyebrow. "I heard that luck was well oiled at the Woodland festival. Sounds like your son should never have been driving."

"Oh, he had a couple beers, but he was okay to drive. Don't jump to conclusions."

"Sheriff, I've overlooked a lot of things, but this time, your son was a danger. He could have killed someone."

"Ellie, please…" Roger looked up as he moved forward in his chair.

"Sheriff, for the sake of your son and the others around, you'd better see that he gets off the booze. If not, his running afoul of the law won't be covered up by our paper—or anyone. His problems will only multiply."

The sheriff raised his voice, "What do you mean, Ellie?

My son is not a drunk." His face was turning red. "He just needs to learn how to handle it. All men go through this stage."

"Call it what you want, Sheriff, but something has to change. Your son needs help. There are ways he can address his problems, and the sooner the better."

Ellie marched to her office and waited for the sheriff to leave, then she stomped down to Roger's office, blocking his door with her small frame.

"Roger Ferguson, how long can you let this go on? That boy could have killed someone, and no one is making him responsible for his actions. It's just criminal. The sheriff might continue to sweep this under the rug, but our paper publishes enough details about infractions of the law that it makes people take responsibility."

"Ellie, you don't understand the politics of doing business in this town."

"I understand a lot more than you think I do. There's politics and there's professional journalism. In a small town like Hawthorne, the newspaper serves to hold people accountable for their actions, and you are ignoring the actions of Richie Richardson. I know you cover up a lot of stories that involve your friends, and you hide things that should be addressed. The good ol' boys' club around here needs to find some integrity."

She started to walk away but turned back to Roger. "And about that good ol' boys' club," she said, forcing a smile. "I think it's time they get to know this good ol' girl."

"Sure, Ellie." Roger clenched his jaw as he nodded. "Sure."

As Ellie went back to her office and sat down to write up the accident, her shoulders sagged. She gazed at her son's picture and asked, "What would you do, son?"

She wrote down the facts that I had obtained from the deputy who had been at the scene. "I spoke with him while the sheriff was visiting Roger. The deputy told me that Richie was clearly intoxicated and that he'd written out a ticket for a DUI. Whether the ticket made it into the records or not he wasn't sure, as tickets went into a file for the sheriff's signature. Only tickets signed by the sheriff appeared in the paper's 'Weekly Arrests' column."

Ma and I could wait to see if it showed up, or Ma could write up what we all knew to be the truth. She chose the latter approach, though she knew Roger would give her an argument about it.

Later that morning, Roger came to her and asked to see what she had written. She didn't feel obligated to give it to him, but she knew there would be hell to pay if she didn't. Ma invited him to sit down and review it with her.

Roger's jaw tightened and his color slowly reddened. "Ellie, you don't say it, but your comments imply that Richie has a drinking problem. That will not only be a problem for Richie but for the sheriff, too."

"I realize that, my friend, but some innocent people could have paid the ultimate price when they met Richie on the highway. Next time, luck might not be on their side. I'm not trying to punish Richie or the sheriff, but I'd like both of them to see that something has got to change. Young Richie needs to change his habits."

Roger, still flushed, returned to his own office and picked up the phone.

With her article about Richie's accident still waiting for support from Roger, Ellie started to work on her monthly column, this month's topic venturing into new territory—the history of brothels in Iowa. She knew it would never see print, but she also knew it would get some immediate attention from her partner. Brothels weren't new to Iowa. They had been around for many years. Everyone knew of their existence, but their locations were well disguised. As for the patrons, no one knew for sure, but there were many rumors. Ellie couldn't wait to see Roger's reaction.

Once she had completed her column, she carefully placed it on the corner of her desk and went to work on other news. Knowing Roger would see it when he came back to discuss Richie's story, she knew he'd be broaching that topic soon. But Roger didn't approach her that morning, and he was out of the office the rest of the day.

When Ma arrived at Emily's that afternoon, her usual table was set but the chairs were empty. She took her seat and worked on some notes while she sipped her coffee.

She looked up as I arrived. "A quiet day? Not much going on? This is the first time no one showed."

"I might have a clue about that." I told her, "I bumped into Roger, the sheriff, and the mayor while I was running some errands at lunchtime. I was going around a corner as they were heading into the tavern. I overheard their laughter at a comment from Roger." I rolled my eyes. "He was saying, 'Those gals will never know what hit them.' They were up to something. Maybe it wasn't a coincidence that no one came to your Coffee today."

Ma and I thanked Emily and bought two slices of her pound cake to take home for dessert. Ma said she had some things to do, so I headed home to start supper. With a pending storm, it looked like a good night for chicken and dumplings and Ma's favorite buttered carrots. The pound cake would make a good ending to the meal.

Ma went back to the office and made a phone call. Walter Curtin was the editor of the *Clayton Courier* and a member of the County Publishers' Association. She called to talk to him about her "Coffee in the Corner" meetings at Lori's.

"Nice to hear from you, Ellie. I understand you're bringing some new blood to *The Times*. How's it going over there?"

"Couldn't be better, Walter, but it's a struggle at times. We sure miss John Powers. He was so devoted to the paper, and he was a good man. My daughter, Kate, has decided to come on board to try and fill his shoes."

"Well, welcome to the industry. I am sure you have a lot of talent to share."

"Thank you, Walter. I will do my best. Liam always took such pride in his work and consistently talked about the need for integrity in journalism. I try to keep that in mind at all times as I work on stories for *The Times*."

"Your son was known for his principles, Ellie. Your understanding of that will serve you well. If there is ever any way I can be of help, just let me know."

"Well actually, Walter, I wanted to talk to you about one of my activities. Perhaps you've heard that I have been conducting meetings to give citizens a way to bring news to *The Times*. My Coffees—both in Hawthorne and now one there in Clayton—have been quite successful. I didn't mean to step on any toes in your area, and I am wondering if I could share the news with you when something comes up in your town. You'd be surprised at what the ladies share in the beauty shop."

"Kind of you, Ellie. Great idea."

"And Walter... um... Walter, do you fellows share any stories at the County Publishers' meetings?"

"Not stories usually, Ellie. We mostly talk about new printing processes or the cost of paper and ink. Often, we just shoot the breeze."

"Perhaps I could drop in on a meeting sometime."

"I don't see why not, but you're going to have to deal with Roger about that. You know, it's always been a group of men, but you're in the business now. Better see what Roger has to say."

"Thanks for your support, Walter, and have a nice evening."

Ma came in just as I was mixing up the flour for the

dumplings. She had that gleam in her eye that told me she was scheming about something.

Over supper, Ma explained her morning confrontation with Roger and the sheriff and her call to Walter Curtin. "Walter was a good friend to Da and to Liam. I've known him through social or school activities, and he sounded very supportive. I think he might be helpful. A way to get to know the other county publishers, too."

"But Ma, what do you think Roger is up to, and why do you think no one showed up for your Coffee this afternoon?" I asked.

"Be darned if I know. I can only act on what I do know. At least I can hold my head high, but… " She shook her head. "Maybe I'll give Mary Conlon a call tomorrow. Remember her? She attended my first Coffee at Emily's." Ma looked down at her hands. "She lost her son, too, last year. I think he was in Germany. Well, she gets around town and might have wind of whatever happened today." She glanced back up at me and said, "As Liam always said, he wasn't in this business to make friends, even though he had friends everywhere he went. Oh God, I miss that boy." Her chin quivered, and her voice cracked with this last comment.

"He was right, Ma. We can't take sides. I used to tell the girls working on *The Champion* that people should read an article and not know if you are friend or foe of the characters or whether you side with the issues. It's a fine line to walk, and not everyone abides by that principle."

We finished the dishes and retired to the living room, Ma

with *The Robe* and me with *Miss Eyre*. It didn't take long for Ma to nod off, as she'd had a long day, starting with her usual delivery to the church. I didn't know how she did it all, but she seemed to thrive on the distractions right now with Liam always on her mind.

When Ma arrived at the paper the next day, she walked past Roger's office. "Good morning, Roger." His head was bent over some papers on his desk, and he gave no reply. She slowed her pace but continued to her office, immediately noticing that her column on the brothels was gone and the article on the sheriff's son was in its place with some notes on the borders. Shortly thereafter, she heard the front door slam and knew that she was alone in the office. She gazed at Liam's picture and whispered, "I think this is going to be a long day, son."

Why not start with a friendly voice, she thought as she picked up the phone. "Hi, Mary. I haven't seen you in a while. I've missed you at my Coffees. They've been quite popular—that is, until yesterday. It was the first time I had empty chairs. Not much news in town?"

"Well." Mary sounded hesitant, but then continued, "I heard from Karen… who heard from Maggie… Oh, Ellie, Roger Ferguson told Maggie that he didn't think we should share any secrets with you, that he wasn't sure you could handle our confidences. I know I shouldn't believe him, but Karen said that Maggie thought he sounded angry. We didn't know what to do."

"Really?" Ma held the phone out for a minute. "Thanks, Mary. Hopefully, people know me better than that. Perhaps I'll talk with Maggie. Yeah, and Roger, too."

Maggie agreed to meet at Emily's for lunch after Ma finished up with her articles for the week's edition, starting with the article about Richie Richardson. Roger had marked it up, suggesting numerous changes, and had clipped a note to it asking her to see him. She surmised that either he wanted to pull the article or whitewash it to the point of nonrecognition. Ma wasn't ready to settle for either.

With a couple hours to spare before meeting Maggie, Ma decided to take a walk. She headed to the park where she used to take me and Liam on warm afternoons to feed the ducks. There were young moms doing the same thing today. She listened to the laughter of the children and the chatter of the young mothers, talking about the schools and about vaccines for their children. Their conversation made her think of Liam's letter. Ma wished she had met his girl, especially since Liam thought she might be the one for him. She wondered what their future might have been. Ma looked upon these young mothers with admiration and hope. It reinforced her courage to do the right thing for the community.

She followed the path around the pond, breathed in the country air, and reflected on the changes life had thrown at her. She didn't anticipate life as a widow, without a son, and no grandchildren so far. Ma certainly hadn't expected to become the editor of *The Times* but found herself enjoying the newspaper business. It was a challenge, but it was rewarding. Even though she was always involved in the community, she didn't expect to be its voice in the weekly paper.

Ma was feeling melancholic, but she wasn't unhappy with her lot in life. She had her faithful daughter home with her, and her best friend spoke from the pulpit every Sunday. Trusting in God, she knew He had a plan.

Just before noon, Ma headed to Emily's to meet Maggie for lunch. She found Maggie, prompt as usual, sitting at her favorite table in the corner. Emily's chicken pot pie hit the spot as she listened to Maggie and waited for her to reveal her conversation with Roger. As it turned out, he hadn't been very direct, but he made it clear that he thought Ma's followers should avoid sharing any unpopular items of news with her. The one topic on which he *was* clear was the sheriff and his son.

"Ellie, I know his motives aren't in anyone's best interest. We all know that. He just wants to be the one in charge, and I think you're threatening his status. I can see it now, and I think others can, too. You're doing the right thing, and I'm sure your Coffees will be busy again soon."

After a second cup of coffee, Ma thanked Maggie, said goodbye to Emily, and returned to the office.

Roger was back at his desk, and as she passed his door, Ma stuck her head in and said, "I'll be back in a minute."

Before she went to see Roger, Ma sat at her desk for a few minutes with the door closed. She thought about the moms in the park and reflected on her previous conversation with Kate about not hurting innocent bystanders. She felt that this was one time when not pushing the issue would be riskier than facing it head-on. Ma rose from her chair and marched down the hall.

Roger was no longer alone. The sheriff was at his desk. Roger looked at the sheriff, then waved her in.

"Good afternoon, gentlemen."

They nodded in unison before a long pause.

Ma began slowly, "Sheriff, I ask this out of concern. What's the latest with Richie?"

The sheriff peered at the floor and replied, "Not much news, Ellie."

As Ma glanced at the papers in her hands and then at the sheriff, her tone softened. "I don't want to hurt you or your son, Sheriff, but Richie could have hurt himself or someone else—or worse. Surely you see that."

The sheriff, still gazing at the floor, nodded. "I guess you're right, Ellie. I'll see what I can do."

"Well, I've got until Thursday to send this article over to the printer with this week's edition," Ma said, waving her papers. "I would rather not do that, Sheriff, but if I have to, I will."

Roger's jaw was tight, but he said nothing.

"I need to talk to you later, Roger, about my Coffees at Emily's. It appears as though my audience is dwindling."

"Yes, and I need to talk with you about your latest... uh... *proposed* column."

Ma paused and looked from Roger to the sheriff, then headed back to her office without further comment. She didn't see either of them the rest of the day and left the office early, stopping by the parish office on her way home. Father Declan was meeting with someone, so she picked up some notes he'd assembled for the next Altar Society meeting. She waited a while, but he seemed to be quite involved with the parishioner.

I was having a cup of tea by the fire when Ma came in. Her shoulders sagged and her steps were slow. At first, I thought she might be ill, but she peered at me with a tiredness in her eyes.

"Kate, my dear, there is so much more to this work than writing a story. I hope we're both up to it." She sat down without removing her coat.

"Give me your coat, Ma, and I'll fix you a cup of tea. The water is still hot, so it will only take a minute."

We dined on leftovers and passed the evening in relative silence. Ma retired early, and I read a few pages from *Jane Eyre*.

Roger was at his desk when she arrived at the office the next morning, and without looking up, he barked as she walked by, "Get in here as soon as you can, Ellie."

She hung up her coat, put her purse in her desk and, nodding her head, stared at Liam's picture for a few minutes before she headed down the hall. The office still bore the overnight chill, and she shivered as the floor creaked under her shoes.

Ma had barely entered his office when Roger growled, "Have you lost your mind? Where did you come up with this story?"

"Just doing some research on topics of interest... things pertinent to Iowa's history... perhaps exploring some little-known issues."

"Well, I think this should go into the Kill File. It's not appropriate for our community paper. It's a cock-and-bull story if I ever heard one. Why don't you stick to stories of interest to the ladies in our community?"

"On the contrary, Roger," she said slowly. "I think a lot of our ladies—and gentlemen—would be interested in this topic. There's a lot they could learn by my doing a little research."

"Ellie, really? You're creating enough trouble by focusing on the sheriff's son. Why go into this topic?"

"Well, Roger, I could set it aside for a while, but I'm quite certain there's a lot to be gained by exposing this issue. I think it hits closer to home than some people would like it to, and mind you, I plan on doing a little more research on the brothels. I also intend to keep a close eye on the facts related to Richie's DUI and to ensure that there is a follow-up plan."

Roger clenched his jaw and got up, as if to usher Ma out of his office.

She didn't budge. "If I might broach another topic, I

spoke with some of the ladies who usually attend my Monday Coffees. They said you have discouraged them from coming down to see me at Emily's. If their words are accurate—and I believe they are—your comments are bordering on slander, and I'd like to hear no more of it. Don't forget my place with this paper. We don't have much time left under the current arrangement."

Ma started to leave Roger's office when she remembered her discussion with Walter Curtin. She turned back to face Roger and said, "Oh, by the way, I talked to Walter Curtin yesterday. I've always respected his work with the *Clayton Courier*, and I thought it would be good to get together with him as a professional colleague and continue to keep in touch. He was open to my joining a publishers' meeting… even said something about accountability."

Roger, jaw agape, offered no response.

Ma walked back to her office, smiled at Liam, and sighed. "There's more than one way to skin a cat."

She pored over her work for a couple hours and then left for a little lunch at Emily's. When she saw her friend, she winked at her and told her to plan on a good turnout for next week's Coffee.

CHAPTER 16

"Hi, Ma," I called as I entered the back door. I could hear her talking, but she didn't answer me.

When I walked into the living room, she quickly said, "Well, my Kate is home, so I must go. It's been nice talking to you."

I inquired about the caller, and she stammered a bit. "Just one of the la… people from the Altar Society." Ma sounded strange. I was puzzled but let it go.

"So how was your day?" I asked.

"Argh! Men are such strange creatures, and some of them are so predictable. I can't imagine Liam would have been like that, and your da wasn't, at least in my presence. Some men sure don't want women privy to their world. They seem kind of threatened or even intimidated."

I smiled as we both shook our heads. "At least Mike Cunningham is not like that. I had supper with him tonight."

"His father was never like that, either. He and your da enjoyed many years of friendship and confidences as our family lawyer."

I continued, "Emily's lamb stew was delicious. I would

love to get her recipe." I glanced over at my mother. "But let me tell you why I met with Mike. The word around town tomorrow will probably be that we are dating. Not so, Ma."

"Oh, dear, I did think it was a social outing." Ma gave me a half smile with one eyebrow raised. "He is a nice lad, you know."

"I had heard a rumor that something was amiss at the hospital… that something was going around about the recent inspection."

Ma's eyes grew steely. "Why, hell's bells! That might explain why I never see Lil Cauley much these days. She and Jim must be worried sick." Jim was Ma's cousin and the director of Hawthorne's hospital. His wife, Lil, had been a nurse when they married but had since spent more time with the hospital auxiliary.

"It's just rumor right now. I heard about it when I was at Perkins' General Store getting some flour. I was in the back aisle, and I don't think they knew I was there. But Jimmy O'Brien was talking to Earl Connors. Anyway, I told Mike. He hadn't heard anything, but he said he'd try to get some information without raising any suspicions."

"Ha! That's hard to do around this town. Hard to keep any secrets in Hawthorne."

"Yes. People even share stories that aren't true… like my being with Mike tonight. People will probably have us engaged, especially if they saw me having coffee with him last week, too. And the ladies will have a time with my seeing Paul—at the same time, too. I really don't have feelings for either of them." I laughed. "My prince charming just hasn't come along yet."

"Maybe you're being too picky, Kate. Your head may be outweighing your heart, dear girl."

"You might be right, but perhaps I just have too much going on right now. I'll know when the right one comes along. You know, I sometimes find myself comparing the guys to our Liam. He was a pretty special guy, even if he was my brother. I can just hear his laugh. His voice had that Irish lilt, and his eyes sparkled when he laughed. And he always looked you in the eye. Not a lot o' guys like him."

I paused as I saw tears form in her eyes. "Oh, Ma, I'm sorry. I just got carried away with memories. I didn't mean to upset you."

She shook her head and opened her mouth, but no words came out. She swallowed as she dabbed at a tear. We sat in silence for a while, and then Ma got up and walked upstairs.

I went into the kitchen. Ma had left some dishes in the sink, as if she had been interrupted by her phone call. The hot water felt good on my hands, and my thoughts wandered. Sometimes Ma puzzled me with her evasiveness, but she had always held some things close to her heart. Maybe I did, too. Perhaps everyone does. I guess that no matter how well you think you know someone, we never really know what is going on inside their heads. Even family—those with whom we've lived all our lives—carry secrets in their hearts.

Sleep came slowly as I thought of the events and conversations of the day. There is so much to follow up on, and I knew Ma needed my help with some of her things. I had barely gotten to sleep when I heard old Rosie outside my window. That darn, old bird never overslept.

Ma was already puttering around the kitchen, and I could smell the coffee. It was Friday, and she'd be leaving early so that she could pick up the altar cloths. I threw on my old robe and went down to the kitchen. I wrapped it a little closer as the chill in the house confirmed that fall was in full swing. Remembering Ma's tears from the night before, I wondered what the holidays might bring.

After a little breakfast, Ma headed out the door. She paused and smiled as she inhaled the crisp, fall morning. She was in bright spirits, even though she was looking forward to a hectic day. We were both happy to see the weekend coming and enjoyed the change in the weather.

I went upstairs and pulled a wool skirt out of the back of the closet as I prepared for my day. Later, when I got to the car, I was happy to have the warm wool between me and the cold seat. I knew colder mornings were ahead and that soon I would have to go out and warm the car before my last cup of coffee.

The outdoor temperature seeped into the office, and I left my coat on for a while. The old furnace creaked as it forced out warm air. The smell of the heater and a cup of tea provided some welcome warmth. I pulled out some files for review.

As I wouldn't hear from Mike until at least Monday, I would have to dig into the town's vital statistics for some news. Reviewing the birth records kept me apprised of the families of old friends. The death records weren't usually surprising as the gossip chain spread that word rather quickly. My job would be to get details about the deceased and the information about funerals. I disliked approaching the families for this purpose, but usually they welcomed the opportunity to talk about their loved one and to share details about the funeral.

Ma didn't arrive in the office until after ten, saying that she got caught up in some of the ladies' activities at the church. They were putting together information about the fall dinner and needed an extra hand, which, of course, Ma was happy to lend, along with a little of her advice and expertise. She always came back after her Friday morning stops armed with a few tidbits of gossip. She also used this visit as an opportunity to resolve any rumors that were going around. This morning, one of the ladies had asked her about my seeing Mike Cunningham.

I laughed at that one. "What did I tell you?"

"I just let their imaginations go on this one." She smiled and shook her head.

Friday was followed by a crisp, fall weekend. Ma and I took a long walk, talking about the days and seasons ahead.

"Are you feeling up to some Christmas decorations this year?" I asked, glancing at Ma from the corner of my eye.

"Not much, really, but I guess we should have something for the neighbors to see."

"Maybe we could have Uncle Joe and Aunt Nell for Thanksgiving?"

"Sure," Ma said, nodding slowly, "and maybe their girls will come, too."

"And then there's Christmas…" She sighed.

"Let's talk to Aunt Nell," I offered, hoping Ma's sister-in-law would invite us to their house.

"And after that"—her tone brightened—"we start a new day at *The Times*."

Roger would step down after the first of the year, and Ma would try her hand at the helm of the paper. She held her head high, and her eyes sparkled as she talked about the challenge awaiting her. "It will be a new life for us and a new day for the paper… as soon as we get through the holidays."

When I arrived at the office on Monday, the phone was ringing. It was Mike, wanting to meet for lunch. He asked me if I could get there early and secure the table in the back corner.

"Of course, thanks." I watched the clock all morning as I read through all the vital statistics reports, filtering out the ones I had previously known through rumors and sorting them into births, deaths, marriages, and divorces. Funny how those four statistics seem to define our lives. So much happens in between those dates, but they encompass all there is to life, all that our descendants will read about us.

It was only eleven o'clock, but I straightened my desk and headed for Emily's. I walked the few blocks, taking in the chilly air and exercising my legs after a long sit at the desk. I made a beeline for the back table and ordered a cup of coffee.

Emily had a new helper today who introduced herself as Peggy. She was a short, dark-haired girl about twenty years of age. She seemed a bit timid, perhaps nervous on her first day on the job. She brought my coffee and offered cream or sugar. As I declined both, I wondered how long it would take for her to learn everyone's preferences. Probably not long at all.

When Mike arrived, we both ordered the chicken salad sandwich. It was one of Emily's specialties and was always on the lunch menu.

Mike's news was a mixed bag. "The hospital was reviewed by the state licensing board two weeks ago, and they needed to respond to some issues, but there's no word on what the issues might be. In fact, Doctor Leary took a couple days off, almost unheard of in his years here in town."

"The rumor is that he made a trip to Des Moines for some personal matters, leaving the new, young doctor, a Doctor Hagerty, in charge. That's really all I know."

Puzzled, we finished our lunch in silence. Afterward, we walked down the street together, crunching the leaves underfoot. Mike offered me a ride back to the office, but I opted to ponder the news with a walk. As we parted, I asked Mike to let me know if he heard anything more.

Ma was sitting at her desk when I returned to the office. Roger was in his office with the sheriff, the door closed. The floor still creaked beneath my shoes, but the office was warm.

The news from Mike kept eating away at my mind. Where could I get more information? Perhaps Doctor Leary would share some information when he got back into town, but that would have to be done through Ma.

At home that evening, Ma talked about her meetings with Roger and his irresponsible approach to sloppy publication. She looked up from the gravy she was stirring and said, "That man can't get it through his head that times are changing. It isn't the same old system that he's grown up with. I don't know how Liam got along with him or some of his old cronies." She beat the spoon on the side of the pan. "The people of our town deserve better, and I know we can give them better."

As we ate, I updated her on the hospital situation and told her I thought I'd try to reach Jan Haley.

"So Doctor Leary did go to Des Moines. Hmm... I don't know how to approach this one, Kate, but I think he might tell us in time. I just don't know when that time might be."

Together, we decided not to call Jan, lest it appear that we were trying to get privileged information. If we or the town needed to know, we'd find out when the "powers that be" decided to share the information.

The rest of the week seemed to drag as we waited to hear more. The only thing we knew was that Doctor Leary hadn't come back to work yet, not even by Friday. I saw Jan Haley at Perkins' General Store, but she was in a hurry and just said "hello."

On Sunday, Doctor Leary was at Mass, as was his new colleague, Doctor Hagerty. They were both friendly, but Doctor Leary didn't stay around long after Mass as he normally would have. His three children were there, all visiting from out of town. That event alone would sometimes rate a brief article in *The Times*, but we hadn't heard they were coming and weren't aware of any family celebrations. They sort of stood together at Mass, shoulder to shoulder, as if presenting a united front. Something was going on, and it seemed pretty serious.

CHAPTER 17

When Ma arrived at Emily's for her Monday Coffee, she had the usual ladies back at the table. Maggie Higgins wanted to share the news of the latest accomplishments of her daughter, Mary. Mary was a bright and studious young woman who took on difficult projects and challenges. Ma put something in *The Times* whenever appropriate.

A new addition to the table that day was Jan Haley. Ma encouraged her to wait until the others had gone. Jan seemed anxious yet hesitant to share. Ma ordered more coffee and offered Jan some of Emily's lemon cake.

"I think you know," Jan started, "that the hospital had its annual review by the state last week."

Ma nodded. "I heard that was going on. That must be a tense time for everyone."

"Yes." Jan paused and closed her eyes. "We all go on about our business, but you can feel the tension in the air. Anyway, I know something is amiss." She looked at Ma, shook her head, and bit her lip. "I don't know what, but I think it's serious. Doctor Leary was gone last week. He came back today, and he seems worried. I heard there are going to be some changes. Please don't tell anyone that I let you know, but I think you might be able to help somehow. Everyone trusts you, Ellie. Maybe you could talk to Mr. Cauley or sit in on one of his reports."

"Thank you, Jan." Ma reached across the table and took her hand. "I appreciate your concerns and your confidence in me." She smiled and said, "I'll see what I can do."

Ma walked out of Emily's with her head down and drove to the hospital. She sat in the parking lot and looked up at the entrance, a short flight of steps that led to double doors emblazoned with the words, Hawthorne Community Hospital. The painted words were fading, but they still hailed the town's place of healing. This small, brick building had been around since before Liam and I were born. Most of the town's younger generation were born in this hospital, and my da had died there. Now something was amiss behind those doors.

The administrator's office was dark, but Ma decided to visit the hospital anyway. The doors were always open, and there would be nurses around. As she entered, the smell of ether brought back memories of her previous visits. One of the nurses nodded at her, but Ma didn't go to the patient area. Instead, she walked down the other hall to the chapel.

The lights were dim, but there was always a candle burning near the altar. Ma sat in one of the four pews. She gazed at the familiar altar and said a silent prayer. Father Declan said daily Mass here. Visitors and family members sought a moment of peace and comfort here… sometimes in pleading or sorrow, sometimes in thanksgiving. Ma was familiar with every picture and every statue. She often took her turn at cleaning the altar and straightening the prayer books. It was a special part of the hospital.

Tonight, she prayed not for herself or a patient but for this little hospital. "Dear God, please let everything be okay. Whatever this crisis is about, let us pass through it and continue the work that has been so vital to this community."

After supper that evening, Ma sat in her chair with a recent copy of *The Times* in front of her and appeared to be examining every section of the page.

I broke the silence. "Ma, do you think we might change the layout of the paper starting the first of the year? You know, it would be a visible signal that *The Times* is going to be a new and different paper. Maybe even change the name of the paper?"

"I want people to know there's a new management in charge, but I plan to keep the name the same for Liam's sake. I don't want people to forget that this was his dream, and his blood will carry on. But, yes, it might be a good idea to change the appearance." She went back to her book.

"Everyone knows we'll be in charge, but I thought it might be a good idea."

"Sure, sure. Maybe I'll talk to Hector after the layout goes to him next week. He might have some ideas for us."

Ma rose and took care of some things in the kitchen. She cleaned out the refrigerator, dumping anything more than three days old, her usual cutoff point for leftovers. Every now and then she would pause and stare out the window, wiping her hands on her apron. There wasn't much to see in the dark, but she appeared to be gazing beyond the dark. At nine o'clock, she turned off the light and headed upstairs. "I'll see you in the morning. Sleep tight."

When I went up around ten, her light was still shining under the door.

The next morning, Ma was up early, dressed in her navy-blue, wool suit. When I came down for coffee, she was almost ready to leave. She said, "I'm going to call Jim Cauley this morning and see if I can meet with him. Maybe I can find out what's going on at the hospital and what we might share with the town. Too many stories going around. I think it's time for some truth. But you know Jim. Not much of a talker. He might not want to tell me anything, but I think he'll want to squelch the rumors. Wish me luck."

"I know you'll do well." I gave her a hug. "Jim's not only your cousin, he's also your friend, Ma. He knows you well and trusts you, certainly more than he trusts Roger Ferguson."

"Thank you, dear. I couldn't be doing this without you." She smiled, held her head high, and marched out the door.

Ma was the first one in the office that morning and immediately turned on the heat. She left her coat on for a while and put some water on for tea. By the time Roger came in, the office had reached a comfortable temperature.

He stopped in her office with his coffee. "You look nice today, Ellie. Anything special going on?"

"Not really, Roger. This old suit is warm and comfortable and feels great when I have to leave the office for a while. You might see it often this winter."

Roger shrugged and went back to his office. Ma waited until 9:30, then closed her office door and rang up the hospital, asking for Jim Cauley. He wasn't available, but the secretary agreed to ask him to return her call. Ma had plenty of other projects to occupy her morning but kept an eye on the clock. Jan had thought there might be a meeting today to let some of the hospital nurses know what was going on.

Shortly after ten, Jim returned her call. "Good morning, Ellie. How're you doing over there?" After some brief comments about her new job, She asked about the hospital. He sighed and invited her to meet in his office after lunch. "You might as well hear it from me."

"Sure… thanks, Jim," she said, though she was not so sure at all.

Jim had attended The Academy with her and Father Declan. After college, he came back to Hawthorne and married his high school sweetheart, Lillian Brady. Lil was from Woodland and was a year or two behind Jim in high school. After high school, she went to nurses' training in Des Moines. Jim and Lil had been involved with the hospital ever since they got married. Lil was often at the hospital to participate in activities. She was there the day my da died, and she was probably there during the recent inspection.

Ma arrived promptly at one o'clock. Jim's face was pale, almost gray, as he rose to greet her. Doctor Leary was there, too, looking as if he hadn't slept in days. "Come in, Ellie." Ma took a chair and sat in silence as she glanced from Jim to Doctor Leary.

Doctor Leary was a short, little man, a bit on the heavy side, and balding. Today, his usually sparkling eyes were red and tired.

"Ellie, you know we had this state inspection last week," started Jim. "Their inspectors examine every aspect of the hospital—go through patient records and look at staff information, including licenses and such. Well…"

"Let me explain," broke in Doctor Leary. His hands trembled as he rubbed his temples. After a pause, he continued, "I bungled up, Ellie. You see, I'm supposed to renew my license every two years. Well, in '42, I simply let the date slip by. It was a busy year with the flu, and so much was going on with me personally that I forgot to renew on time. Somehow, I got away with it, and when my renewal date came around in '44, I didn't get a renewal notice. I figured… well, I guess I figured I'd better not call it to their attention. I should have owned up to it right away, but I didn't know what would happen." He bowed his head and wrung his hands. "I don't know what in bejesus got into me." His cheeks flushed, and a fine sweat appeared on his brow. "Paperwork has always been secondary to me."

Ma, her mouth slightly open, looked from one to the

other. "Uh, what, I mean, what..." She couldn't even form a question.

Jim, shaking his head, replied, "Doc has been fined and put on probation with the state medical board. The hospital has had to come up with a plan to review his old cases since 1942, and we have to get another doctor to cover while Doc is on leave. Trust me, Ellie, no patients have been harmed. You know that Doc always does what is best for his patients, but the State of Iowa doesn't have that same amount of trust."

"Bloody hell," Ellie muttered quietly as she put her hand to her lips. "What is the plan?"

Jim explained further, "Doctor Hagerty, the new, young fellow from Omaha, can take over, but he'll require help. He's been with us for the last six months, and he's very talented, well trained, and sincere, but he doesn't know the town and all the folks Doc has been treating for years. We also need to bring in an outside doctor—one or two—to review Doc's patient records." Jim rattled his fingers on his desk. "Doc will be off duty for at least six months, possibly a year."

"Ellie, this whole feckin' mess is inexcusable," interjected Doctor Leary with a trembling lower lip. "I'll do anything I can to make it up to Jim, the hospital, and the town."

"With Doctor Hagerty taking all the calls, both here and in the office, word will get out fast," Jim continued. "It's not something I want to see in the paper, but I think it would be better coming from you, with the truth, in as kind a way as you can think to do."

"Who else knows?" Ma queried, glancing from Jim to Doctor Leary.

"Lil, of course, and I've asked her to work with Madeline, who oversees the nurses. The other nurses and staff know that something is up, but they don't know what. Doctor Hagerty has known since the state people were here."

Ma looked from one to the other and asked, "Do you have a plan for letting people know? I want to do what is best for everyone. I'll work with you on this."

"Thanks, Ellie," said Jim. "I'm glad you're on at *The Times*." He took a deep breath. "I know you'll handle this with care. Can we get back together in the morning? Back here in my office, say nine?"

"Sure, I'll be here."

Jim and Doctor Leary rose together, both nodding and mumbling their goodbyes.

Ma ambled slowly down the hall and through the front doors, those same doors that welcomed her for the birth of her children and consoled her when Da was dying. Hawthorne Community was more than a building. It was life and death to our town.

That evening, Ma was more quiet than usual. She picked at her dinner and washed the dishes without any conversation. Afterward, she roamed about the house, touching some of Liam's trophies and picking up some of our family pictures. Every now and then she would stop and peer out into the dark evening, pulling her cardigan tightly around her. She declined a cup of tea, so I fixed one for myself, picked up a book I'd recently chosen at the library, *A Tree Grows in Brooklyn*, and took my chair in the living room.

The next morning, Ma was up, dressed, and ready to leave the house before I came downstairs. "I have things to finish early today, Kate. I'll be on my way."

"Be careful out there, Ma," I replied, "it looks a little slippery." I watched her as she pulled through the drive and headed onto the road leading to town.

No one else was at *The Times* when Ma arrived. She immediately turned on the heat and warmed the kettle for tea. The light was already on in her office. Did she forget to turn it off when she left yesterday? Something seemed amiss, but she didn't know what. She had come back to the office after her meeting with Jim Cauley, but she didn't make any notes about their discussion. The only evidence she left was a note on her calendar about today's meeting at the hospital. As she rummaged through her top drawer, she heard the back door and Roger's footsteps lumbering down the hall.

"Good morning, Ellie. I didn't think you'd be here yet."

"I got up with the chickens. I have a busy day. What brings you in so early?"

"Just the usual," he replied. "Let me know if there's anything I can help with. You know, we do need to meet more often now that we're approaching the end of the year."

"Sure, Roger... uh... thank you."

Clearly, something was up. Roger must have gotten wind of the hospital issue. Ma doubted that he had much real information, but he seemed to know that she was in on something.

At 8:30 a.m., she straightened her desk, locked her drawer, turned off the desk light, and walked out of the office, saying goodbye to Roger as she passed his door.

Arriving at the hospital early, she stopped by the chapel. Father Declan was there, putting away the holy oils and candles. He had just administered Last Rites to a dying patient.

"An elderly farmer from Bickford who'd been in the hospital for several weeks. That new Doctor Hagerty was there. He seems like a nice, caring, young man."

"Yes, I have heard that," Ma replied. "Pray for him, Father Declan. It must be a challenge to live up to Doctor Leary's reputation."

"It's good he's here. Doc carries a big load, and like us, Ellie, Leary's no spring chicken."

Ma took a seat in one of the pews near the altar and pulled out her rosary. Father Declan nodded and went on his way. Ma's shoulders sagged as she sat for a few minutes longer.

At 8:55 a.m., she headed to Jim's office. "May I come in?" Ma asked as she poked her head around his door.

"Of course, Ellie. The docs aren't here yet. I understand this was a busy place last night."

"Yes, I just saw Father Declan as I passed the chapel."

Ma took advantage of the wait time to ask about Lil and the hospital staff.

"Lil is fully informed on the issue. Other hospital staff seem to be questioning the results of the review and Doc Leary's sudden withdrawal from his routine. I'm sure the nurses have some suspicions. I need to get some word out to them soon, and I think Lil can help."

"How is Lil taking this?" Ma asked.

"Not so well. I don't think she's been sleeping much. It will be good for her, as well as us, to have her participate in the resolution. Ah, here come the docs."

Jim and Ma rose together as the doctors entered the office. Both doctors sported red-rimmed eyes. Doctor Leary looked down at the floor, while Doctor Hagerty glanced from Jim to me. Doctor Hagerty appeared to be about thirty and was almost a head taller than Doctor Leary. He had deep-blue eyes and a head of dark, curly hair. He nodded as Jim introduced us, then took a seat, stretched his head back, and rolled it from side to side.

"Let's begin," said Jim. "I brought you each a copy of the report, and I thought we might go through it line by line. Then we can put together a plan."

After about an hour, they came up with a strategy. Doctor Leary would contact the state licensing board and get the renewal process started. He hoped not to have to take an exam. Both he and Doctor Hagerty would work with the state to get one of their doctors to assist with record review, and Doctor Hagerty offered to call one of his contacts at the college to see if there might be a resident available who would be interested in some clinical hours. Jim would discuss a plan with Lil to inform the staff. Ma's job, of course, would be to draft an article for *The Times*, hopefully ready for release on Friday.

Doctor Leary's shoulders sagged, and his eyes were teary as he left, thanking them all for their support. Doctor Hagerty said a quick goodbye over his shoulder and headed down the hall. Ellie agreed to bring a draft article over to Jim as soon as she could get it ready.

On her way back to the office, Ma stopped in at Emily's to see if there was any new gossip, especially about the hospital. The place was quiet, and Emily was busy in the kitchen.

"Hi, Ellie."

"Good morning, Em. It's pretty quiet in here. I guess I don't get in here in the middle of the morning very often."

"I'm glad for the lull. It's been busy," said Emily as she wiped her hands on her apron and stretched her back. "Even your partner was in here today, talking around to everyone."

"Really? Roger?"

"Yes, I don't know if he was looking for you or what."

"Have you got a minute for coffee? You look like you could use a rest."

Emily filled two cups and took a seat near the kitchen. "It feels good to sit a while." She paused. "You know, Ellie, I don't much like that man. It will be so good when you're on your own over there. People trust you. I can't much say the same for him."

Ma didn't get much news other than to hear that Roger was snooping around. He must have heard something, but Ma wondered who else was talking. Who would know?

She returned to the office and started working on her article. It took her a while to get started. When she heard Roger enter through the back door, she peered at Liam's picture, turned her papers over, and picked up the list of daily statistics that were waiting for me.

"Hi, Ellie. You were out for a while."

"Yes," she replied without looking up. "I guess it helps to know most people in town, doesn't it?"

"Yes, Ellie, that makes your job easier. When do you want to meet? We need to start planning for next year."

Ma nodded her head, still not looking up. "Yes… sure. How about early next week?"

"I have some time today or tomorrow." He tapped his foot as he stood in her doorway.

"No, next week is better for me. I'll check in with you later."

Roger bit his lower lip and nodded. "Let me know what's a good day for you."

"Sure thing, Roger, and would you close the door as you leave? I need a little quiet."

He hesitated for a moment but then did as she asked.

Ma looked over at Liam and sighed as she returned to her article. She remembered his words, *"It's our job to accurately, honestly, and objectively inform the public without shaming, blaming, or defaming the subject."* That rule was certainly appropriate in the case of our revered hospital. She finished her report and called Jim. He was available and asked her to come over right away.

Just as she was putting on her coat, Roger called out, "Do you have a minute, Ellie?"

She paused and sighed. "It will have to wait 'til later. I'm on my way out."

At the hospital, she and Jim reviewed her article. "I don't always give my subjects a preview, but in this case, I want to know if you are comfortable with it."

"Thanks, Ellie, and your words are perfect. This hospital means so much to our community. You've told them what they need to know. I don't think you'll create any alarm. Thank you."

Now, to assure that Roger doesn't intervene, Ma had an idea. As soon as she returned to the office, she stopped by and offered to meet with Roger in the morning.

CHAPTER 18

The house was warm and the table was set when I arrived home that evening. Ma was humming an Irish tune and putting a tuna loaf in the oven.

"Hi, Ma." I smiled as I hung my coat in the closet and returned to the kitchen. "Something tells me you had a good day."

"Well, sometimes sad events produce good opportunities."

"So what's the event and what's the opportunity?"

Ma told me about the hospital review… at least, I think she told me all the details.

"I'm surprised word hadn't leaked out," she said.

"Me, too," I replied. "I guess this town can keep a few things quiet."

"It's driving Roger crazy. It's not like him to offer to meet, especially to discuss moving forward with handing things over to me." Her eyes had a mischievous sparkle. "I think this is a good time for me to start dealing directly with the print room. I'll talk to Hector about a new format. No approval needed if it's from me."

We ate slowly as we discussed ideas for working with

Roger and moving forward with Ma's role at the paper. After supper, she jotted down some things in her notebook while I did the dishes.

Once the kitchen was clean, I went into the parlor, picked up my book, and relaxed in my favorite chair. Ma resumed her Irish tune and walked about, looking at Da's old books and some of Liam's pictures.

She was nodding and talking to herself. "I need to get my name in the editor's section. Most people know I'm there, but they don't know that I'm about to take over. I have a faithful following with my Monday Coffees, but I need to get more into my column."

I didn't try to butt in. Her mind was moving quickly. It was good to see her enthusiasm, just like the confident woman I'd always known.

I went to bed before Ma that evening and barely heard her trudge upstairs after midnight. When I came down in the morning, she was in the kitchen, dressed in her navy-blue suit, drinking her coffee.

"Well, I've decided that I will approach Roger respectfully, but I'll be ready to take charge if he doesn't agree. I'll let him know that I am not asking for his opinion or agreement, and I plan to take the hospital article directly to Hector myself tomorrow."

With a chuckle, I replied, "I know you, Ma. You'll hit him right between the eyes."

The office was already starting to warm up when Ma arrived. Roger's light was on.

"Good morning, Roger," she said as she stepped into his doorway. "I can meet this morning, if you're still available."

"Sure. Let's meet around ten o'clock. I have a few things to finish up here."

"Great. How about my office?"

Roger paused and finally nodded. "Um… okay."

Ma proceeded to her office, straightened her desk, and organized some papers into three neat stacks. She placed her hospital article in the drawer, then reviewed her notes from the night before. Having a few minutes left, she fixed a cup of tea.

Roger stepped through her office door at ten o'clock sharp. "Before we start, Ellie, I just want to know if you've heard anything about what's going on over at the hospital. I understand they had their certification review, and there are some problems."

Ma took a deep breath. "Well, yes, I talked to Jim Cauley yesterday."

"What did he have to say? We need to be in on this, Ellie. It could be a good story."

Ma's jaw tightened as she stared Roger in the eye. "Let's talk about our changing roles first."

"But, Ellie, this is important, and we need to get something to Hector by noon tomorrow."

"Right, Roger. And that will happen."

His eyes widened. "So you're working on something?"

"Roger let's take this one step at a time. First of all, in order for me to be prepared for January 1, I will be doing certain things on my own. I've been working with this paper and in this office for several months now, and after all, I know most of the people in this town, most of the resources that I need."

"Sure, Ellie, but there are ways of doing things that you only learn after years in the business. When there's an important story out there, we need to be the first ones to get it out to the readers. If we're not 100 percent accurate, we can correct it later." He sat on the edge of his chair, holding his palms upward. His oily, dark hair hung over his right eye.

Ellie swiveled in her chair, and she glanced at Liam's picture. "Not everyone works the same way, Roger. Our credibility is of utmost importance." She turned again to peer at Roger. "We need to be responsible not only to our readers but to those about whom we write. For instance, our little hospital is vital to us and to a community beyond the town of Hawthorne. It is a resource for life and death for people beyond our own borders, and its reputation is golden. Roger, this is not just a story for the purpose of selling newspapers."

Ma looked him in the eye as she continued, "Yes, I have talked to Jim Cauley. I have worked with him and the doctors and put together an article that I will take directly to Hector this afternoon. I'll be damned if you're going to change one word or decide on its location in the paper. As a matter of fact, all of my articles will go directly to Hector from now on. That will be one step in the direction of my new role. We can discuss other changes later." She glanced down at the papers on her desk.

Roger sat with his jaw gaping. "But, Ellie, I... I ... "

Ma glared at him with steel in her eyes. "There'll be no buts this time, Roger."

After a moment, Roger rose, stepped toward the door, hesitated, then stomped down the hall.

Ma wrapped her hands around her warm teacup, closed her eyes, and sighed. As she looked over her shoulder at Liam's picture, she knew her son was smiling.

On Friday, the article about the hospital, exactly as she had written it, was positioned on the lower half of the front page—not to be sensational but to emphasize its importance. After reading it, Ma exited through the back door and went down to Emily's.

The place was abuzz with comments, questions, and statements of concern. Several people approached Ma. She confirmed what she'd written in the paper but also noted that Jim Cauley, the doctors, and the staff appeared to have it under control and that care would be provided as usual. She received several thanks and pats on the back.

"When there's more to share, I'll do so," said Ma. "But meanwhile, please be assured that the hospital will continue to provide excellent care as usual. Everyone there is taking part in the resolution."

The phone was ringing as she returned to the office. It was Jim Cauley.

"Good morning, Ellie. Thank you. Your article was great. The nurses and other staff seem to be reassured that everything will be all right. I'm wondering if you might consider coming over and talking to the staff. I believe you could be a spokesperson as part of our team and give some credibility to our plan. I meet with them next Wednesday. Think you can join us?"

"Sure, Jim, I will make time. Do you want me to prepare anything? And what time would you like me to be there?"

Ma immediately took out some paper and started making some notes. Then she called Jan Haley and asked if she could meet at Emily's after she got off work. "I need to know what rumors might be going around or what the nurses might be worried about. Could we get together and talk?"

Jan arrived at Emily's right after four. She had also attended The Academy but was about ten years younger than Ma. She was a pretty woman, sturdy looking, with short, blonde hair and deep-blue eyes. She sighed as she said, "I could use a cup of tea. It's been a long day, but I was so pleased to get your call and to read your article in the paper this morning. The nurses have been so worried. They haven't known what was going on."

"Well, I'm glad I could help. I asked you to join me for tea because I will be attending a staff meeting with Jim Cauley at the hospital next Wednesday. Could you fill me in on the concerns of the nurses?"

They chatted for almost an hour, and Ma left with a pretty clear idea of what she would talk about next week.

On her way home, she stopped at the church and picked up the altar cloths. Father Declan was putting something away in the sacristy. "Hello, Ellie. How are things going?"

"I've finally crossed a bridge today, Declan, and I believe our Liam would approve. Did you read *The Times* this morning?"

He smiled broadly. "Of course, first thing. Great job! Didn't sound censored, either. I'm so proud of you, and I am sure Sean and Liam would be, too. Congratulations." Father Declan's words and calm demeanor always gave Ma comfort and courage.

It was my turn to have dinner ready when Ma arrived home. She deserved a break. Since it was Friday, I didn't have many choices, but I knew Ma would be happy with anything she didn't have to fix. Grilled cheese sandwiches and tomato soup hit the spot.

"Kate, my dear, I think I made some real progress this week. We can start to do some planning for January."

Ma and I spent the weekend making plans for the holidays. She invited Uncle Joe and Aunt Nell for Thanksgiving, and Aunt Nell, in turn, invited us to their house for Christmas. Ma got a little teary as we talked about some of our holiday recipes, especially if they had been Liam's favorites.

"I sure miss him, Kate, but after last week, I think he's here with us in some way. And somehow, together, we can fulfill his dream, don't you think?"

"Yeah, yeah... sure." I tried to smile, but my shoulder muscles tensed. Ma was gazing out the window. "Sure, Ma. Liam's dream."

Ma invited Father Declan for Sunday dinner and fixed a pork roast and applesauce. She also made an apple pie. She hadn't made a pie in a long time, and the aroma made me smile. It was Grandma Cauley's recipe with raisins, walnuts, and, of course, cinnamon. The combination produced a warm, melt-in-your-mouth mixture. A few summers before, her recipe had won a blue ribbon at the county fair, and it was just as good today.

During dinner, she told Father Declan about her interactions with Roger.

"Well, Jaysus, Mary, and Joseph, it's about time. You're ready for the job." He smiled broadly. "You're ready for the whole shebang, Ellie. *The Times* will be much better under your guidance. Keep it up, dear friend. When is your official takeover date?"

Ma laughed. "January 1 is the big day. I've a bit of fear and trepidation, but I'll take it one day at a time. After this past week, I'm confident that I'm ready for it, but"—she sighed—"it won't be easy."

"I hear from everyone about how much they like your Monday Coffees and how much they trust you. The townspeople loved our Liam, but now they are ready and waiting for you."

"We'll trust that Liam will be watching o'er us." Ma bit her lower lip and looked away.

"Ready for pie?" I offered as her pastor put his hand on Ma's. I picked up the dinner dishes and started some coffee. While I was in the kitchen, I could hear them chatting quietly. I think Ma was crying as Father Declan tried to comfort her.

"No, Ellie, the pain will never go away. Sometimes the happiest of events will bring that pain to the surface. It won't go away, but you'll get better at dealing with it. It's the Lord's way of keeping us strong."

"Aye, but I so often wonder if I'll ever have a day without the ache in my heart. Why our Liam…" They grew quiet as I returned to the table.

The pie was perfect. Ma hadn't lost her touch. Father Declan even had a second, but smaller, piece before he had to return to the church.

"Thanks for a nice evening and a great meal, ladies." He gave us his blessing before he left.

CHAPTER 19

November passed quickly. Ma, and probably the entire town, awaited news from the hospital. She checked in frequently with Jim Cauley, and townspeople checked in frequently with her.

Her Monday afternoon Coffees were attended mostly by people asking if Doctor Leary was doing okay. They inquired about his absence from the hospital and wanted to know when he would return. Most people liked Doctor Hagerty, though he could never replace Doctor Leary. On the other hand, they questioned almost everything about the young resident who was assisting him. Even Jan Haley confided in me that the resident approached things differently than the other two doctors, but she noted that his patients did well. Things were otherwise calm at the hospital. The staff nurses were going about their routines as usual, and patient care was not interrupted.

We made it through Thanksgiving without much difficulty... that is, until Ma served the pumpkin pie. When she passed the whipped cream, she broke down and left the table, followed closely by Uncle Joe. Nell and I stayed at the table, silently, slowly eating our pie and sipping coffee. We could hear Uncle Joe and Ma talking in the parlor.

"Ah, Ellie, I miss him, too. The holidays won't be the same—ever—but we have to move on and trust God's will."

"I just don't know how to go on. First it was Sean, now Liam. My life just isn't the same, and it never will be. They both used to love the Thanksgiving meal, especially the pie. Liam always had seconds, even when he was stuffed. I used to laugh and tell him, 'You'll be as big as the turkey,' and he'd have it anyway."

When they returned to the table, Ma's eyes were red but she was trying to smile. No one else had anything to say. We cleared the table and did the dishes.

Uncle Joe went into the living room and picked up last week's *Times*.

"So, Ellie, will a new edition come out tomorrow?" he called out.

Ma dried her hands on her apron and walked into the living room. "Never has in the past, Joe, maybe next year. I find it hard to believe that two weeks go by without any news. I might do things differently, but it will be difficult to retrain everyone to work the day before Thanksgiving. Then we'll have the same issue at Christmas when it falls later in the week."

"You'll have your hands full, my Ellie, if you decide to stick with it."

"Oh, I have to stick with it, Joe." Ma smiled. "Not only to fulfill Liam's dream, but so much happens in this town, and people need to be honestly informed. That, in itself, will be a change. Besides, what else would I do with my time?"

"It seems to me that you'd be quite busy, what with this big house and your work with the church and other activities in this town."

"True. This old house needs quite a bit of attention from time to time, but I can put most of those things on simmer. *The Times* is my new priority. And having Kate here is such a help to me."

I looked over at Ma and smiled. She was such a strong woman, but I again wondered where I fit into her big plan... her big plan being my brother's dream.

The rest of the holidays went by more slowly. Fortunately, the hospital issues seemed to be resolving themselves. Doctor Leary did not have to take an exam. He was a good doctor, but not necessarily on top of all the latest theories in the medical books. Doctor Hagerty and the resident were fitting into the community with relative ease.

The one thorn in Ma's side was Roger. He tripped her up whenever he could, but Ma was stubbornly determined, and when she had her eyes on a goal, no one could stop her. Many evenings, she came home exhausted. Perhaps it was a good distraction from the loneliness brought on by the holidays.

We put up a small Christmas tree and strung lights around the front door.

"No sense taking the joy out of Christmas for anyone else." Ma sighed.

Several neighbors brought gifts over during the weeks prior to Christmas—mostly food, special recipes passed down within their families. Father Declan came by a couple times. Not being a cook himself, he enjoyed all the neighborhood offerings and, of course, a glass of sherry. We enjoyed a quiet dinner at home on Christmas Eve and then went to midnight Mass. A light snow fell as we entered the church with the bells sounding above.

When we came out in the wee hours of the morning, a full moon shone above and the new snow crunched under our feet. The white covering was romantic on Christmas Eve, but it made for a treacherous drive to Uncle Joe and Aunt Nell's on the twenty-fifth.

Their house was warm, and Uncle Joe was in a jovial mood as he led us in a few Christmas carols. Aunt Nell had plans for all of us in the kitchen. It was a good break to be with them. Ma smiled as Nell assigned her the task of preparing the gravy. It was another recipe for which Ma was famous. We stayed with them just a few days as Ma felt the need to get back to the paper.

We attended the New Year's Eve party at The Grange in Woodland. The Cunninghams were all there, and I enjoyed dancing with both Mike and Peter. Paul Kelly was there, too, but he spent most of his time with another young woman.

Doctor Leary joined us. "Ellie, I look forward to the new day at *The Times*. You and Kate will be such an asset to our community." It was the most relaxed I'd seen him in a few months.

Doctor Hagerty and Doctor Lyons joined us, too. I had not previously met Doctor Hagerty or the resident, a young doctor from eastern Nebraska. Ma had told me that Doctor Hagerty was tall and dark-haired, but she hadn't mentioned that he was handsome. His dark hair and deep-blue eyes revealed some strong Irish roots, and his smile was shy but sincere.

He asked me to dance to one of my Perry Como favorites, "Sentimental Journey."

"I have heard a lot about you from Doctor Leary. I guess he's known your family for a long time. I'm glad to finally meet you." He had surprisingly soft hands for a man but a firm touch as he held me throughout the dance.

"He has been around a long time… brought most of the younger Hawthorne generation into this world, including me and my brother."

"I've heard about your brother, too. I'm sorry. It sounds as though he's been a big loss to you and to many folks around here."

"Yes, yes, thank you."

I visited with him and Doctor Lyons for the rest of the evening. We had much in common. Doctor Hagerty had gone to school in Omaha. Doctor Lyons, a thin, wiry, and boyish-looking guy, went to Iowa. It was reassuring to be with young, professional singles in our little town. Paul and his date joined us for dessert and the midnight toast. Before the evening was over, Doctor Hagerty had asked me to go to the cinema with him on the following weekend, and I gladly accepted.

Ma had circulated around the hall throughout the evening, talking with friends. Close to midnight, she had returned to our table. She joined in the toasts, but I could see the sadness in her eyes as she raised her glass. The year-end celebrations were filled with melancholy reflections but optimism about the future.

The sheriff was there with his son, Richie, both appearing sober and subdued. Roger and his wife sat with the sheriff, and he was his usual aloof self. Neither Ma nor I knew Roger's wife very well. She was never seen around town without Roger. She looked kind of frail, perhaps timid, wearing a black dress over a thin frame. I had never seen her socialize with any of the townspeople. Even tonight, everyone at their table appeared to be in a somber mood. The coming year, 1946, was going to be a new year for the Fergusons, too.

The next day, Uncle Joe and Aunt Nell came over for our traditional New Year's buffet brunch. Father Declan joined us as he had done in years past. Since the young doctors were new in town and on their own, Ma had invited them to drop by, too. Emily and her husband stopped in with some of her lemon cake and a bottle of sherry. It turned out to be a celebration of the new year as well as a launching for Ma's coming role with the paper.

We toasted the end of the war and the beginning of peace.

We toasted Liam. Father Declan said a brief prayer with a tear in his eye. Ma bit her lip and nodded.

We toasted *The Times*... out with the old and in with the new!

PART THREE

CHAPTER 20

It was snowing the first day that Ma was the editor in chief. The streets were icy, and it was bitter cold and windy, but a team of mules couldn't have kept her away from the office. She didn't have any appointments, but she wore her best suit and held her head high as she entered the building, turned on the lights, cranked up the furnace, and heated the water for tea.

Per agreement, Roger had cleaned out his office before the end of December, but Ma's space was just as she'd left it, or so she thought. She hung up her coat and rubbed her hands together. It was going to feel good to hold a warm cup of tea. She stared at Liam's picture and smiled. "Well, son, I'm here to carry on your dream. Your father and I are so proud of what you started, and I hope I never let you down."

Ma surveyed her office, feeling something was amiss, but couldn't see anything out of place. Roger already knew about the hospital issues, though he wasn't in on the meetings with Jim Cauley or the doctors. He also didn't have the contacts Ellie had with Lil and the nurses. Over the last couple months, Roger asked a lot of questions about the hospital and offered to join her at the meetings, but she declined his offers.

When she heard the kettle, Ma sauntered down the hall and fixed her tea. As she returned to the office, she saw it—her top drawer, which she'd kept locked, was slightly skewed, and the wood around the keyhole was scratched. The lock stuck a little as she turned the key, but the drawer opened. The folder with this week's articles was there, but the latest hospital update was missing. Even though she was sure she put it in the folder, she rifled through the rest of the drawer. It was gone. She could rewrite it in time to get it to Hector today but wondered what Roger might have done with it.

Ma paced around her office, stared at Liam's picture, and then traipsed down to Roger's office. He had cleaned it out completely. There was nothing on the shelves and the drawers were empty. Even the waste basket was empty. She went to my office. Nothing in sight.

Her jaws tightened as she marched back to her desk and began to sip her now-lukewarm tea. She thought to herself, *How am I going to deal with Roger in the future? He'll continue to be on the board of directors, and he owns half of the building. I can't just change the locks—at least to the outside doors. But to the office doors? Maybe so. And should I move into his old office or not?* It was larger, but she had grown accustomed to her current space, which had been Liam's office. It worked for him, but he was second in charge. *Do I need to make a statement by moving into a larger space?*

I entered through the back door, and Ma startled when I stuck my head in to say "Hello." I could tell she was distressed as I walked over and hugged her. "Congratulations, Ma, it's finally yours."

I stepped back as Ma shook her head and slammed her paper down on the desk. "Bloody hell! That man won't be leaving us alone! I think he had the gall to break into my desk." She told me about the missing article and asked if, by any chance, she had left it on my desk.

"No," I said, shaking my head slowly. "No, we discussed it, but you didn't give it to me. I don't think you even brought it into my office."

"This must be his farewell trick for me. I could call him, but I'd have to outright accuse him of breaking into my desk, even though that's what I think he did. I guess I'll begin a rewrite. That mean, old buzzard." Ma stomped down the hall, threw out her tea, and started over.

After a busy morning of getting the paper together, Ma and I went to Emily's for lunch. Em's New Year's specials were delicious, though probably made from leftovers. The café was busy, but there was one table left. The turkey noodle casserole did not disappoint.

Everyone who came into the café said hello to us and congratulated Ma on her new role. There was always a friendly atmosphere at Emily's, but today seemed especially lively and joyous, busy with folks starting out the new year.

Hector was there, eating with some of the local merchants. Ma thought it might be a good idea to let him know we would be cutting it close to get everything to him on time.

"Don't worry, Mrs. Hurley. Roger brought the article over this morning, so I'm sure we can get a paper together before the usual deadline."

"Roger what?" Ma held her breath and her eyes widened.

"Roger brought you an article? Um… could I stop over on my way back to the office?"

"Of course, anytime. I have to get some things from the hardware store, but I'll be back in the shop by half past one."

Ma smiled and made a little small talk with the other men present. She also stopped and said hello to one of her usual Coffee attendees, then returned to our table.

"Did you hear that, Kate?" Ma whispered, "I think I know what happened to my article. Can't wait to see it, and I'll set Hector straight on who determines what goes into the paper. The gall of that man!"

Ma was quiet as we finished our lunch. She didn't order dessert, even though Emily's lemon cake was one of her favorites. Before we left, she stopped to thank Emily for a great lunch and to assure her that she would be in on Monday for her usual Coffee hour.

Emily dried her hands and gave us each a hug, congratulating Ma on her new role. "It's going to be a new day in this town, Ellie, and I'm so glad you've got Kate here to help you. The Hurley women will be changing how things are done around here." Ma smiled and we all laughed.

We walked back to the office in the sunshine, cautiously traversing the glistening snow. Ma worked on a few other items for the paper while I finished up the latest demographics. It had been a busy week with two new babies and one death. Sadly, a young farmer had passed away on New Year's Eve. I had heard it was from pneumonia.

At 1:30 p.m., Ma donned her coat. "Well, I'm going over to see Hector. I'll let you know what gems Roger brought him this time."

Hector had just returned with his hardware purchases and

took them to the back room. "So, Mrs. Hurley, I understand you're officially in charge now. Congratulations." He shook Ma's hand.

"That's right, Hector. Thank you, and please call me Ellie. No need to be so formal."

Hector looked down at the floor as he nodded.

"So Roger brought you an article this morning?"

"Yes, first thing. You and he must have worked on it over the holiday. You're taking this job pretty seriously."

"May I take a look at it, Hector? We didn't talk about the final version, and I... I don't want to duplicate it."

"Of course, Mrs. Hur... I mean, of course, Ellie."

Sure enough, it was Ma's article. As she took a closer look, though, she noticed that it had some changes.

"I'll need to take this back to the office, Hector, and work it into the rest of this week's submission. Do you mind? I'll have it back this afternoon."

"Well, Roger said it was important, but I guess you're in charge, so you go ahead and take it with you."

"Yes, Hector, and yes, I'm in charge. Thank you." Ma smiled, took the article, and headed back to the office.

I could hear the anger in her footsteps as she stomped down the hall.

"Kate, you won't believe what that dirty, old buzzard did. I'm so glad that I caught it. It's my article, all right, but it appears to have minor changes—changes that alter the gist of the article. Jim Cauley is being painted in a negligent light, as is Doctor Leary. It's practically defamation, and it was submitted under my name. That dirty, old buzzard!"

Before Ma started over on the article, she called the locksmith. Once she completed her rewrite of the hospital article, she pulled out the other one she'd been planning for the first edition of 1946—"Greetings from the New Editor in Chief."

She and I had had several long talks about the future for *The Times* and had come up with a short-term plan. Now that Roger was gone, I had committed to one year as the managing editor–column editor. Hector would serve as the copy editor as had been his role in the past. We could go on that way for a while, but we knew we would require more help. We discussed hiring an additional person, perhaps a copyboy or maybe another writer, at least on Wednesday and Thursday when we're finalizing the week's submission. We decided to hold off on hiring until we evaluated our workloads and finances. We set the end of January as the deadline to assess the need.

Ma had outlined quite a detailed plan for her first year as editor in chief. She looked at all the requirements, responsibilities, and expenses of running the office, from the utilities to the staffing and contracts. She set financial, subscription, and personal goals for her first year and must have stayed up into the wee hours.

Her first official meeting with Roger and the board would be the middle of January, and she wanted to be totally ready with a plan that would overwhelm them. I doubted that Roger had ever done that kind of detailed preparation. If Ma needed to get approval for a loan to maintain the business, she would be fully prepared and, most likely, highly successful.

We had defined my role. I agreed to a full year, even though it would put my teaching career on hold and possibly limit my options for returning to Omaha. At the same time,

I was getting more comfortable back here in Hawthorne. I'd found more unattached people who were my age, and I was enjoying the newspaper work, although I longed for a little more challenge. I was confident that 1946 would bring that challenge.

Doctor Hagerty's invitation had been a bright spot, but he'd called back on Wednesday to let me know we'd have to go to the cinema another time. The new intern had received an urgent call and would have to be out of town for a couple days.

CHAPTER 21

"*Greetings and Happy New Year! As of January 1, Eleanor Hurley is the editor in chief of* The Hawthorne Times. *She welcomes her daughter, Katherine Hurley, as the managing editor. Both women are lifelong Hawthorne residents and have been working at* The Times *for the past year. Mrs. Hurley's son, Liam, had been a co-owner of the paper until he gave his life for his country on the soil of Germany in February 1945. It was a sad day for the Hurley family, but it was a turning point for Eleanor and a new day for* The Times.

"We welcome the opportunity and the challenge to serve our community and to share the news of the day in a timely, fair, and honest manner. We are committed to integrity and professionalism in journalism. And we are committed to the lifelong dream of Liam Hurley. We thank you for your trust and confidence and welcome your input at any time. It's a new year and a new day for The Hawthorne Times*!"*

The first edition of 1946 went to press on time, and every word was reviewed and approved by Ma. After taking it to Hector, she and I grabbed a quick lunch at Emily's and returned to the office to start on next week's paper. We talked about her plan as we walked down our narrow hallway. Neither of us wanted to move into the larger space previously occupied by Roger.

"What if we set his office up as a conference room, or perhaps a workspace where we can lay out each week's paper for preview," suggested Ma. "Of course, we'll have to change the lock on that door, too." She inhaled deeply and shook her head. "Ralph is sending a young fellow over from the hardware store in about an hour. I think I'll have him change all the door locks and our desk locks, too."

We arrived home a little late that evening but had plenty of leftovers to reheat. While they were warming, we toasted our new year with a glass of sherry. "To whatever comes our way in 1946!"

On Friday, we picked up our copies of *The Times* at the front door of the office and brought them to our respective desks. Everything was printed as planned. Ma swiveled in her chair and read her column aloud to Liam's picture, smiling from ear to ear. "I've done it for you, son!"

We went to lunch at Emily's and were greeted warmly by so many of our friends and neighbors with well wishes from all.

Doctor Leary stopped in to pick up a sandwich and came over to me and Ma. "Congratulations, ladies, and best wishes on this endeavor. I am so pleased and confident that you will give this town—this entire community—something to be proud of, something to trust."

After most of the others had left, the sheriff, who had been dining with some cronies, came over and shook Ma's hand. "Congratulations, Ellie, and thank you!" Then he lowered his voice and added, "You know, I didn't appreciate your butting in when you hassled me about Richie, but you made me face the truth about my son." He swallowed and nodded. "We addressed his problems together and... well, you've given me back my son." The sheriff beamed. "He's been sober for sixty days, and I couldn't be happier." He paused and continued, "As for the paper, I think you'll do a great job. If there's ever anything I can do to help, let me know. Best of luck to both of you."

We hardly had time to eat our lunch as everyone who walked in the door came over to greet us and wish us well. Ma was relaxed. Her chin was high and her eyes sparkled, reminiscent of years gone by. As for me, I felt suddenly taller, stronger, and ready for a new day.

We took the afternoon off. Ma stopped by the rectory and picked up the altar cloths. I couldn't see how she got that chore done every weekend, but she insisted on doing it. While at the rectory, she stayed for a cup of tea and warm wishes from Father Declan. She often confided in him about her plans and progress. As her pastor and best friend, he served as kind of a sounding board—or perhaps a stalwart of confidence—to reassure her that she was on the right track.

At home, we again dined on leftovers and then relaxed with our evening reading. Ma wandered through the house, browsing through the parlor, occasionally brushing off some of Liam's trophies and dusting the old family photos using the sleeve of her sweater. She had dry eyes and a satisfied smile on her face when she returned to the living room.

The weekend brought some fresh snow and bitter winds. We stayed in most of the time, except for Sunday Mass. Ma did her church laundry and cleaned out the refrigerator, trying to get rid of some of the leftovers. I did the other laundry and some badly needed dusting and vacuuming.

Together, we took down the last of the Christmas trim. Even the removal of the decorations didn't dampen Ma's spirits.

There were still many unknowns in the coming days and weeks, but between us, we had a plan and a direction, plus the support and trust of our community. Yes, it was a new year and a new day for *The Times*, but it was also a new purpose in life for Ma and, maybe, a new career for me.

The snow had let up by Monday, but the cars were moving slowly. Ma and I drove to the office together. It took a little longer to warm up the office, so we kept our coats on for a while. Something told me it might be a long winter.

Shortly after we got settled, Ma's phone rang.

"Hello. Good morning to you, Jim. Yes, we've got time this morning. Here? That would be great. I'm not much for driving on these streets. Perfect. I'll see you at ten thirty."

Ma called out to me, "Jim Cauley has an update on the hospital's review. Do you want to join us?"

"Sure. Did I hear you say ten thirty?"

"Yes. I'll bring another chair in here, but now I'm thinking that maybe I do need a bigger office, or we could convert Roger's old space into a conference room of sorts. Hmm …"

I made my usual calls to the county services, the coroner's desk, and the hospital to get the vital statistics from last week. Then I called the sheriff's office to check on accidents or arrests. Things had slowed down now that the holidays were behind us, but life goes on and the people want to know who was born and who died, as well as any kind of trouble in town.

Jim was right on time and in good spirits. He shook hands with both me and Ma. "I know I've said it before, but I am so pleased that you two are in charge. I think our town is going to benefit from your commitment. I liked your column in last week's edition, and I hope you'll continue to keep the community informed about your progress."

"Well, Jim," said Ma, "we hope to measure our success not only by the numbers and the increase in subscriptions, but also by feedback from the community, so your comments are always welcome."

Before we start, Jim, would you like some coffee?" I offered.

"That would be great. Thanks Kate."

"While I brewed a fresh pot, Jim and Ma talked about the holidays and the winter weather.

"According to the *Farmers' Almanac*, we may be in for quite a winter," said Jim.

"Oh, brr!" shivered Ma as I returned with the coffee.

"Well, let's hear the latest about the hospital," Ma started.

"It's good news, ladies. The medical society gave me an update on Doc Leary's follow-up. He's been submitting all the required reports and, as you might know, he doesn't have to take or retake any exams, which he's relieved about. And perhaps a bonus in all of this is that Doctor Hagerty might stay on with us. He was looking for a place to settle and develop a practice, and he rather likes the hospital and our community."

"Great news, Jim," Ma said. "I think Doctor Hagerty fits in nicely, and he and Doctor Leary seem to get on quite well. What about the young resident?"

"I'm not sure about him right now. Not sure if there's

enough work for all of them once Doc is back in business."

"I've heard a few comments," said Ma, "things like, 'He does things differently,' or 'He's a little too independent.' Perhaps that's just because of the theories he's learned from a different school or experience."

"Yeah, I've heard that, too. Maybe it's just his personality. We'll learn more in the next few months, waiting for Doc to return to practice."

As I listened to their conversation, I could see the product of the years of friendship. Jim's trust in Ma was obvious. Her experience with our town was such an asset, and she had a reputation for integrity. I was so proud of her.

Ma agreed to write another update to assure the town that the hospital was doing well and that its future was in good hands. It seemed a fitting way to start the new year.

Later that morning, we received a surprise visitor—Doctor Leary himself. I don't think he'd ever been in the office of *The Times* before. He tottered down the hall, peeking into Roger's office first, then into Ma's where she was busy writing.

"Well, good morning, Doctor Leary."

When I heard his voice, I was initially startled, but their conversation quickly assured me that it was just a social call... well, at least until Ma closed her door. He stayed about fifteen minutes and then started back down the hall. Before he left, he stuck his head into my office with a cheery, "Hello, Katie."

"Good morning, Doctor Leary." He brought me into this world and treated all my childhood illnesses, trips, and falls. He was there, too, when Da was ill and when he died.

"Congratulations. How are you doing?"

I told him how excited I was to be part of this new venture and how proud I was of Ma.

"Does this mean you're going to stay here in Hawthorne?"

"Quite possibly, at least for Ma's first year. I'm beginning to get comfortable being back here. Hawthorne's changed a little since I was growing up, but mostly for the better. More young people and things to do."

"I think our young Doctor Hagerty is pleased to see you here in town. I believe he'd like you to stay."

I felt a warmth rise to my face and didn't know what to say. "He seems like a very nice man, and I hear good things about him. I... I'm glad he's here to help out."

"Well, I hope I can convince him to stay on. I'm no spring chicken, you know, and one of these days, I might like to retire. Not too soon, though." He winked at me through his smile.

"I hope you'll be around to take care of us for quite a while. I can't imagine going to anyone else." I wished him good luck with everything as he turned to leave. As he strolled down the hall, I replayed his comment about Doctor Hagerty and felt a smile cross my face.

Ma had brought lunch for both of us that day, and we decided to stay in the warm office. We ate in the little back room where the tea kettle was.

"Well, Kate, having squeezed a couple meetings into my office, I think we'll need to make better use of Roger's old space. What do you think?"

"I can't quite see either of us using it as an office. It might be haunted!"

"Glory be, you might be right." She shook her head and laughed. "But I like the idea of a library or resource room. I think we need to subscribe to a couple other newspapers. Walter Curtin's *Clayton Courier* would be a good one, and maybe the *Des Moines Register*. The *Register* is very progressive and would certainly be a good model for us. It's time to get some broader ideas to keep us up with the industry."

"Good idea. We might want to check out the teleprinter, too, and get the Associated Press releases. Roger kept it hidden in his office, and, well, I don't even know what it does or how to use it."

"Kate, my girl, I think we have an exciting future," Ma said with a warm sparkle in her eye, "but first, I have to go over to Emily's for my Monday Coffee to see if we're missing out on any news right here."

Prompted by a phone call from Emily, I asked if I could join her.

Emily's was almost empty on this snowy afternoon, but there were seven ladies waiting at Ma's table. Emily had made her January special—fruit cake cookies. Somehow, the cookies tasted so much better than the original product, the *proverbial fruit cake*. They went especially well with afternoon tea, but today, we noticed an additional beverage at the table. There were crystal glasses filled with sherry. As Ma approached, all the ladies, previous Coffee attendees, stood and applauded. "Congratulations, editor in chief!"

Ma started to open her mouth but swallowed hard, momentarily speechless. Granted, they were a small representation of the town, but they were her faithful supporters and followers. Ma shook hands with each of them and then took her place at the table. I sat across from her, and Emily came over and joined us.

We talked about the weather and the forecast for more snow. We talked about the feel of the new office, absent any males. We talked about the war being over and how it had changed our town. So many losses. We talked about the new roles of women who had taken over their family businesses, many of whom are now being asked to step back into their household roles, and the others who needed to stay in the businesses. I saw Ma nodding, appearing to make a few mental notes as the ladies all shared their thoughts.

As we strode back to the office, Ma reflected on their conversation. "There are some voices out there we've not heard from—the ladies who are working in their family businesses. I'll bet they have a totally different take on things."

"Right, right, Ma. I'm sure they have a lot to offer."

Before we arrived back at the office, Ma had a plan in mind. "What about an evening meeting, something that starts after business hours or maybe even after supper? I'm not sure where or when we could meet, or if the working ladies would have time or even be interested. Guess we could find out."

Back in the office, she got busy on her hospital update. I finished up my vital statistics notes, and then I made another cup of tea. While waiting for the tea to brew, it struck me that this might be an opportunity for me.

I broached the idea with Ma. "Got a minute, Ma?"

She looked up from her writing.

"What do you think of me taking over the new meeting? I could meet with the business ladies, perhaps here in the office in the new conference room."

Ma paused only briefly, then replied, "Why, hell's bells, Kate! I think that's a grand idea."

"I don't have all the details in mind, Ma, but I can work on that and come up with an agenda."

I wandered down to Roger's office, soon to be called the conference room, and browsed around, considering some rearrangements. The desk would have to be replaced with a meeting table, one that would seat six or eight. We'd probably need to use folding chairs to fit a group and to make the table available as a work area during the day. And the art that had hung on the wall for years had to go. The blinds needed cleaning but were otherwise okay. Just a little elbow grease, and this place would be transformed. It would be fun to banish the ghosts and make this a product of the new management.

At home that evening, Ma built a fire and we sat quietly with our books, but so many thoughts were going through my head. Sleep didn't come easily that night, either, as I mentally rearranged Roger's office, found a new home for his desk, and put together an information sheet to distribute to the businesswomen. I decided that Monday evenings would work best for our schedule. I finally drifted off to sleep, despite details swirling in my head.

I arrived at the office before Ma the next morning, and by ten o'clock, I had my plan written up and approached Ma. I labeled the meetings, "A Word After Five." I stood tall as my mother reviewed my outline, nodding and smiling.

"Great plan, Kate. I think you can make this work. How soon do you think you can get it together?"

I immediately started working on a notice to advertise "A Word After Five" and compiled a list of places to distribute it. I decided to give each businesswoman at least two copies so they could share it. Then I went to work replacing the furniture in the conference room. In addition to furniture, it needed some new art. Perhaps something from home would be good.

The following weekend, Ma and I searched the attic. We came across several family pictures. After gazing at them for a while, we set them aside. I found a large picture of Iowa fields that was in sepia tones and had a windswept look, very peaceful.

I collected my finds and went to the office. It didn't take long to get the conference room together. I put a couple old pictures of Iowa on top of the bookcase, dusted everywhere, cleaned the blinds, and moved the teletype machine to the back corner. In no time, the conference room looked spick-and-span and very welcoming. Then I put out the notices. Now I just had to await the first meeting.

Emily assembled a tray of mini sandwiches and added some small mint cookies. I put fresh water in the teapot. Ma agreed to stay in her office. Perhaps she would come in to say "Hello," but the meeting would otherwise be my responsibility.

By ten after five, four ladies had arrived and were chatting away. They knew each other from church and their children's activities. Their families did things together before the men had gone off to war.

The first to speak was Myrne, a slightly plump woman of about thirty who ran the dry goods store. She had premature wrinkles at her eyes and a touch of gray in her dark hair. Her voice was flat as she began, "Now that the war is over, families are reunited and the men are back home. I'm not sure how I will fit in without a husband. I have to run the store until I can afford to hire someone. My boy is only ten, and he tries to be helpful. He's a strong lad, but I worry about him growing into manhood without a father."

Rita spoke next. She was a tall, slender woman with dark-red hair and intense, brown eyes. Also a war widow, she had taken charge at her husband's bank when he left for the war. "I have had a hard time getting people—especially the men—to trust me. I always helped Paddy with the bank and know as much about the business as he did. It's going to be even harder now that the other men are back home. I'm happy for the lucky wives whose husbands have returned, but I need to make a living for my family, and I don't want to let go of everything Paddy built. I don't know if people will continue to accept my role."

Jo and Charlotte listened as the other two spoke. Their husbands had returned home, safe and healthy, but they acknowledged that things were different now. They were going to leave their positions—Jo from the dry cleaners and Charlotte from the feed store.

"I know I'm one of the lucky ones, and for that I am so grateful, but at the same time, I'm going to miss being a part of the community," Jo started. "I'll miss my regular contacts with the customers, but I know I have to turn my job over to Leo. The men in our community need the jobs to support their families."

Charlotte nodded. "Yeah, I'll be leaving my job soon, and I will miss hearing the daily chatter, especially news from some of the neighboring towns. The farmers come in at least twice a week, and they've always got some news." She looked at me. "I'm sure glad you and your ma will be doing the reporting. I think we'll get the real scoop and hear about things that matter."

"Thanks, Charlotte. Ma and I will do our best. We are very committed to providing a professional newspaper."

Despite their different circumstances, the women had something in common. Their viewpoints did indeed differ from those of the women who attended "Coffee with the Editor." These businesswomen had a greater sense of ownership over their activities and their opinions. They also had ideas for how to solve some of their concerns. They got in on a different line of gossip than did the Coffee women. But at the core, their concerns were about the same things— they cared about their children, the schools, the hospital, and they cared about our town and the changes they were witnessing.

As the war had come to a welcomed close, these women were hearing about the status of the POWs who had been housed in a camp in a nearby town. Where would these men settle? Would they go back to their home countries, or might they scatter throughout the surrounding area? If they stayed, how would they fit in? How would they support themselves? Many of the men had proved themselves to be useful on the local farms and as builders for some construction projects.

These women, for the most part, saw the men as people other than a "bunch of Krauts," as some of their neighbors called them. They had skills that were helpful to the communities that housed them.

As I listened, I made some notes for further reference and research. The women didn't have suggestions as to how we might react to the situation, but they were open to different ideas. I agreed to do some research and see what I might learn.

The women left right at six thirty, and I tidied up the room. Ma was still in her office, so I dropped in and we discussed the meeting.

"Ma, these are a different breed than the women you see at your Coffees. They are responsible for running the home and supporting the family. They take on a whole new set of worries and concerns. Rather than providing me with gossip or leads for stories, they're asking questions and wanting information. I see a different role here."

Ma nodded. "Hmm... this sounds like an opportunity as well as a challenge. How would you have handled something like this at Saint Anne's?"

I laughed. "Well, I would have assigned my brightest students to gather all the facts. Without those students, I guess I have to do the homework. I'll get to work on it first thing in the morning, but you know, we may possibly need an assistant sooner than we'd planned. And it might have to be someone who can do more than just run errands."

"You might be right, Kate, but perhaps not full time until we have our feet a little firmer on the ground. I'll start asking around. Maybe your After-Five ladies will know of someone."

CHAPTER 22

On Wednesday, I drove over to the POW camp. It was about twenty-five miles down the highway, and I'd never been there.

The property was much larger and more developed than I had expected. The numerous buildings could house two thousand to three thousand men, and I'd heard that they weren't all German. The acreage was bigger than some of the surrounding farms.

The woman at the desk looked up at me, without smiling. "Can I help you, miss?"

"Good morning, ma'am, I am Kate Hurley with *The Hawthorne Times*. I'm wondering if there is a way to learn more about the camp. I think there might be a story here that would interest the people of the community."

"December was very busy here, and we're just getting back to our usual routine. I'll have to check with the commander to see if he is willing to schedule you, but it certainly won't be today." She continued, "Our men here don't just sit around. They have itineraries, too." She got up and proceeded down a hallway leading away from the lobby. I heard her unlock and then close a door.

I surveyed the lobby. The gray walls and unfinished wood

floor looked cold, but the display case along the wall told another story. There were hand-carved, wooden toys and some small paintings of foreign countrysides. A Bible lay flat at one end of the case, open to Psalm 23. *Though I walk in the valley of darkness...* I was immediately intrigued and welcomed a tour and a meeting with the commander.

The woman returned and offered me an appointment. I agreed to return on Friday, weather permitting.

On the way back to Hawthorne, I made a mental list of questions for the commander. I also thought about what to wear. Something warm, for sure, as it was cold outside and cool in their front office at the camp. And I thought a hat might add to my official look.

By Friday, the weather had cleared. It was warmer, though the wool suit still felt good, as did my heavy coat and overshoes. I found my gray cloche in the closet and added a gray-and-red-plaid scarf.

I arrived at the camp just before ten, carrying my notebook and sporting a pencil in my hatband. The commander, a tall man with thin, graying hair and steel-blue eyes, came to the front office and greeted me with a polite smile. "Welcome to the camp, madam."

"Thank you for seeing me, sir. I am Kate Hurley from *The Times* in Hawthorne."

"So I'm told, madam. And you want to see how we treat the prisoners?"

"I've heard many good things about the camp, Mr.... uh ..."

"It's *Commander* Brownlee, madam."

"Of course, Commander Brownlee. I have heard good

things about the camp, but quite frankly, I am not at all familiar with it. Can you tell me how large it is, as in how many men are housed here? Are they all Germans? How do they spend their days?"

He hesitated, as if taking a count. "We have room for two thousand, but we're just a little over half full. Most are Germans, and they do a variety of things during the day. We also have prisoners from Italy and some Japanese."

"Japanese? I didn't know that. How many Japanese men are there?"

"Not many but enough to cause trouble. The Japs are not very welcomed by some of the men. I guess the news about the Japanese has been somewhat harsh. It might be rather frightening to know some of them are here in our facility, right here in your backyard."

After learning about the prisoners' activities, I broached another subject. "So can you tell me what the postwar plan is? Where will the men go?"

"As far as I know, most will be repatriated to their home countries or other European countries as laborers. I doubt that many will stay here in the US, though they have been useful here in our towns. We've tried to help them maintain any skills they brought with them as well as cultivate new ones. You'd be surprised at their cultural interests and capabilities—music, art, literature…"

"Really? I am surprised at all of this. Most people don't know anything about what goes on here, nor are they aware of anything about the men who've been living here in our midst, men who have been working in our communities."

Commander Brownlee took me around the grounds and through part of the facility. I saw where the men ate their meals, and I noticed a workshop, a room with musical instruments, and a library. I knew the commander didn't show me everything, but what I did observe looked quite comfortable and well organized.

At the conclusion of our tour, the commander asked me what I thought, what I was going to write.

"Well, I am positively impressed, and I think we have an opportunity to educate the community regarding the program. Is there anything else you'd like to tell me?"

Commander Brownlee paused for a minute, glanced down at the floor, and then looked me in the eye. "Most of these men didn't want to go to war, and many have welcomed their placement here. It's a better living situation than they had before being captured and shipped here. The Geneva Convention has much to do with the conditions here, but their contentment here is, in part, due to their previous experiences in the war. If there are any escape attempts, they would be men trying to find a better life here."

I thanked Commander Brownlee and headed back to my car. The drive home gave me time to think about how I might convey my findings. The After-Five ladies would appreciate the information, and I could easily share it with them at our next meeting, but what might I write for *The Times*? Neither *The Times* nor the other local papers had discussed much about the camps before, but they've always been right here, in our backyard, as the commander put it. It would answer the ladies' questions, but there was much more of a story here... something people would like to know.

At home that evening, I opened a new book, *Goodbye Mr.*

Chips, a book from 1934. I tried to read, but I found my mind wandering. I went to bed early. I tossed and turned and finally got up and proceeded downstairs for a cup of tea.

Sauntering through the parlor, I looked at things we no longer used—Liam's trophies and Da's books. Da was always on top of the news, both local and national and worldwide as much as possible. What would he want to know about the camp?

I picked up one of his books, one he read shortly before he died, a book of poems by Langston Hughes. I didn't know Da had read poetry, but this was on his shelf. One of the pages had a folded corner. The poem there was *Dreams*. I clutched my pendant as I read it.

I wondered what Da saw in these words. He was a deep thinker and came out with some profound comments at times. Was he thinking of me or Liam? Or someone else? Perhaps himself? He was always a gentle man, always concerned about others—not just his family and friends, but those less fortunate. Oh, how I missed him. He might have reached out to the POWs or gotten to know what was going on in their environment.

Even with Liam going to war, Da would have cared about the captured men. He saw them as people... people with families back home, people with personalities, cares, and needs perhaps different from ours, but real feelings just the same. Maybe he could see that Liam, or any of our American boys, could end up in a similar situation on enemy soil. Not many people had the same compassion as Da. I wondered how he would advise me if he were here.

Saturday was crisp and clear and just barely warm enough

for a walk. Ma and I strolled about a mile down the lane and then back. She was full of excitement about the new arrangements in the office. "Kate, I think things are going to work out all right. Perhaps Liam is watching over us. I feel positive about our future. All the women are supporting us. Some of the men, too. Roger has his cronies and will always be trouble, but some of the businessmen have come by the office or stopped me on the street and wished me well."

I nodded, but I was pondering an article about the POWs. I didn't discuss it with Ma but asked myself, *Do I need her permission to work on it?* I knew she'd have to okay it for publication, but I wanted my first article to be complete before I broached the topic with her.

Perhaps she was reading my mind. "Any new ideas about the After-Five women?"

"They offer a unique perspective, different things to think about. The end of the war is changing their lives, and they have concerns about their own futures as well as the future of our community. They seem to have developed a bond, even though they haven't had time to get together very often. I think our evening meetings will be good for them—and for me—in more ways than one."

"Good for you, Kate. I think you've started something."

We continued on in silence and welcomed the warm house when we arrived back home for another cup of tea. Ma went downstairs to launder the altar cloths. I retreated to the living room with my book and a notepad, the notepad being for my ideas for *The Times*. I had to start over on page one in the book, and the notepad was filling up quickly.

I arrived at the office ahead of Ma on Monday. I reviewed

my notes about the camp and had an outline for my article. Time was an issue for this article, as the prisoners would be released or returned before long, and I wanted to get this out well in advance. It took me another hour and a half to fill in the blanks and have a rough draft. I asked Ma if she had room on her schedule to get together. We agreed to meet after her Monday Coffee, allowing me time to work on my usual local statistics.

Ma returned later than expected. I gave her a few minutes to hang up her coat and remove her snow boots, then I approached her door.

"Oh, yes, you wanted to get together. What's on your mind?"

"Well, I told you the After-Five ladies asked a lot of questions, so I decided to follow up on one issue that I think has interest beyond their little group. Are you familiar with the POW camps?"

"Well, of course. Everyone knows about them."

I informed her about my tour with Commander Brownlee and what I had learned about the camps, the men, and their possible releases coming up in the next few months.

Ma commented, "A lot of people around here don't like those prisoners being in our midst. Some people think they were responsible for many of our boys and men not coming home. They're part of the reason we have to ration goods and supplies. They've changed our lives, you know, according to some folks around here."

"Sure, we've seen many losses in our community, Ma, but these men are not the ones responsible for that. You told me that yourself when the camps were first set up. Many of them didn't want to go to war. They're not really enemies. They have worked in our communities, been helpful to our families, worked on our farms—"

"Yes, but... well, let me read this, and we can talk again later."

I moseyed down the hall and sat down at my desk, shaking my head. I peered at my notes on the local stats. I could finish them up in the morning. For the moment, I needed a walk. It was almost dark, so I decided to leave quickly.

I went out the back door and headed toward town. I pulled my coat closely around me and treaded quickly. I soon found myself in front of the bank where Rita was just locking the door.

"Hi, Kate. What brings you this way? Not much open right now, and it's pretty chilly for a stroll."

"Hi, Rita. Just trying to clear my head in this refreshing air."

"I suppose your work requires that once in a while."

We stood and talked for a few minutes, but the chill was starting to set in and Rita said that she needed to get home.

"Kate," she said as she started to turn toward her car. "I've got some lamb stew to heat up this evening. Would you like to join me for supper?"

I hesitated, then replied, "Sure. I need to go back and get my car and let Ma know I won't be home for a while, but we didn't have much planned."

Ma was still at her desk, and I quickly gave her my message.

Without looking up, she responded, "That's fine. Have a nice evening."

Rita's house was just warming up. She had put the stew in the oven. We sipped a cup of tea in the kitchen while we waited.

"So how is your new job going, Kate? We ladies told you about the changes the war brought us, but I guess it brought changes for you, too."

"Yes, yes it did. When we received the news about Liam, and having lost my da just a couple years ago, I couldn't stay with my life in Omaha." I hesitated as I remembered my apartment and the friends I'd made at Saint Anne's. "I knew I needed to be here with Ma. Now Ma's life is taking shape, and I'm not sure what my future looks like. It seems I go through each day not taking the time to look ahead."

"Do you have a beau?"

I laughed. "No, not really. I've gone out with a couple of the local guys but haven't been interested in any one of them. Small town, you know."

As I told Rita about my life in Omaha, I realized that what I missed was my independence and my private space. I missed my social life, too.

"Ma isn't so needy anymore, but she still wants me around. It's been almost a year since we got the news about Liam, and she has settled into following his plan. She's doing a good job. Better than she expected of herself."

"She certainly is, Kate. I hear that from lots of folks. I guess the question is, 'Where do you fit in,' right?"

"You're right. I sometimes wonder what's ahead."

We sat in silence for a while and then moved on to some lighter topics, enjoying our evening together. Her stew was excellent, containing some different spices than mine or Ma's... cinnamon, nutmeg?

I went home, pleased with the idea that I had made a new friend, someone whose lifestyle might be similar to my own.

CHAPTER 23

Ma was up early and busy in the kitchen when I came downstairs. She was frying bacon and scrambling some eggs. I wrapped my hands around a cup of coffee as I waited. It was going to be another cold day, but there was no snow in the forecast.

"About your article on the camp," she began as she tapped the fork on the frying pan. "I read it again last night. I think you can go ahead with it as long as you keep it neutral. Just don't take sides or try to create sympathy. We might get some backlash, but if we're neutral, people can only criticize the situation, not the author. I'm sure you know all of that, but I always ask myself, 'What would Liam do?' That question seems to point me in the right direction."

"Sure, Ma." *What would Liam do?* I swallowed the lump in my throat, thinking about my brother, his dream, and Ma's plan. I wondered how I would have fit in had he come home to us. Would I be here? Still in Omaha? Would I have ever had a place with *The Times*?

By noon that day, I had revised the POW article and finished my weekly stats. As I was putting the papers on the work desk, we received a call about an accident on the highway. The ambulance had been called and transported someone to the hospital. I offered to go over and check it out.

The emergency room was busy when I arrived, and there were some visitors pacing and crying in the waiting room. No one I recognized. I introduced myself, and they gave me their names and told me about the accident. Icy roads seemed to be the cause. Fortunately, no one was killed, but the seriousness of the injuries was still uncertain. I asked if there was anything I could do. Would they like some coffee? As we talked, they gave me the details about the injured parties and their reason for travel. They were from eastern Nebraska and going to Dubuque for a college tour. Their son was the driver.

Just as they sat down and relaxed a bit, Dr. Hagerty came out from the ER exam area.

He glanced at me and then went over to the parents, speaking in a soothing tone. "He's not quite out of the woods, but it appears that he'll be okay. It could have been worse." He took the woman's hands and looked her in the eye. "Do you hear me?"

The woman's lips trembled and her chin quivered. "Yes, Doctor. Thank you. Can I go in and see him?"

Doctor Hagerty took her by the elbow and headed toward the examination room. The husband followed.

I sat down to take a few notes and then packed my things together. As I was about to leave, Doctor Hagerty came out of the examination room.

"Kate, do you have a minute?"

"Sure," I said, pulling out my notepad.

He led me aside. "I'm sorry I haven't gotten back to you,

but it's been very busy around here. May I give you another call?"

"Sure, sure." I could feel my face flushing as I looked around to see who might overhear. "Of course. I'm at *The Times* pretty much eight to five and at home other times."

"Great. I'll be in touch."

I returned to the office to summarize a report on the accident. I started, then restarted, the article. I rose from my desk and walked around my office, dusting off the picture of me and my da. I touched my Irish pendant. "Things might be looking up, Da."

The week went by quickly. The paper had come out that morning, and our articles appeared as expected. We positioned my POW article on the lower half of the front page. My write-up of the accident also found a small place on the front page. The victim's injuries were not life threatening, and he was expected to recover quickly. It was a good reminder to all of us to be careful on the icy roads. Some accidents, but not all, could be prevented with a little extra caution.

Having read the paper cover to cover, Ma and I went to Emily's for lunch.

Myrne was there dining by herself. She nodded as we walked over to our usual back table. After we ordered, Myrne came over to us. "Gosh, Kate, it sounds like you had an interesting tour of the camp. The prisoners have it pretty easy, don't they?"

"I wouldn't exactly call it an 'easy' life for them, but they are treated humanely."

Her eyes narrowed and her lips quivered as she said, "At least they're alive and can go back to their homes, their families, and their jobs." She turned around and went back to her table.

Ma and I looked at each other.

"I lost a son," Ma said. "I know how much pain she is experiencing. Your article may have stirred up some angry feelings. We'll have to keep our ears open."

I felt a knot in my stomach, and I tried to breathe as quietly as possible. I wanted to go over to Myrne but didn't know what to say. I decided to wait and stop by the store later in the day.

As Ma and I returned to the office, I thought about Myrne's comments and wondered about others in town. Did other people have a similar reaction? Maybe Rita could give me some insight.

I left the office around three-thirty and drove over to the dry goods store, hoping to find Myrne. The young clerk who assisted her was out front. He told me that Myrne was in the back room and offered to get her. He returned without Myrne, said she was busy right now, and could I come back later.

"Sure, but please let her know Kate Hurley was here." As I turned to go, I heard Myrne come out from the back room.

"Hello, Kate. Did you want to see me?" Her face was drawn, and her eyes were red.

"If this isn't a good time, Myrne, I can come back later... or tomorrow?"

Myrne led me to the back room. It was small and served a

dual purpose. Cans and boxes were stored along one wall, and there was a desk and two chairs in the corner, abutting the other wall. Though crowded and a little cluttered, the room was spotlessly clean.

"Have a seat, Kate."

"Myrne, I just wanted to say that I'm sorry my article upset you. Perhaps I should have discussed it with you and the other ladies first. It just seemed that the word needed to get out. The POWs are going to be released soon."

"Yes, I know, Kate. I just can't get over the fact that we have been harboring the enemy and..." Her voice trailed off as she glanced down at her desk.

"I guess I should have looked at it through your eyes. Ma had concerns about my article—you know, after losing her only son—but she agreed that people needed to know about the government's plans."

"Yes, yes. I'm sure it's something we need to know. It's just so hard sometimes, and I never know what will trigger the memories, the sadness. Robert has been gone almost a year and a half, and I still ache for him every day. Sometimes I wish that he was a prisoner in their camp and would someday come home to me. It's selfish of me, I know, but I miss him so much."

"Oh, Myrne, I know. I miss my brother, and I can see Ma's pain, too. I hope you'll forgive me."

"You didn't do anything requiring forgiveness, Kate. It's just me and, I know, others like me. Please continue your work. I realize you and your ma are good people, and I'm sure you'll do what's right."

We sat in silence for a few minutes, then Myrne looked up. "I'll be okay, Kate. Thanks for stopping by."

I returned to the office and called Rita. We agreed to meet at the bank a little after five. She sounded cheerful but reserved. Perhaps she was busy. Just as I was about to go out the door, the phone rang.

"*Hawthorne Times*," I answered.

"Just who do you think you are, writing about the POW camp as if you knew anything about what's going on over there?" shouted a male voice.

"Excuse me, but who is calling?" I asked as calmly as possible.

"They're just a bunch of Krauts and Japs! You make it sound as if they're decent citizens whom we should welcome with open arms," the man roared.

"I would be happy to discuss this if you would tell me your name."

With that, the phone went dead. I stared at the receiver and sat down at my desk.

"Whew!" I guess I didn't realize the reaction people might have. Ma and I missed our Liam dearly, but we didn't hold it against the POWs. I suppose not everyone feels the same.

It took me several minutes to compose myself, and then I left the office and headed to the bank. Rita was still at her desk doing some paperwork. She waved me in and motioned to a chair. "I just have to finish up this receipt."

"Sure, sure." As I took a seat and glanced around her office, the most prominent item was the photo of her husband, Paddy, in his military uniform. Next to that was their wedding picture, and alongside that was a photograph of Paddy and three other men in uniform. While Rita worked, I took out my notepad and tried to look busy.

She finished her work and took it to another desk out in the bank. When she returned, she asked, "What's on your mind, Kate?"

"Well"—I paused and swallowed—"I'm sure you saw my article in *The Times* about the POW camp."

"Yes, I did," she replied with a cold stare.

"Well... uh... did it answer any of the questions you and the ladies asked last week?" I didn't know where to begin.

"You might say that." After a pause, she asked, "What did you really think about the camp? How did you feel hearing that these men were treated so 'humanely' while our men were crawling on the ground in their country or being shipped back home in boxes?" she asked as she glanced at the photo of the four men in uniform.

My heart was heavy. "I'm sorry, Rita. I guess I wasn't looking at it through the eyes of others. When I met the commander and toured the camp, I was impressed with the civility our country showed these men, most of whom were not at war by their own choice."

"See these men?" Rita asked as she picked up the picture behind her desk. "This is Paddy, his two brothers, and my brother. Except for Paddy, the others came home, but their hearts, their minds will never be the same. These men were not treated 'humanely' on the battlefield." She bit her lower lip and returned the picture to the shelf.

"Oh, Rita, I am so sorry. You know that Ma and I are living through the pain of losing Liam, too. I never meant to upset anyone. Perhaps because Ma and I have each other, we've been able to deal with our pain in other ways. Please forgive me, and I hope others will, too."

"I look forward to your friendship, and I am sure we can get beyond this, but I know I am not the only one upset by your report."

"Thank you, Rita. I, too, hope we can be good friends." I let myself out the front door and went home to dinner.

"Hi, Kate," Ma called as I came in the door. She looked up from setting the table. "Oh my, dear, what's wrong?"

I guess it was written all over my face. "Oh, Ma, I think I've made quite a bad start." I shook my head as I removed my coat. "Why didn't I take my time and talk to the group before I put this in the paper? I was so anxious to get something in, I convinced myself it couldn't wait. I've offended so many people." I told her about my talks with Myrne and Rita and about the man who called on the phone.

"I'm sorry." She gave me a gentle hug. "You'll have an uphill road for a while, but you'll get back in their good graces. The ladies will get beyond this. But the man who called… did he give you a name?"

"No, and I didn't recognize his voice. He was clearly angry."

"I don't give much credence to someone who won't give a name, but he could rile up others, depending on who he is and who he knows." As Ma said that, I wondered if Roger had anything to do with the call.

"Myrne and Rita were forgiving, but I feel like I took twenty steps backward with them. As for the man who called… well, who knows what will come of that." My hands felt icy, and I had to struggle to eat Ma's pork roast, usually one of my favorites.

I stared out the window as I washed the dishes, letting the water warm my hands. It was dark and not much was going on around our neighborhood. A car drove slowly past the house, turned around at the corner, and came by again. Someone lost? Another angry reader?

That night, I tossed and turned and eventually got up long before Rosie called to me. I chose my old, gray skirt and cardigan, ate a light breakfast, and headed to the office on my own. The building had just started to heat up, and I was still on my own when I heard the front door open. I could tell the footsteps didn't belong to Ma.

"Hello?" I called.

"Good morning, Kate," said Roger. "I just thought I'd stop in and see how things are going for you ladies."

"Things are okay, Roger, and we are doing just fine. How are you doing? Are you enjoying your leisure?"

"Well, I wouldn't exactly call it leisure. I'm keeping busy… uh… but I wondered if you needed my help with anything."

"No, Roger," I replied, clenching my teeth, "but it's nice of you to ask."

"Well, I just thought maybe… You know, I worked in this town a long time, and I have lots of contacts. Perhaps I could help pave the way for you with some of the men."

"Hmm… thanks, Roger, but as I said, we're doing okay."

Roger fiddled with his hat a bit and stared down at the floor.

"As I said, thank you, Roger. It was nice of you to drop by."

"Sure, Kate." He went back down the hall and out through the front door.

When Ma came in, I told her about Roger's visit. "I think I know the source of the anonymous call last evening, Ma."

"Crikey! Perhaps one of Roger's 'contacts,' you think?"

"That man is disgusting, Ma, but it's better to get a call from one of his 'contacts' than to get one from someone who was truly an offended townsperson. Guess I'll continue to tread lightly."

"Yes," agreed Ma, "and carry a big stick!"

I dug into my usual work, following up on community statistics, and started to prepare for my next After-Five meeting, hoping I would get a good turnout.

CHAPTER 24

Over the weekend, Ma prepared for her first board meeting. It would be Roger and two other men from town, a trio of cronies. This was going to be an interesting day.

"What do you want to bet, Kate? The first thing they'll do is ask me to make the coffee."

"Ha! I'll bet you're right."

"Surely, they've been in the office before. I'll tell them where the break room is." Ma wrote up her goals and plan for the year, identifying some challenges as well as reassurances and opportunities. She had some accomplishments to report. "I don't know if I'll make copies of my report or just tell them what my plans are. What do you think?"

"Either way, they'll be gobsmacked! They've probably never planned farther ahead than their next beer at the bar."

Just then, the phone rang. It was Doctor Hagerty inviting me to go to the cinema on Sunday afternoon. He assured me that the young resident would be able to cover for him, and Doctor Leary was available for consultation as needed. He was ready for a relaxing afternoon and wanted me to join him.

"Sure, I would love to go." I felt a slight flutter in my chest as Ma raised her eyebrows and looked up at me.

After Mass on Sunday, Ma and I had our usual breakfast and I tidied up the kitchen. Then I went upstairs to get ready for my date. I put on the navy skirt and white blouse but changed my mind and donned the gray. No… I changed into the maroon, my favorite.

Doctor Hagerty arrived right on time, wearing gray slacks and a black sweater. He looked relaxed and, well, quite dashing in something other than a white coat.

"Good afternoon, Kate, Mrs. Hurley. Nice to see you socially for a change."

"And you, too, Doctor Hagerty," said Ma.

"Please… please come in," I said.

We visited with Ma for a few minutes and then left for the cinema. His car, a year or two newer than mine, was still warm.

He had little to say on the way to the theater, and I tried to fill in the silence with some of the news that was printed just yesterday. He admitted that he hadn't read the paper but had heard some of the stories via the grapevine. He apologized, saying he knew how hard Ma and I had worked on it, how hard we worked on it every week.

"Really, it's quite all right." We both laughed as I accepted his apologies that sounded like they were coming from a schoolboy who hadn't finished his homework.

The movie was a rerun of *The Philadelphia Story*, but Doctor Hagerty hadn't seen it. I had seen it but loved it and was happy to see it again. About halfway through, my date was getting a little sleepy. I produced a gentle cough, and he jerked his head up. He made it through the movie without falling asleep, while I enjoyed every minute of the story and viewed the credits.

Afterward, we went back to our house for coffee and a piece of Ma's apple pie. Like everyone else, Doctor Hagerty loved her pie.

"It was a great movie, Mrs. Hurley. You might like to see it sometime."

"I'm not much for the cinema, Doctor Hagerty, but Kate always likes to see the latest. She has her favorites, too, ones she'd see over and over," Ma replied.

"Maybe she can direct me to some others. And please, Mrs. Hurley, you can call me Kevin now," Doctor Hagerty said.

"How about 'Doctor Kevin?' It only seems appropriate," reasoned Ma.

I nodded, enjoying their comfortable exchange. Doctor Hagerty seemed quite at home in our kitchen. I wondered how he managed in his own.

Ma went to the living room as he and I sat at the table a little longer.

"I hear you might consider staying on here in Hawthorne."

"I'm getting more comfortable with the idea. Ma seems to like having me around, and I'm enjoying my work at *The Times*... well, mostly." I told him about some of the reactions to the POW article.

"I'm sorry. I didn't read it, as you know," he said, rubbing his forehead and smiling. "I had no idea what the POWs were doing over there, and I didn't know there were men other than Germans. I need to make *The Times* part of my

Friday morning routine so that I know what's going on around here. Guess there is life outside of the hospital. I hope their comments don't discourage you. I haven't read your writing, but you seem to do such detailed research."

"I'll hang in there. Some of the concerns were expressed by women whom I consider friends."

"But the caller who wouldn't give his name?"

"You know, Doc... Kevin, Ma and I think he may be one of Roger Ferguson's cronies, and that Roger may have put him up to it."

"That Ferguson guy sounds like a pretty low character. How often do you have to see him?"

"Ma meets with him on a monthly basis and needs him to help her keep in touch with the good ol' boys' club. But other than that, we see him when he drops in the office, always unannounced, and usually looking for Ma, not me, thank the Lord. He has to watch his Ps and Qs around her. He thinks he can get away with more around me. I'll have to earn his respect."

"You appear quite capable of that," Kevin said, grinning.

"So..." I felt myself blush a little at his compliment, and I hesitated to call him by his first name. "Kevin, what do you do when you're not at the hospital?"

"Hmm. I don't get a lot of time away from the patients, especially with Doc Leary off duty right now. When I do get a break, I like to take long walks or ride a horse now and then. At home, I read. What about you, Kate?"

"I have always loved to write. Journalism was my goal, even though I went to teachers' college." Without thinking, I reached for the Trinity knot that hung around my neck. "I think I liked writing more than my brother. Ma and Da talked me into the teaching route. It worked for me, especially since I was able to take charge of the school newspaper.

"Now, to come home and help Ma with *The Times*... well, I like the challenge and I enjoy meeting the people this way. It pretty much takes up my time—that and helping manage this house. I loved working with all the girls in Omaha, and I liked being on my own. Sometimes I miss it, but I don't think I'd feel right not being here with Ma, at least right now." I sensed that I was rambling on, so I paused. "How do you like it here compared to Omaha?"

"Well, I lived on a farm outside of West Point until I went away to college. Omaha was okay, but I enjoy being back in a small town. Hawthorne has a lot going on, and you have all the services you need here. And I don't have to milk cows!" He chuckled quietly, then went on, "It's a great little hospital. It's quite modern for a small place, and everyone is friendly and truly dedicated to their work. Doc Leary is a tough act to follow, but I like the old guy. He's still very competent, and everyone loves him."

"He—actually, all of the community—is glad to have you here," I said as our eyes locked for a brief moment. "Uh, would you like more pie?"

He was blushing as he replied, "No, no, that's fine. And tell your ma it was delicious. I really must go. Thank you for joining me this afternoon."

"Thank you... Kevin." I don't know if he could see me melting into his blue eyes. "It was a lovely afternoon."

Kevin donned his black overcoat and fumbled with his hat. "Well, okay. Um... perhaps we could get together again sometime soon?" It was hard to believe, but this handsome, talented man seemed a bit shy.

"Of course," I gushed. "I'd love to."

I watched him walk to his car and drive away. When I started to pick up my book, I remembered the dishes on the counter. I went back to the kitchen and washed and dried them, recalling the afternoon. It had been one of the most enjoyable days since I had returned home.

CHAPTER 25

Monday morning greeted us with some lightly falling snow, but not enough yet to stick to the roads. Ma was up early. "I have lots to do today, Kate. I want my desk in order prior to tomorrow's meeting. I don't want to be worrying about things on my list."

"Yeah, I know what you mean." I was still thinking about my date with Kevin, speculating how long it might take for him to get some more free time. "See you in a bit. I wonder how many babies were born last week?"

Ma didn't reply. She rinsed her dishes, got her coat, and was picking up the altar cloths that had been folded neatly across the chair. "I'll see you there. Drive carefully."

I enjoyed a second cup of coffee, washed and dried the few dishes, and straightened the kitchen.

As soon as I arrived at the office, I picked up last week's paper and reread my POW article. I sighed, trying to see it through the eyes of Rita or Myrne.

My calls to the county offices revealed only one new baby born last week, in Woodland, to a name I didn't recognize. It was later in the morning at Emily's that I heard a baby had been born the previous afternoon, and that the young resident had gotten there just in the nick of time. Fortunately, the nurses had assisted with so many deliveries, mother and baby were in good hands. It must have been in the middle of the movie or maybe while we were eating pie.

The day went by quickly, and I prepared the conference room for my evening meeting. Jo, Charlotte, and Rita arrived promptly at 5:00 p.m. Jo and Charlotte had read the POW article and were discussing their surprise at the activities of the men imprisoned there. Rita listened quietly. By 5:15, Myrne had still not shown up.

We moved on to other topics. The hospital was always on their list, and Charlotte had heard about the late arrival of the resident last evening. "What is going to happen when Doctor Leary retires? Everyone seems to like Doctor Hagerty, but this new one isn't very popular. Doctor Hagerty won't be able to do it all alone. I hope he stays on."

"That gives me an idea... maybe Jan Haley would like to join this group," suggested Charlotte. "She's always interested in the town's activities and wanting to participate in whatever's going on. Do you want me to ask her, Kate?"

"Well, sure. Anyone is welcome." I wondered to myself if having Jan at our meetings would be okay with Ma, given that the hospital was her pet project right now. But it was Charlotte's idea, so I let go of my concern.

The meeting came to a natural close about 6 p.m., but Rita stayed around after the others left. "Kate, I want you to know I support you and hope you do well with *The Times*, but I'm not sure I am ready to be a part of this group. Losing my dear Paddy still hurts so much, and some of the discussions are painful. I hope you understand."

I found myself forcing a smile as I replied, "Sure, Rita." I placed my hand on her arm. "I understand. Please know that you're always welcome, here at the meeting or any time you want to talk."

Rita lowered her eyes and mumbled, "Thank you, Kate. I'm sorry."

I started to clear the table as I listened to Rita walk slowly down the hall. When I heard the door close, I sat down and stared at my notes. A million thoughts ran through my head. *Maybe this group wasn't such a good idea... maybe the POW article wasn't a good idea, either... maybe I need to back off altogether.*

I wondered what Ma would do, or Liam. He never seemed to let anything get him down. He always looked ahead, not back. Would I ever gain Ma's trust the way Liam had? Would I ever hold my own in this town? I reflected on Sister Edward Joan's words and those of my da. After a few minutes, I took a deep breath, held my head high, and said to myself, "You can do this, Kate Hurley!"

The house was warm, and Ma had saved some meatloaf for me. She joined me at the table as I ate. "So how was your meeting tonight?"

"Not as productive as last week." I paused, remembering their faces. "Actually, it was a little subdued. They talked about my POW article and about various things going on around town. They had heard about the baby born yesterday and the new doctor being late." I looked at Ma and sighed. "And, oh... the ladies plan to ask Jan Haley to join us."

"Jan Haley? Hmm." Ma glanced at me, frowning. "She doesn't share much news, you know, and she's mum when it comes to hospital gossip. I mean, she might talk to me, but she doesn't share much with other people."

"I know, Ma, but I didn't want to discourage the group. I

guess we'll determine if she's interested and then see how she would participate."

"I can talk to her, Kate, if you'd prefer."

"Thanks, Ma, but I'd like to let the ladies take care of it."

Ma gripped her teacup. "Sure, Kate," she said as she looked the other way. "I was just trying to be helpful."

"Ma, I need to do some things by myself if I'm to establish my own credibility with *The Times*."

Still gazing out the window, she nodded. "I understand."

"I'm not sure you do, Ma." I tried to control my voice. "I loved my work in Omaha. I had the confidence of Sister Edward Joan and the other teachers. We had a lot of teamwork in our projects, and I had great friends after school. I'm getting comfortable back here, and I genuinely love being here with you, but... but I need to be trusted to do my own work." I sighed, fearing I had said too much.

"I know, Kate, I know. Just give me time. It's not easy for me, either." She turned and ambled to the living room.

I cleaned up the kitchen, then went in and joined her. She didn't offer much conversation as she was settled with her book. Rather than pick up the book I had been reading, I decided to look through Da's old book that I had noticed a couple nights ago. I ran my hand over the soft, aged leather of his chair. "Da always had a book by his chair, didn't he, Ma?"

"Uh-huh." She nodded without glancing up.

Funny, Ma and I rarely sat in his chair, but I knew it would never leave our living room. It had a depression in the seat, and the leather was shiny and thin in some places. It still smelled a little like his tobacco. I picked up the book, *The Heart Is a Lonely Hunter*. It was one of his favorites. I think he'd read it more than once. The edges were frayed, and the corners of several pages were folded down. I read the first ten pages, then closed the book and rubbed its soft cover.

"Ma, did you and Da ever read the same books?"

"No, not really. We had quite diverse tastes in books. I was never interested in his books, and he didn't care much about mine. I guess men and women are different that way. If he liked a book, he always read it more than once." She shook her head. "I never did that."

"This looks like one he probably read several times. It must have been meaningful to him," I said as I peered at the book in my hands.

I gazed at the fireplace and at Ma, who didn't look up from her book. I couldn't concentrate on the book in my hands. I finally got up and went to the kitchen for a cup of tea. "Do you want a cup, Ma?"

Her reply was prompt. "No, thanks."

As I heated the water, I noticed a car driving slowly by the house. It looked like the one I'd seen drive by a week ago, but I couldn't be certain. All cars seemed pretty much alike to me, especially in the dark. But it was moving slower than necessary, given that the streets were dry.

Before I left the kitchen, it went by again, headed in the same direction. A chill ran down my spine, and my hands turned cold as I stared out the window. I pulled my sweater tighter around my shoulders as I returned to the living room, deciding not to mention it to Ma.

We finished the evening reading in silence, or at least staring at our respective books. Before I went to bed, I sat by my bedroom window for at least a half hour but saw no further sign of the mysterious car.

I arrived at the office a bit late the next morning and started working on my stats. The phone rang a little after nine. It was Commander Brownlee. "Kate Hurley?"

"Yes," I replied.

"I read your article about my camp," said the commander, "and I don't want to see any more write-ups about it. It's really none of your business."

"Er, what did you say, Commander?"

"You heard me. No more articles about my camp!"

"*Your* camp, Commander? Isn't it a function of our federal government?" I felt the hair stand up on the back of my neck.

"Listen to me, miss. I don't want to see any more written about it."

"I'm afraid I don't understand your concern, Commander, and the people of our community like to know what's going on around us."

"Perhaps they want to know, Miss Hurley, but I don't want—or expect—to see anything more written about my camp."

"Thank you for letting me know, Commander," I replied without making a commitment to comply with his orders.

He hung up the phone.

"Wow!" I said to myself, puzzled at the fierceness of his 'orders' to me... his 'orders' about *his* camp. It sounded like there was something going on that he wanted to keep quiet, or maybe he had a crony who talked to him.

I returned to my work, finished the stats, and decided to

walk to Emily's for lunch. Ma was working on some of the hospital issues. The brisk walk felt good, but I was thankful for my gloves and wool scarf.

On my way, I thought about Commander Brownlee's phone call. I couldn't imagine what prompted his strong words, his "orders" to me. Doesn't he know that a private citizen does not have to follow his commands? I wasn't about to be intimidated by the stripes on his uniform or his large frame.

Emily's was warm and busy when I arrived, but there was a table available near the back corner. I could smell the roasting chicken and knew pot pie was on the menu. Her chicken pot pie was very popular, and I thought I got the last available portion. It warmed me to the bone as I relished my first bite. My thoughts drifted to the past weekend.

"May I join you?"

I glanced up from my thoughts to see Kevin Hagerty standing by my table.

"Of course. It's nice to see you here. I didn't think you got out of the hospital very often." A familiar, warm sensation coursed through my body.

"Well, not often, but the resident is on call today, so I thought this would be a nice change." He stared at my chicken pie and said, "That looks divine. Is it as good as it looks?"

"Yes, it is, but I'm sorry to say, I think I got the last serving." Fortunately, I had already eaten a few bites and was not tempted to share.

"Oh, just my luck." He shrugged. "I'm used to eating what is left at the hospital since I rarely get to the dining room in time for the main course."

Just as he sat down, Peggy arrived at our table. "Would you like our last serving of the chicken pot pie, Doctor Hagerty?"

"Well, faith and begorrah! I'm a lucky man. Yes, I would." His smile reminded me of the saying, "The way to a man's heart…"

We chatted about the movie we had seen as well as other movies.

"Have you read anything interesting lately, Kevin?"

"You mean anything other than patient records and medical journals?" He smiled, then said, "Not really. Most recently, I reread one of my favorites. Are you familiar with *The Heart Is a Lonely Hunter*?"

"Yes," I replied, my heart skipping a beat at the coincidence. "I just picked up that book last evening. It was one my da had read more than once, and it was on his shelf."

"Really? I read it twice. It's one of those books that makes you think differently about so many things, about people, about life."

"Uh-huh." I had been at a brief loss for words. Kevin was like no other man I'd ever met.

"My da often reread books that he liked. You can tell by the worn pages. I think that was one of his favorites."

We finished our lunch, continuing with small chatter, before Kevin said he really needed to get back to the hospital.

"I hope to get Saturday evening off. Could I see you again?"

"I'd like that, Kevin." I nodded my head.

After Kevin left, Peggy came and offered me more coffee. She had a knowing smile.

"Sure, anything, Peggy." I sat at the table completely unaware of anyone else being in the café.

Despite the chill in the air, I sauntered back to the office slowly, noticing snowflakes that I hadn't seen before. They'd just collected in small drifts along the walk, as if they were making way for me to pass by. I laughed to myself at the silly thought.

Ma was at her desk when I returned. "Welcome back, Kate. Did you enjoy your lunch?" She sighed as I walked past her door.

"Yes, Ma, I did. How is everything here?"

"I had my first official meeting with the board, as you know… or at least I thought you knew."

"Of course I knew. I'm sorry, I guess I was a little distracted. How did it go?"

She clenched her jaw as she replied, "That Roger is continuing to be a bugger. He keeps bringing up hospital issues—things he knows nothing about—and then he wants to follow up on it. But I'll be damned if I'm going to let him interfere."

"What is he onto this time?"

"He says he heard that Doc Leary was having to rewrite his licensing exam. I know it's not true, but he thought someone should investigate further and, meanwhile, alert the community. Crikey! He's a devious, old buzzard!"

"What did you…"

"I told him I was well aware of the state of things and that I would not put such slander in my paper. That really got his goat. He reminded me that he still owns half of *The Times* and that I had to answer to the board. The other board members didn't say a word. I think they're all afraid of him. No wonder he's run the paper any way he pleases. Well, no more. There's a new editor in this town, and I won't put up with his shenanigans. And I told him so. I told the board the same thing." She slammed her paper down on the desk.

I walked over to give Ma a hug, but her steely eyes peered down at her desk. "Damn him!"

"I know you can handle him, Ma. You've got more grit than he does, and you've a lot of support in this community."

I saw her jaw relax. "Like you, I just want to do my job and do it well. Your brother had so much of himself invested in this project. We can't let him down."

"I know, Ma, and we're not going to let him down. As a matter of fact, I think you'll stand up to Roger just as well—maybe even better—than Liam. The men expected Liam to be part of the good ol' boys' club, which put him in a difficult position. You don't have to take their guff, and neither do I."

Ma gazed at me. Her eyes softened, and her shoulders relaxed a bit. She smiled up at me and said, "Thanks, Kate. Together, we can do this."

We worked on our respective projects the rest of the day and then agreed to go home around five. I followed Ma in her car as a light snow was beginning to fall. A blizzard was predicted for later in the evening.

The house was chilly when we entered. Ma turned up the heat, and I started a fire in the living room. I warmed the leftover pot roast and added a few more potatoes. By the time we finished supper, the house was warm and the fire was going. Ma fetched the brandy from the back of the cupboard. It hit the spot.

She picked up her book but soon put it down. "So I've thought about your comments last night. You have been a great help to me. Are things going okay for you?"

"You mean at *The Times*, Ma?"

"Well, yes. What else would I mean?"

"Huh." I chuckled as I thought about Kevin. Then, remembering her reaction to my After-Five ladies wanting to invite Jan Haley to the group, I decided to tell her more about the POW camp issue and Commander Brownlee's call.

"Hell's bells, Kate! These men sound like they all come from the same breed. They think they can run everyone and everything. But it does make you wonder what's going on over there."

"What would you do, Ma? I was respectful to him, but I didn't make any commitment… didn't say that I wouldn't do any more articles or follow-up. And he kept referring to it as *his* camp. The gall!"

"Let's think about this one, Kate. As a matter of fact, let's put our heads together on more of our issues. Perhaps it's time to get back to our weekly meetings, our planning meetings."

"I agree. It's time."

We picked up our snifters and nodded.

"Here's to the Hurleys!" I offered.

"Sláinte!" said Ma. Da and Liam used to toast with that Irish phrase, and I think they were listening in that evening.

CHAPTER 26

The blizzard arrived as predicted. The wind blew, and the snow fell all evening and night. In the morning, a large drift blocked our drive and the entrance to the street.

"Think we could take a day off?" I asked Ma.

"Huh. I think we'll have to. I don't believe the plow has been by yet. I've got plenty of work I can do right here. Maybe later in the day we can venture into town."

I wrapped my robe tighter and poured a second cup of coffee.

Ma, already dressed in her gray wools, went to the parlor desk, got some paper, and then settled herself at the dining room table.

I warmed my hands by washing the dishes, then marched upstairs and got dressed. I decided to read a bit of *The Heart Is a Lonely Hunter* to see what it was that intrigued Da and Kevin.

Ma stayed at the dining room table until noon. I checked on her once, but she was deep into her notes, maybe stopping once for more coffee. At noon, I offered to make sandwiches.

Ma stretched her arms up over her head, then left her work on the table as she joined me in the kitchen. "You know, I presented my plan for the year to the board yesterday, and now I've been going over our books and my schedule for the next few months. It's a bit overwhelming, but having analyzed the numbers, I think we can go ahead and look for the assistant we need."

"I believe we're more than ready for a little help. What do you see someone doing?"

"Perhaps some of the copy setup, running things over to Hector, a little office cleanup. Just odds and ends."

"Sounds like a great start."

"And Emily knows a lot of people. Perhaps Father Declan would know of someone, too."

"I can ask my After-Five ladies next Monday, if you're ready to go ahead that soon."

"Let me think on it a little more, but I believe the time has come… sooner than we'd planned."

Ma went back to the dining room table, and I spent the afternoon doing some cleaning. By suppertime, Ma had put away her papers and cleared the table. I had thoroughly cleaned the pantry cupboards and was ready for a few minutes by the fire before eating.

Ma took over in the kitchen. I heard her mumbling as she browned some onion and ground beef. Her spaghetti wouldn't meet the approval of my Italian friends from Omaha, but it was a favorite in our house.

Over supper, she announced that she would talk to Emily and Father Declan the next day and see if they had any ideas.

"Good luck, Ma."

The following week, she had three interviews on her calendar.

One young man came in with an exaggerated limp, dressed in wrinkled trousers and a ragged sweater. He had come home from the war missing his lower left leg but was able to walk with a prosthesis that had been made for him by the VA specialist. He didn't smile once during the interview, and he told Ma that she should hire him because he had given so much for his country and it was time for the country to give back to him.

The second man was from Hunter Creek. He had not gone to the war because of a medical condition, he said, mumbling something about flat feet. He had worked briefly at the hardware store in Hunter Creek and had done odd jobs around his town. Unlike the first guy, he smiled and laughed frequently during his interview, telling stories about things that had happened in his town.

The third candidate was a young woman named Lisa. She was about twenty-two years old, from Clayton. She wore a simple, beige dress that matched her straight, honey-blonde hair. She had a pretty face and a sweet smile. Lisa was quiet, perhaps a bit shy. Father Declan had known about her through another church pastor. She was not married and had a baby at home.

"I really need the money, Mrs. Hurley, to take care of my boy." She smiled softly but didn't offer much conversation.

Ma had to pry a little to get her to talk about her experience. Finally, she shared a bit of helpful background. "I worked at the dry goods store until my Billy was born. His daddy was killed in the war, and we live with my parents. They help me out as much as they can. I'd really like to give him a good home. I will do anything you need done, and I'd like to learn more skills."

After meeting all the interested parties, Ma and I talked about the three candidates. It didn't take long at all to conclude that Lisa would be the best choice. She thanked Ma repeatedly when Ma offered her the job.

Lisa arrived early on her first day, wearing a plain, green, wool dress that brought out the green in her eyes. Her hair was held back with two barrettes on each side. She was an attractive, young woman, but rather somber for her age. Her clunky shoes looked like they belonged on a much older person. I gave her a tour of the office, starting with the back room where we brewed the morning coffee.

"Do you like your coffee strong, or do you prefer it a bit weaker?" she asked.

She took notes on everything as we walked along. After showing her around, we ended at Ma's office. Hers eyes focused on Liam's picture.

"Yes, that's my boy," said Ma. "I lost him in the war,

too." Lisa teared up a bit, and Ma put a hand on her shoulder. "It's been rough for so many of us."

"I know, Mrs. Hurley," said Lisa, not taking her eyes off Liam's picture. "It's just... it just hurts so bad."

"If there's anything I can do to make it easier for you, Lisa, please speak up. It must be so hard for you."

"Thank you, Mrs. Hurley, but I'm here to do a good job for you. So where do you want me to start?"

Ma showed her the conference room and the teletype machine. "This machine provides us with some of the national news. We'll show you how to use it later. You probably know Hector," she continued, explaining the printing schedule. "He does our printing, and we need to have a final copy to him by noon on Thursdays. I think you'll help us keep on schedule by getting things here and there and doing some of the setup in this room."

"I'll do my best, Mrs. Hurley," said Lisa as she wrote down more details in her notebook.

Ma showed her a stack of news articles from the teletype and had her sort them by date received. Before Lisa could discard them, Ma wanted to look at the most recent printouts.

We all agreed on an afternoon schedule for Lisa. "That would be great for me. That way, I can get Billy up in the morning and bathe him. My mum and dad can take over in the afternoons when he naps. I wouldn't miss him so much that way."

"Yes, that's good." Ma nodded and smiled.

After Lisa went home from her first day, Ma came into my office. "Well, what do you think?"

"She's a little quiet, but she seems conscientious. Quiet might be good around here."

"Yes," Ma agreed. "I think she'll work out fine as long as things work out for her at home. Poor girl. She has her hands full with a little one and no husband. It's good she has her parents." Ma hesitated, as if to say more, but then walked back to her office.

As she sat down, she gazed at Liam's picture. "Too bad I'll never see your children, my boy. It would have been so special."

CHAPTER 27

The first weeks with Lisa in the office, Ma and I focused on our normal activities, conducted our meetings as usual, and delivered the post to Hector ahead of schedule. Ma took Lisa to her Monday meetings at Emily's and introduced her to the ladies. During the Coffees, Lisa took notes so that Ma would remember to follow up on everything. She helped prepare for my After-Five meetings by picking up the refreshments at Emily's and making the coffee.

Ma had her review the teletype every afternoon as soon as she arrived. Lisa sorted the printouts and flagged anything that looked important to her. Of course, Ma reviewed every printout at first, but surprisingly, Ma agreed with all of Lisa's selections.

Lisa arrived right on time every day—sometimes even early—and worked hard every minute. It wasn't until early February that she called in one day, saying that she was unable to come to work. She was not feeling well. Ma said she sounded tearful. We both hoped that her work had not become a burden for her household.

Ma didn't mind being alone in the office that day as it was the first anniversary of Liam's death. She and I had gone to church that morning where Father Declan was offering Mass for Liam. She stayed a while and had a cup of tea with our pastor.

Much of the day, her eyes were red and she sat at her desk without working on anything. I went by her office to tell her that Jim Cauley had phoned, asking to meet with her.

"Sure," she said, nodding her head as she moved some papers around on her desk.

"Is there anything I can do, Ma?" I offered, knowing what day it was.

"No… no, no. I'll take care of it."

She went home early without returning Jim's call.

As we entered the office the next morning, the phone was ringing. It was Jim Cauley.

"Ellie, I think we'd better meet sometime today, if you can."

"Of course," said Ma. "What time works for you?"

They agreed to meet at the hospital right after lunch. I stayed in the office and caught up on my weekly statistics, while Lisa cleaned the conference room and sorted the teletype printouts. You'd never know she was in the office because she was so quiet, but her work was obvious.

"Lisa, can you take a break?" I asked. "Let's have a cup of tea."

She went to the utility room and filled the kettle. I joined her when I heard the whistle.

"No sugar, right, Miss Kate?"

"Right, Lisa. Thank you."

She blushed slightly and smiled, nodding her head.

"So what is little Billy up to these days? I'll bet he keeps everyone busy."

She beamed as she told me about his expanding vocabulary and his ability to climb out of his crib, even though it was an activity she discouraged.

"He's in good hands with my parents. They love him so much, even if at first they didn't approve."

"Didn't approve? Why on earth would they not?"

"Well... uh... with his daddy being away at war and all, they thought it would be too much responsibility. But they love him to pieces now." She looked away as she spoke.

"It will get easier as he gets older."

She nodded.

"You're not married, are you, Miss Kate?"

"No, Lisa. The right one hasn't come along yet, and that's okay. Ma needs so much help here and at home right now. I'm glad I can be with her as much as she needs me."

We finished our tea in silence until Lisa said she needed to complete her teletype sorting.

Around four o'clock, the office door opened, ushering in a chilly gust. I heard Ma's heels strike the wood floor in a sharp, staccato rhythm. I could tell something happened in her meeting with Jim. A minute later, her office door closed firmly.

I waited about twenty minutes and then knocked, opening her door slightly. "Any chance you'd like a cup of tea, Ma?"

"Yes," she spat out. "Yes, as a matter of fact, I would."

I brewed her favorite, an Earl Grey, and took it to her. This was not a time for Lisa's help.

As I placed the cup on her desk, Ma glanced up. Her eyes were steely and her jaws were tight. "Kate, that Roger is going to drive me crazy."

"Uh-oh. What is he up to now?"

"I told you how he wanted to follow up on Doctor Leary's issues with the state. Well, he tried. The dumb fool went to the state medical board, as if he had any right! But no one would give him any information. Stupid of him to try, really. Doesn't he know better? The state will only give information to Jim Cauley or to Doctor Leary himself. You'd think anyone would know that, but Roger thinks if he yells loud enough, he can get whatever he wants. That stupid, old buzzard!"

Ma cupped her tea in both hands and drew a deep breath, shaking her head. "Something has to change."

I briefly placed my hand on her shoulder and then returned to my office to work on the stats. Lisa worked quietly in the conference room, and Ma leafed through her calendar and other papers on her desk. We all finished our day by five o'clock and locked up the office.

On the way home, Ma grumbled some more about Roger.

"I have half a notion to string him up by his manhood! That devil!"

I knew she was angry, and I tried not to laugh. "I can just picture that, Ma."

We laughed so hard, I almost drove off the road.

We continued to talk as we prepared dinner. Ma glanced up as she turned the pork chops over in the pan. "I wish there was a way to buy him out, but I don't see that coming for years. I think the best I can do is go around him and work with the other two board members. Trouble is, I'd have to get them both on my side, and they're either afraid of Roger or, God forbid, they agree with him. Tom Burton has always agreed with him, so all decisions have been made by at least a two-to-one vote. Now I'll be lucky to get my ideas beyond a two-to-two stalemate."

"I still have my inheritance from Da, though it's invested in the cattle he had. Maybe we can find a way to liquidate it, but Roger would never sell. What about the board of directors? Can you add a new member? It seems to me a board should have an odd number anyway."

"Hmm, maybe, Kate. I'll think about that. Buying him out would be knotty, but adding another board member might be possible. It would have to be someone they all respect, but I sure don't want one of their *trusted* cronies."

I could see Ma's wheels turning as she nodded her head. "Good idea, Kate."

"But, Ma, let's think about my inheritance. That might be the best plan in the long run."

She nodded but offered no comments.

During supper, Ma opened up about her meeting with Jim Cauley. "It looks like Doctor Leary will be coming off suspension by the end of the month—a real relief to Jim and to Doctor Hagerty and, by the way, contrary to gossip being spread by Roger Ferguson. Doctor Leary was there today. He just stopped in for a minute, and he looked so rested and relieved. Everyone will be happy to see him back, but I think he'll be the happiest of all."

"Ah, glory be, Ma. It will be wonderful to put all of this behind us."

Ma went to the office early the next morning, and when I arrived a little after nine, she was on the phone, sharing her thoughts with Roger Ferguson. "That's a bunch of gobshite and you know it, Roger. For one thing, the state is not allowed to give you any information, and you're spreading falsehoods. You'd better keep your trap shut with those lies, or you're going to be slapped with a lawsuit!" She took a deep breath. "No, the suit wouldn't be from me. Your lies could be harmful to Doctor Leary or the hospital. You'd better watch what you say. You're bordering on slander, and your words can get you in a lot of trouble."

Ma got busy with paperwork when she hung up the phone. She stood up from her desk now and then, pacing the office.

"Lisa, could you get me a cup of tea? Earl Grey, please," she called out.

I heard Lisa hurry down the hall and fumble with the kettle in the back room. "Of course, Mrs. Hurley." She walked back to Ma's office, holding the cup over a saucer. "Anything else, Mrs. Hurley?"

"No, no thank you."

Ma picked up the phone and dialed.

"Good morning, Bob. This is Ellie Hurley. Yes, fine. How are you? I was calling to confirm that you'll be at the next board meeting. Yes, great. Do you suppose that we could meet at Emily's for coffee before that date? I have a suggestion that I'd like you to think about. Sure, Friday would be fine. Thanks, I'll see you there."

Ma came down to my office and sat down. "I'm going to meet with Bob Burger on Friday and plant the seed about adding another board member to see how he reacts. He's a little more open-minded than Tom Burton. If he seems receptive to it, I'll ask if he has any suggestions. I'm thinking perhaps someone from the hospital—maybe Jim Cauley or even Doctor Leary. What do you think? You're the one who gave me the idea."

She had the old sparkle in her eyes that showed me her wheels were whirling.

"Great idea. I think either Jim or Doctor Leary would be a good addition. With Doctor Hagerty on board, Doctor Leary might have more time, and he'd be a great support for you. It seems that the recent focus on the hospital would make them likely choices. I'll bet Bob would back that up, too. If you bring up one of their names, Bob might welcome the idea of another board member."

"Right, but I'd better be sure Jim or Doctor Leary would be willing to serve. This could backfire if we ended up with the wrong person. If Bob is open to it, maybe he could broach Tom Burton with the idea. I can do a little behind the scenes work with Jim or Doctor Leary."

"You can do it, Ma. You have the integrity and a lot of friends in this town."

"Thanks, hon. I really appreciate your support, too."

After Ma returned to her office, I sat and thought about her for a while. She'd been through a lot in the last few years. First, she lost Da, and that was after watching him suffer for so long. Then to lose our Liam. She didn't show it very often, but she still carried a heavy heart beneath it all. She was a survivor and a fighter. When she had a challenge facing her, she stared at Liam's picture, took a deep breath, sat up straighter, and forced a smile. My mother amazed me sometimes.

I thought back to the days when Da was here. He was the head of the household, but Ma was the one who made sure everything was done according to her beliefs. I had to smile as I thought of times when she finagled things behind the scenes. No one intimidated her. She was using those same skills at *The Times*, and I knew she could make them work.

Friday morning rolled around quickly. We'd had a busy

week, and we were both thankful for Lisa's help in the office. Ma was anxious for her meeting with Bob. She had spoken with Doctor Leary and Jim Cauley, both of whom were very willing to participate in anything to support *The Times*.

Ma wore a kelly-green, silk blouse, gray skirt, and tweed jacket as she left the house for Emily's. Arriving early, she secured her favorite table in the back corner. She could carry on a relatively private conversation in the corner, and from there, she could see everyone who walked in the door. She never liked to sit with her back to the door.

Bob arrived right on time and ordered coffee and a blueberry scone, one of Emily's best creations.

"So how are you this morning, Ellie?"

"Just fine, Bob, although it's good to see the week coming to a close. It's been a busy one. I'm so thankful to have the new girl around. Lisa is a great help. You should stop by and meet her sometime."

"I'll do that. Besides, I'd like to see how things are running now with you in charge." He paused briefly and looked around. "So tell me, what's on your mind today?"

"To get to the point, I've been thinking about the makeup of the board. You, Roger, and Tom have been it for several years. Of course, Liam was active when he was here. I'm wondering if we might benefit from an additional member, some new blood, so to speak. And this town is growing. I think it's time to reflect that growth on our board."

Bob rubbed his chin. "Hmm… I wonder how that would go over with Roger and Tom."

Ma nodded as she looked him in the eye. "I guess we won't know until we ask, but we've had some issues come up with the hospital recently. We might consider giving them a voice on the board."

"You may have a point," Bob said, nodding his head.

"Jim Cauley has been coming to see us quite a bit lately. He might be interested in serving, and I think he'd be an asset."

"How about I talk to Tom Burton?"

"Great, Bob." They chatted about other goings-on around town. Bob still had teenagers attending The Academy, and they were active in the school play and sports. His stories reminded Ma of the days when Liam and I had been there. Not much had changed. Sister Mary Joseph still ran things with an iron hand.

Just as they were about to leave, Tom Burton walked in. Bob looked at Ma and asked, "Shall we approach him now?"

"Well, why not," replied Ma.

Bob waved him over. "If you have a minute, Ellie and I were just discussing an idea. Can you join us?"

As Bob explained the idea, Ma sat back and watched the two men interact. Tom nodded a few times. "Well, you know, Roger has always been of the mind that we got things done more easily with just the three of us," said Tom.

Ma's jaw tightened, but she kept quiet.

Bob pressed the case that the town was growing and talked about the hospital issues.

"Now, with an even number, there might be delays trying to come to an agreement. So another member might be good for several reasons, and someone from the hospital. Yeah, I think that's a great idea," said Tom.

"Let's discuss it at our next meeting," Bob concluded.

They all agreed to put it on the agenda.

On her way out, Ma picked up a couple pastries and brought them back to the office. She came in from the cold and walked down the hall with a bit of a lilt in her step.

She stopped by my office and offered me a pastry. She had a gleam in her eye as she smiled. "I think it's going to work. Thanks for the idea. It was a much easier sell than I'd thought. Of course, we have Roger to deal with, but hell's bells! If Tom and Bob are both for it, I don't think it will be too difficult to bring him around."

We finished things up early that day, and Ma stopped by the parish office on her way home to pick up the altar cloths. Father Declan was at his desk and invited her to sit for a minute. She shared the news about her plan.

"This calls for something more than a spot of tea. Could I tempt you with a little brandy?"

Ma gladly accepted, and the two of them talked for an hour or more.

CHAPTER 28

The next board meeting would be the first meeting in the newly designated conference room. Ma thought about picking up some meat and cheese but opted not to appear to be a hostess. The board members arrived promptly at 5:00 p.m., and the editor in chief was ready and waiting. She did offer coffee and asked Lisa to serve it, then she told Lisa she could go home.

Ma had prepared a written agenda and distributed it to the board. The last item was labeled "Board Expansion." She saw Roger skim down the agenda and look around at the others. He fidgeted a bit in his chair and then leaned back, looking from Bob to Tom.

As the meeting went on, Ma dragged out a few items. She went into detail about the bank's statement regarding an opportunity to change the loan restrictions for the old loan for *The Times*. She had discussed banking issues with Da over the years, understood their processes, and knew the terminology.

"Regarding Hector's notice of an increase in his fees," Ma began, "he hasn't raised his rates in over four years. I checked with printers in two other towns, and Hector's requested fees are right in line. His work is excellent, and he's always flexible if we need to change our schedule. I propose that we approve his increase without any exceptions."

"Well, Ellie, I don't think—" started Roger.

Bob interrupted, "I agree, Ellie."

Tom nodded.

Roger glanced from one to the other and grumbled, "Okay, all right, but we need to keep a close watch on the budget."

That brought them to the last item, "Board Expansion."

Roger growled, "What's this all about?"

Bob and Tom hesitated, so Ellie spoke first. "In recognition of the growth in our subscriptions, perhaps it's time to consider adding an additional person to the board. I had an opportunity to mention this to Bob and Tom last week, so they have had a chance to think it over. I certainly didn't mean to catch you off guard, and it's not something we need to decide tonight. Just for discussion, unless we all agree."

Roger responded, "I don't think it's necessary at all. It's hard enough to get four of us to agree."

Bob leaned forward. "Well, that's part of the reason I believe another member might be helpful. We may resolve things easier with an odd number."

Tom interjected, "I've been thinking it over, and it came to me that with everything going on at the hospital, perhaps a representative from the hospital might be a good addition. Someone without a direct tie to the paper... someone who would have knowledge of what's going on in town and who would want to see quick resolutions. Hospital folks are good at keeping things quiet, too."

Roger's face reddened as he continued to stutter, "I-I-I just don't see the need."

Their discussion went on for some time, when Tom finally said, "Well, I guess we don't need a unanimous decision to at least give it more consideration. What if we put out some feelers to Jim Cauley or Doc Leary?"

Roger's eyes bored into his colleague. "I think that's a bit premature. Let's decide first if another member is even needed."

Ma offered another idea. "If we agree that someone from the hospital would be good, perhaps one of the nurses would be interested."

Bob casually put his hand over his mouth as he glanced at Tom. Their eyes met, and both struggled not to smile.

Roger slammed his fist on the table, got up from his chair, and headed for the door but turned around. "Ha! We certainly don't need one of the nurses on the board. I doubt any of them would know anything about running a newspaper or any other kind of business." He left the room and started down the hall but soon returned. He peeked inside the room, shook his head, and left again.

Ma peered at the other two. "Well, maybe he'll mull it over and come up with an idea that we can agree on. Tom and Bob looked at each other and said in unison, "Good idea." They appeared to have caught Ma in her mischief.

"There's more than one way to skin a cat," Ma stated as she reviewed her notes. She knew Roger wouldn't hear of one of the nurses—or probably any other woman—on the board. Bob and Tom knew that, too. Formally, she suggested the topic be tabled until a future meeting. Ma knew her *Robert's Rules* and used them to keep the meetings formal.

The men went home, and Ma took the dishes to the break room and left them in the sink.

When Ma came home, she told me about the meeting. "You should have seen Roger's face. When I suggested one of the nurses, he was fit to be tied! Bob and Tom didn't know what to think, either. Hell's bells! If they agree on Jim or Doc Leary, Roger will probably think it was his own idea. It may take longer than I'd thought, but I believe we'll see some changes."

Ma astonished me over and over with her ways. She knew how to get things done and how to get around, or perhaps through, the obstacles.

The next morning, Lisa called. Her mother had become ill during the night and went to the hospital. Her dad needed to be with her, so there was no one to take care of her Billy. "I'm so sorry, Mrs. Hurley. I don't know if I can find someone else to watch him, but I'll try." Ma could hear the tremors in her voice.

"Don't worry, dear, we'll get by. You have to take care of your son."

"But I was behind on the afternoon sorts yesterday. I won't be able to catch up, and…"

"Don't worry, we'll do okay, really." She could hear the distress in Lisa's voice and paused for a moment.

"Unless, if it's Billy's naptime in the afternoon, maybe I could bring him with me for a couple hours," Lisa suggested. "He sleeps anywhere. It would give me time to work on the sorts and keep me from getting too far behind."

Ellie hesitated, then nodded. "Well, let's give it a try. We'll see you this afternoon."

Ma and I weren't in the office when Lisa and Billy arrived, so Lisa took him into the conference room and cleared an area on the floor where she laid out a large, thick blanket. She sat down with her son and read him a story while he snuggled with his favorite teddy, a brown, threadbare, cuddly animal he'd had since he was six months old. He quickly drifted into slumber before Lisa finished the story. "Thank you, my little man. Your daddy would be so proud," she said as she covered him with a small, blue blanket.

When we returned from lunch, there was no evidence of a little boy's presence, and Lisa was busily sorting the daily printouts.

Then Ma looked in the corner. "Oh, you did bring him in. How sweet. Lisa, he's beautiful," whispered Ma as she reached out to tousle his curly, dark hair and touch his turned-up nose. She stopped herself and paused. Her face softened, and her eyes grew moist. "It's nice to have a little boy around."

Ma tiptoed out of the conference room and went back to

her office where she picked up Liam's picture. "You know, son, it's not about how many papers you sell or whether you're the first to print a story…"

Lisa appeared at Ma's door. "Can I get you something, Mrs. Hurley?"

"Not right now. I hope I didn't wake him."

"Oh, Mrs. Hurley, he sleeps so soundly. You won't wake him." Ma smiled as Lisa beamed.

"You come and get me when he's awake. I want to meet this little treasure. For now, I'll make myself a cup of tea. May I get you something?" Ma asked, realizing she didn't even know what Lisa drank. "Tea, coffee?"

"Oh, no, Mrs. Hurley. I have a glass of water here, and that's all I need. Thank you."

I arrived a half hour later, and Ma greeted me with a finger to her lips. "Shh, Kate. We have a sleeping boy here today. And he is so adorable."

I smiled inwardly at Ma's turnabout from her all-business demeanor to her soft, grandmotherly side. *Maybe someday, I can bring that smile to her face.* Just then, we heard a cooing from the conference room and approached slowly. Our little mother was lifting a bundle of curly, dark hair off the floor. Billy turned abruptly and stared at us, as if opening a surprise. He gazed into Lisa's eyes as he clung to her neck.

"Hello, my little boy," said Lisa. "These are some very important people in our world."

"Hello, Billy. Did you have a nice nap on our floor?" Ma smiled at him as she peered into his big, blue eyes and touched his chubby, little hand. He drew his hand back as his bottom lip quivered.

"He's going to be a handsome lad, Lisa," I said as I watched the interactions between them.

"Thank you, Miss Kate. He takes after his daddy, but… er… I guess…"

I knew not to ask any questions.

"He's lucky to have such a good mum and grandparents who help," said Ma.

"I just have a few things to finish up, and then, if it's okay, we'll go home."

"That'll be fine, Lisa. Have you heard anything about your mum?" Ma inquired.

"No. Dad hasn't called or come home since this morning, and I can't take Billy into the hospital. I hope I'll hear soon."

"I'm sure things will be all right. You let me know if you need anything." Ma started to lift her arms and move toward Lisa but paused and stepped away. She looked at the two of them and then returned to her office. Her moist eyes went to Liam's picture. "I remember you at that age, my darling. If only I had one more day…"

That evening over supper, Ma and I talked about Lisa and Billy.

"What a beautiful child." Ma sighed. "It's such a shame that this old war robbed him of his daddy. He won't even know him. I hope Lisa finds someone new who will be there for Billy."

"Has she ever mentioned his daddy, Ma?"

"Only vaguely. Every time she sees Liam's picture, she looks a little teary, as if it reminds her of her soldier. She's never mentioned him by name or ever said that they were planning to marry or anything."

"She's never said anything to me, either, except today, she said Billy looks like his daddy."

"I hope her mum comes through okay, or she'll really be in a fix. I don't know how much help her dad is. You know, some men are more work than a child." Ma chuckled. "I loved your da, but I had to butter his toast or he wouldn't have been able to eat his breakfast. Kate, when you get married, don't wait on your husband. Start out waiting on him, and you'll do it all your life." Ma shook her head and half-smiled.

I remembered my da. He was a wonderful man, but Ma was right. He didn't do anything in the kitchen or in any part of the house. He worked hard at his job and made sure Ma, Liam, and I had everything we needed. He went to our school events, especially Liam's football games, and was involved with our town council, but once inside the front door, it was all in Ma's hands. I never saw him cook anything or dry a dish. I never thought anything of it, either. It just seemed to be a man's privilege to be waited on by his wife—even on a day when Ma had helped him at the bank all day or assisted with the town dinner.

Now that Ma and I spend our days working at *The Times*, neither of us really has the time or the energy to do all the cooking and cleaning. It would be nice if we could get some help around home, too.

CHAPTER 29

Lisa called again the next morning. "I'm afraid my dad won't be here again for Billy this afternoon. I called my aunt, but she has a doctor appointment and my neighbor has to go over to Woodland this afternoon. I could bring him in for his naptime again if you want me to."

"It worked well yesterday, so let's give it another try." Ma looked forward to seeing the little guy again.

Lisa arrived promptly at one o'clock, carrying little Billy and everything he needed for naptime—a soft, blue blanket, a bear named Baba, and a cushion for the floor. When I arrived, Billy was sleeping quietly with everything arranged around him, and Lisa was finishing her sorts. Having caught up yesterday made today's work much easier. She was dressed more casually than usual in a navy, tweed jumper, and her hair fell in loose strands around her young face. Her brow was furled and her lips were tight.

"Is everything okay, Lisa?" Ma asked, guessing it was not.

Lisa glanced up and gave a half smile. "Mum was doing better when I saw her. Dad and I went to the hospital this morning. He waited outside with Billy. She's doing better, but I have never seen her suffer before. She was pale and in pain and looked so... so helpless and confused."

"Oh, I'm sorry, dear. Just take it one day at a time. Sometimes progress is slow. And remember, we can get along if you need time with her. You've been such a big help to us, and I really appreciate all you do. But we got on before you arrived, and we can make do again if you need to be with your mum and dad." In the background, little Billy was sleeping soundly. He looked right at home here in the office.

"Thank you, Mrs. Hurley."

Ma asked me into her office as we left Lisa and Billy. She suggested that we have that meeting we'd talked about—a much-needed time to discuss what we were doing and what our plans were for the paper. We agreed to stay late in the office that afternoon and go over ideas and issues.

After Lisa and Billy left and I had cleared most of my daily items, I walked down to Ma's office. She was putting away a few papers.

"I think Lisa's short hours will be a test for us," she began. "She's been great, and I was getting more done with her help, but going back to a tighter schedule will help me set my priorities."

"Me too, Ma."

"I think I need to meet with Jim Cauley on a regular basis. The hospital is so important to our community. I hope I can finagle getting Jim on the board. At the very least, it would keep Roger honest." Ma laughed to herself. "My Monday Coffees are so valuable, but I have a hard time squeezing them in some weeks."

"Maybe I could be of more help. If I occasionally filled in for you at the Coffees, I might be able to tie things together with my evening meetings. It would help me to hear from other people about things like my article on the camp. Perhaps get another point of view." I offered this suggestion carefully so as not to tread on Ma's project. I knew the Coffees were special to her.

Ma hesitated. "Hmm... I guess you could give it a try. Actually, next Monday is a really busy day for me. We could let the ladies know ahead of time that there would be a change. That one day only, of course. Let me think about it, and then I could post a note at Emily's."

"Sure. I'd love to give it a go. Ma, the ladies won't have the confidence in me that they have in you, but it's time I start getting more involved, more visible."

There were high winds and a chilly rain on Monday. We blew into the office looking like a couple of shattered scarecrows. We knew Lisa's mum had returned home, but we didn't know if Lisa might need to stay home and help with her. But she arrived as usual, just as I was heading to Emily's and Ma was returning from her meeting with Jim Cauley.

Ma's regulars showed up for coffee but had little to offer. As they sat staring at me and trying to make small talk, I decided it was my opportunity to get feedback from them. I thanked them for coming and acknowledged my role as a substitute, knowing they would never give me the trust and openness that they easily conferred on Ma. I told them about Ma's involvement with the hospital and how she had been meeting with Jim Cauley and Doctor Leary. Maggie Higgins turned and looked around the café, then turned back and asked in a hushed voice if I thought Doctor Leary was going to retire.

"Oh, no, I certainly don't think so. He appears to be ready for a full return to his practice and hospital activities. He was on call over the weekend," I replied.

"So that meant the new, young doctor… er… had a little time off, right Kate?" asked Mary Conlon as she toyed with the fork on her plate. The ladies looked at each other and then turned their collective gazes on me.

I felt my face warm as I stood up. "Let me get more coffee, ladies."

I came back with a fresh pot, set it on the table, and as I returned to my seat, asked, "Did any of you happen to read my article about the POW camp?" Maggie's head jerked and her eyes moistened as she stared at me. This topic wasn't going well, either. I had briefly forgotten that her son was killed overseas.

Mary let out a sigh. "Yes, Kate, I think all of Hawthorne read your article."

"I hate to tell you, but I didn't appreciate it, Kate," said Maggie. "We don't owe those Krauts anything, and I don't want them free on our soil."

I took a deep breath and glanced at Karen, hoping for a little support.

"I understand that it's news and people need to know what is going on over there, but I'm sure you know people have painful feelings about their own losses. They ache for the sons who didn't come home. Your timing might have been off, dear."

Soon after, the ladies excused themselves, one by one, and the Coffee broke up, with Emily's poppy seed cake left uneaten on the table. I forced a smile as I said goodbye and thanked them for coming, but inside, I cringed.

Establishing trust in this business takes a long time. Just being a Hurley isn't enough. My shoulders sagged as I dragged myself back to the office to summarize the Coffee discussion. It wouldn't take much time.

Lisa was just leaving. She had tidied up the conference room and cleared the worktable. "I'll see you in the morning, Miss Kate."

"Thank you, Lisa," I mumbled.

Ma sat at her desk, head down, writing rapidly. She didn't respond as I walked by and said "Hello."

I let out a sigh as I closed my door and slumped into my chair. Here I was in my hometown, feeling like an outsider, struggling to fit in. My experience with the school newspaper was a fairy tale compared to Liam's and Ma's work with *The Times*.

CHAPTER 30

I got home before Ma that evening, so I peeled some potatoes, opened a jar of Aunt Nell's green beans, and breaded the pork chops for the cast-iron skillet. Everything would be ready to turn on the minute Ma walked in. Meanwhile, I changed into a pair of slacks and my old Aran sweater, the one Da had liked. As always, it warmed me as soon as I put it on and connected with its Gaelic roots. It seemed to retain the look and feel of the lamb who offered its coat for me. I built a fire in the hearth, picked up my book, and waited for Ma.

By seven o'clock, Ma still hadn't arrived. I didn't see anything on her calendar, so I called the office. No answer. After making sure the fire screen was secure and the stove was off, I got in my car and drove to the office. Ma's car was still there. I could see the light on in her office.

"Ma!" I screamed, as I saw her slumped over in her chair. She didn't respond. She was breathing and drooling from the left side of her mouth. Her skin was cool and pale. My hands trembled as I picked up the phone and dialed the operator. "Quick, I need an ambulance. It's Kate Hurley here at *The Times*."

It seemed like hours as I waited, trying to get Ma to respond. She mumbled a few unintelligible words and moved her left hand a little.

"It's okay, Ma. You'll be all right. The ambulance is on its way."

It was the same medic who came when I'd found John last year. He was quick, calm, and reassuring. As he wheeled Ma to the ambulance, I agreed to follow him in my car.

We arrived at the hospital at the same time. Kevin greeted us in the emergency room. "Give us a few minutes with her, Kate, and I'll let you know what's going on."

I could think of nothing to do except call Father Declan. He came over immediately. I explained what I knew as we waited together, sitting side by side on the cool, metal chairs that lined the faded, green walls of the waiting room. There were three other people in the waiting room. An elderly man cradled his left arm, holding it close to his body. On the other side of the room sat a young mother rocking an infant. The baby's face was flushed, and a few brown curls were pasted to his forehead. He looked sleepy but would occasionally bring forth some deep, raspy coughs. The youthful mom appeared as drowsy as her baby.

Father Declan jumped as Kevin came out to greet us.

"It looks as though she may have had a stroke. She's awake but groggy. We'll have to watch her and run more tests until we know how serious it is."

"Can we see her?" asked Father Declan.

Kevin glanced at me and then at Father Declan. "Of

course, Father. I'm sure your blessing will do her good, but keep the conversation short. Come along, Kate." Kevin placed his hand on the small of my back. His calm voice and strong hand were warm and reassuring.

"Oh, Ellie," Father Declan started as he took Ma's hand. "I'm here, Ellie. Please be okay."

"Hi, Ma," I said softly as I approached her from the other side. Her face was gray, and her mouth drooped a little to the left. I knew she was aware of our presence as I could see her squeeze Father Declan's hand. She turned her head toward me and gave me a crooked smile.

"It's okay, Ma. Don't try to talk. Just rest."

We stood there a few more minutes in silence. I looked at Father Declan and then asked, "Were you going to give her your blessing?"

"Oh, yes. Yes, of course." He took a deep breath and continued, "Ellie, may Almighty God bless you. May He give you strength, healing, and forgiveness. In the name of the Father, and of the Son, and of the Holy Ghost."

As he said these words, I signed myself with the sign of the cross. Ma didn't move. Father Declan rubbed his thumb on her forehead, lips, and heart.

Kevin placed his hand on my shoulder. "Let's let her rest. You can stay right here with her if you want. I'll ask the nurse to find you a chair. When we are ready to transfer her to a ward, I will let you know."

As he left Ma's bed, he motioned to the woman with the

baby. "Bring the little one in, ma'am. We'll take a look at him."

I held Ma's hand as so many thoughts went through my mind. I couldn't lose Ma. She'd been through so much the last few years, and she had been so strong. Surely she would pull through this, too. I wouldn't know what I'd do without her. I rubbed the Trinity knot that hung from my neck and wished Da was at my side.

Soon Kevin came back, looked into Ma's eyes, and asked her how she was doing, but Ma gave no reply. Holding her left hand, he asked her to squeeze his hand. Ma tightened her jaw and grimaced slightly, but her hand didn't move. Kevin tried the same with her right hand, and she moved it weakly. "That's good, Mrs. Hurley." He placed his big hand on her shoulder. "You keep moving your right hand, and we'll work with the other. It's more important to get some rest now. The nurses will come in soon to take you up to a ward. And your lovely Kate is right here. You're in good hands."

The nurse and an orderly entered with a gurney and, pulling on the sheets, smoothly slid Ma over from the bed to the gurney. "It's time to take you to the ward, Mrs. Hurley. It will be quieter there, and you'll get more rest."

I looked back for Kevin, but he was on the other side of the room, leaning over the baby with his stethoscope, his eyes focused on the baby's chest. His hands appeared so big as they cradled the baby's tiny body.

The nurse and orderly wheeled Ma to a room down the

hall. The nurse was right. It was much quieter. No one was around, except for the gray-haired woman sleeping in the next bed.

I stood by her side and spoke quietly, "You're going to be okay, Ma. You'll be back to yourself in no time. You just rest and you'll be fine. Please, Ma?" Father Declan was at my side. He didn't say a word, but I was comforted by his presence, and I know Ma was, too.

After what seemed like forever, another nurse came in. She checked Ma's blood pressure and pulse, shined a flashlight in Ma's eyes, and asked her to squeeze her hands. She looked at me and said, "You must be her daughter."

"Yes, I'm Kate. How is she doing?"

"She's about the same," replied the nurse. "Progress is slow at this stage. The physical therapist will be here in the morning and start working with her. The sooner the better. You should go home and get some rest."

I knew the nurse was right, but I was afraid to leave. I walked back to the emergency room. Kevin was standing among the beds, studying a chart. "Hi, Kate. Is your ma settled?"

I gave him an update and said that I might go home.

"You need to rest, dear. I'll be here all night, and I'll call if anything changes."

I started to reach out to him, but I squeezed the edge of my jacket instead. "Thank you, Kevin. Thank you for everything."

When I returned home, I had to throw away the pork

chops that I'd left on the counter. I put the beans and potatoes in the icebox, hoping I could revive them the next day.

As I headed toward the stairs, I got a chill down my back. This old house was so quiet, so big when you're the only one home. How had Ma done it these last few years after Da had passed and Liam was away? It must have been so lonely for her, but she never said. She always did keep herself to herself. Sometimes I think I hardly knew her.

After I turned out the light and crawled under the cool sheet, I listened to the sounds of the old house. It creaked and moaned, sounding like an old man sleeping in the attic. I tossed and turned much of the night and was just about to fall into a deeper sleep when old Rosie called. Damn bird! Sometimes I really didn't like hearing from her, but she was more reliable than any clock in the house.

I brushed my hair and put on the same clothes I'd worn the previous evening. I decided I could get coffee and something to eat later. I went directly to the hospital. Kevin was coming out to his car as I entered the parking lot.

"Good morning, Kevin. Have you seen Ma yet this morning?"

He turned around and walked with me. "Yes, and I talked to the night nurse. She said your ma did well throughout the night. Let's go see her together." He reached for my hand as we sauntered across the hospital threshold but let go quickly when one of the nurses approached the door.

Ma was awake. She looked more alert, but her color

remained gray. I took hold of her hands and gave her a kiss on the cheek. Her skin was still a little cool and her grip was weak.

Kevin checked her blood pressure and pulse and asked her some questions. Ma responded slowly, between labored breaths. She said she was not having any pain this morning but felt so tired.

"That's okay, Mrs. Hurley. Just continue to rest. You're doing better. We'll run some more tests today, and we'll keep a close eye on you. We need you to stay here a few days while we figure things out and monitor your progress."

He turned to me and explained that they would draw more blood and take another EKG. Meanwhile, she had to stay in bed. No visitors, except family. Just as he said this, Father Declan appeared at the door. "And Father Murphy," said Kevin. "He can visit, of course."

I thanked Kevin and turned back to Ma. Father Declan was giving her a blessing and then offered some reassuring words. "You'll be all right, Ellie. I've seen you come through greater struggles. The Good Lord will get us through this one, too."

After a few minutes, Ma drifted back to sleep. Father Declan and I tiptoed out of the room.

"Have you eaten, Kate?"

"Not yet, Father," I replied.

"Well, I came directly after Mass and told Mrs. Kennedy to hold breakfast until I returned. Would you like to join me? I'm sure she won't mind cooking an extra egg."

As we sat in the rectory dining room, drinking coffee and waiting for Mrs. Kennedy to fix the eggs, Father Declan talked about Ma. "You know, we go back a long way, Kate, many years. She and I grew up together in this town. We were here before most of the businesses that are here today." He gave a half smile as he gazed out the window. "We were here the day the hospital opened. I remember Doctor Leary standing in front of the door beside Father Connelly as he blessed the building. Now it holds so many memories, like the day Liam was born, the day you were born, and the day your da passed. It's really been good to have our own hospital and not have to travel, especially in emergencies. I think it has improved the survival chances for many people, too."

"I hope so, Father," I said. "I need Ma to stay around. I don't think I can make it without her."

Mrs. Kennedy arrived with our breakfast. After Father Declan blessed the food, we ate in silence.

"I'd better get going," I said, "and thank Mrs. Kennedy for the breakfast. I'm headed to the office to see what I need to do. I'll check on Ma at lunchtime. I'm sure Kevin—that is, Doctor Hagerty—will call if anything changes."

Before going to my car, I stopped in the church. It was cold and quiet as I knelt. I asked for God's help for Ma, for me. Where would I be, who would I be, without Ma? She had to survive this, and I knew she could.

I turned on the heat as soon as I arrived in the building. I peeked in Ma's office before going to my own. Her pen and papers were still on the desk. It didn't seem right to read Ma's notes, but it didn't seem right not to. I might need to follow up.

She had stopped writing in the middle of a sentence. It appeared that she was writing an update on the hospital certification issue. A line about Doctor Leary was half complete. It was something about probation. Was it complete or extended? I couldn't tell. A note under the papers had Doctor Hagerty's name on it. I organized her papers as well as possible and locked them in her top drawer. Whatever this was about could wait a day. *If Ma is awake and okay, I'll talk to her. If not, well... I'll see.*

I performed my usual dailies without any interruptions until Lisa called at ten thirty. "Hi, Miss Kate. I was just calling to see if it's all right for me to come in early today. I need to be home this afternoon when the health nurse comes by, which would be about three o'clock."

"Of course, Lisa," I said. "Come in as soon as you can. I'm on my own today, and I'll explain when you get in." I knew I was really going to need her help with Ma being sick.

Lisa arrived an hour later and started on her sorts.

I called her to come to my office for a bit. I explained about Ma. "Lisa, I'm so glad you're here, but I know you're needed at home, so tell me what you can do." I gave her a key to the office. "Come in when you can, whether or not I'm here. Do your usual sorts, and I'm sure I'll be giving you some other things to do. And thank you, Lisa, thank you."

At noon, I drove to the hospital. Doctor Leary was at Ma's bedside. He turned and motioned me out into the hall. Outside the door, he whispered, "Kate, she's sleeping now and she's doing better. Your ma's a fighter, and she'll pull through this, but it's going to be a long road."

I closed my eyes and took a deep breath before I went in to see her. "Hi, Ma. How are you feeling? Doctor Leary said you'll do fine, and I know you will. I know that God, Da, and Liam are all watching over you. You have to get better, Ma." I swallowed. "We have lots to do, but we'll take it one day at a time. First things first, and that means you just take it easy and get better."

Ma opened her eyes, looked at me, and garbled a few unintelligible words. I squeezed her hand.

"One day at a time, Ma. Remember that." I sat by her bed for a half hour as she slept.

Jan Haley came in to check on her. She asked Ma a few questions, took her blood pressure, felt her pulse, and then turned to me. "She's holding her own. The physical therapist worked with her this morning. It's important to exercise her hands, arms, and legs right away in order to maintain the muscle strength. He'll be back again this afternoon. Progress will be slow but steady. Your ma's a strong woman, and we'll do our best to work with her. Try not to worry, dear." She looked me in the eye as she held my mother's hand in hers. I took a deep breath and leaned back in the chair.

I went straight to Ma's desk when I returned to the office.

Knowing Ma wouldn't be able to talk for days, I decided to contact Jim Cauley myself and see what he and Ma were working on. He suggested we meet at five o'clock so he could give me an update. He knew that Ma was going to be disabled for some time.

I arrived at the hospital at four thirty so I could see Ma before I met with Jim. As I walked into the room, I recognized the oily, dark hair and the stiff posture of the man standing at Ma's bedside—Roger Ferguson. I clenched my jaw as I tried to control my voice. "It's family only, Roger. You need to leave."

He turned to me with his phony smile. "Oh Katie, dear, I just want to help. You need to be here with your ma. I can step in at the office."

"No visitors, Roger. You need to leave." I could see Ma grimace and try to say something.

Just then, Jan Haley came in. "Well, hello, Mr. Ferguson."

"He was just leaving," I told her. "He apparently didn't know about the visitor restrictions."

Jan stepped aside and pointed at the door. Roger started to say something but then sauntered out of the room.

"I'm sorry, Kate. There is a sign on the door, but he must have ignored it."

"Family only. Let's keep it that way, at least for now," I said.

"Yes, Doctor Hagerty and Doctor Leary insist."

I took a deep breath and then went to Ma's side. "How are you doing, Ma?" I asked. She gave a bit of a smile but offered no words. After a brief stay, I left and went to Jim's office.

I groaned as I saw Roger Ferguson sitting in a chair. "I'm sorry if I disturbed you, Kate. I heard about your ma this morning, and I wanted to see her. She's a special lady and I—"

"I'll come back later if you're not ready for me, Jim," I interrupted.

"Mr. Ferguson was just about to leave," said Jim, "and I know you have a lot on your schedule."

"But I thought I might be able to help," said Roger.

"Thank you, but Miss Hurley and I have things to take care of," said Jim.

"Well, just call me anytime," said Roger. "I am happy to step in wherever needed."

As I took the chair vacated by Roger, Jim shook his head. "I've worked with him before and learned to be careful with anything I say." He paused and began his update on the status of the hospital inspection. Things were going well, and Doctor Leary's probation had been lifted, a relief to all. I gathered that was to be the gist of Ma's article, and Jim agreed that it was time to let the community know. "Just call me if you have any questions or need more details. I'm sure you'll do a good job, and we'll both keep an eye on your ma."

I stopped back in to see Ma before I left. She was on her

side, propped up by pillows at her back and under her arm. She opened her eyes as I patted her arm. She looked so frail, and I had to remind myself that there was still a strong woman inside her tiny frame. I told her Roger Ferguson wouldn't be back and that Jim and I had met. She moved her head slightly and gave the half smile I'd seen earlier.

"Don't worry, Ma. You have good people taking care of you, and I have good people helping me." As she drifted back to sleep, I tiptoed out of the room.

Kevin was at the hospital door, still wearing his white coat. "Would you like to get a bite of supper, Kate? I will run home and change, and I can pick you up in half an hour."

"I... I don't know. I have so much—"

He placed his hand on mine. "Kate." This kind and gentle man knew just what I needed.

Supper with Kevin was the first time I relaxed since my mother went into the hospital. We talked about her and her prognosis, but we also discussed movies, the weather, just anything that came to mind.

He took me home and gently put his arm around my shoulder as he walked me to the door. As I started to reach for the knob, he held my hand and turned me toward him. "Please know that I am here anytime you need me." He pulled me close to his chest. I could hear his heart beating as he kissed the top of my head.

I leaned into the crook of his neck. "Thank you, Kevin."

I awoke the next morning, rested and ready for another day. I went to the hospital first thing. Ma was more alert, and the nurse was helping her with some sips of water. It pained me to see her struggle with such an ordinary task. She couldn't quite close her lips around the small glass, but she was able to swallow the little bit that made it into her mouth. The larger amount soaked into the towel the nurse had placed under her chin. I guessed that was what was meant by slow progress. Had Ma been more aware, she would have had tears in her eyes, but she just stared vacantly. When I took her hand, she responded by squeezing mine.

"Ma, you're doing well," I managed to say. Her half smile surfaced. She continued to grip my hand as I told her about going to supper with Kevin. I think she was trying to say something, but she couldn't form the words. Her eyes teared as she struggled.

Doctor Leary came in and approached the other side of the bed as Ma was still holding my hand. "You're making good progress, Ellie," he said, "not only in what you can do physically, but your lab results are improving. The physical therapist will keep working on your muscle strength and coordination. He'll be getting you out of that bed soon."

As we left the room together, Doctor Leary said quietly to me, "It's definitely going to take some time, Kate, but her early progress is a good sign. There are some things she may never do again, but we'll take it little by little and encourage even the smallest signs of progress." He went on about his morning rounds, and I started down the hall.

Just as I was about to leave the ward, the physical therapist passed me. I turned to see that he was heading toward Ma's room and decided to stay and see what he did with her.

"Good morning. I'm Kate Hurley, Mrs. Hurley's daughter. Do you mind if I watch?"

"Not at all, miss. We're taking it slow, and your ma is making good progress. I don't like to push her to the point of frustration, but it's a fine line between frustration and progress." He was a tall, strong-looking man with gentle hands and kind eyes.

The therapy session lasted about twenty minutes. Ma was struggling, but I could see she had no intention of giving up. Her inner strength was a good sign.

"Ma, you're doing great. I can tell you're not going to let this get you down."

She blinked her eyes as the therapist completed the exercises. I kissed her on the cheek and said goodbye just as she was drifting back to sleep.

When I arrived at the office, Lisa had turned up the heat and was working in the conference room. "Good morning, Miss Kate," she called out.

"Good morning, Lisa. Thanks for coming in so early."

"My mum is doing pretty well, and Dad said he would take Billy to the park this morning. I can stay most of the day if you'd like."

"That would be great. I have some catching up to do. Let's get together a little later to see what needs to be done."

"Sure. And how's Mrs. Hurley doing?"

I gave her a brief update and then headed for my office. As I turned to leave, Lisa said, rather offhandedly, "Mr. Ferguson stopped in to see what he could do to help."

I froze in my tracks and felt my jaws tighten. "Really? Did he offer anything specific? Uh… just what did he have to say?"

"Not really. He went into Mrs. Hurley's office and sat at her desk for a while."

I felt my eyes open wide.

"Is that okay, Miss Kate? He's a board member and used to work here, right?"

"We'll talk about it later, Lisa. He doesn't work here anymore, and I really don't like him snooping around."

"I'm sorry. I… I thought he was just being helpful."

I went straight to Ma's office. Fortunately, I had locked her papers in the drawer and nothing else looked amiss. She kept a "Ready" box on her desk, and it had several pages in it. I couldn't tell if anything was missing, but I leafed through the ones present. One page had a red pen edit, changing a word from "did" to "didn't," and the school fundraising report was altered to state that $56,000 was raised. I knew it was only $5,600.

"That scoundrel!" I knew this was Roger's work, an attempt to discredit Ma or me. I'm so glad I caught it. I wondered if anything was missing but had no way to find out. I put the papers in a large manila envelope and locked it in Ma's drawer. I would meet with Lisa later, wondering what to tell her. I'm sure she'd be uncomfortable keeping

Roger out of the office, so we'd have to keep our office doors locked, mine and Ma's. I hate to tell Lisa what a scoundrel Roger is, but I didn't think I had a choice. We worked out a plan, increasing her time in the office. I let her know about Roger as tactfully as possible.

Ma was making good progress, and Doctor Leary and Kevin asked to meet with me.

"Come in, Kate," said Doctor Leary. "I think it's time we all discussed your ma's next steps."

I was nervous as I looked at him and Kevin. Both appeared rather somber. Doctor Leary was usually so chipper, but today he wasn't smiling. Kevin glanced down at the floor.

"She seems to be doing quite well, Doctor Leary," I offered. "She was up in the chair yesterday, and she was eating... well, not much, but she was getting it down."

"Yes, Kate, she's made good progress, but she still has a long way to go. It's time to move her to a different setting. She still requires a lot of help getting in and out of bed, going to the bathroom, and even eating."

"Yes, I see that." I hesitated, waiting for further comments from Doctor Leary.

"She could benefit by spending some time in a nursing home."

"Oh, Doctor Leary, no, that would kill her." I glanced from him to Kevin. "She'd never want to go there," I pleaded.

"Kate, they have physical therapy there and nursing assistants to help with everything. She'd get everything she's getting here."

"Then why make her leave here?" I probed.

"She doesn't need the registered nurses to provide her care, and she's getting a little stagnant, a little bored."

"Oh, but please, not a nursing home. Couldn't I take her home?"

"Kate, I don't see how you could care for her," interjected Kevin.

"I'm sure I can work it out. Please, just give me some time."

They both looked at each other, then at me. Doctor Leary suggested we get back together in two or three days.

Kevin walked me down the hall. "I'm sure you'll make a good decision, Kate. Let me know if I can be of help."

I decided not to go back to the office. Instead, I headed over to the church. As I knelt in a front pew, Father Declan came by. He knelt beside me for a while and then asked if I'd like to talk.

He'd been here ever since I was born and was a pillar in our town. He had a reputation for his ethics and his dedication. Everyone loved and respected him.

I told him about Doctor Leary's recommendation for a nursing home. I choked on the words and finally let the tears flow.

He reached over to me and put his hand on mine. His bottom lip quivered, and it took a few minutes before he could speak. "Kate, I agree that your ma would hate the idea of a nursing home. She would either fight it tooth and nail or she'd give up. She's not usually a quitter, but she's vulnerable right now not being able to do much for herself."

"I don't know how I'd manage at home and still be able to run *The Times*. I'll be darned if I will accept help from Roger Ferguson. I've got to think of something."

"If she doesn't need registered nurses, maybe some ladies from the parish could help," offered Father Declan.

"I think I can afford to pay someone for a few hours a day, and I believe her insurance would pay for physical therapy at home. Maybe Jan Haley can help me with a plan."

On my way home, I stopped by Emily's to see if I might take home something for supper. Rita and Myrne were seated at a table. They called me over to ask about Ma. I guess everyone had heard. They had ordered dinner and were waiting. "Would you like to join us?" asked Rita.

"Well, I was going to take it home, but…" I sat down at their table. "It's nice of you to ask me. It's been a rough week."

"Kate, I know we've had some differences lately," said Myrne, "but we're still friends."

For a minute, all I could do was nod. Then I swallowed hard and gave them an update on Ma. When I mentioned the nursing home, they replied in unison, "Oh no, not Ellie, not your ma."

"She's too young and strong to be in a nursing home," said Rita.

"She'd hate it," said Myrne.

I told them about Father Declan's ideas, and they both nodded. "Your ma is so well loved in this town, I'll bet we can easily rally others to help," said Myrne.

By the time my dinner arrived, I was feeling better, more optimistic. "Maybe I can bring her home after all. At least, I can try."

That evening, I called Jan Haley at home. "Hi, Jan. I'm sorry to bother you at home, but I really need your help." I explained the possible sources for assisting Ma at home, and Jan was very supportive.

"I think you may have a good plan, Kate, and physical therapy can be done at home. All it takes is the doctor's order. Would you like me to join you when you meet with Doctor Leary?"

"That would be great, Jan. I have another day to get help lined up. If I have a strong plan, I believe he'll let me give it a try."

CHAPTER 31

I went straight to the office in the morning. It was cold, as usual, but the old heater kept doing its job. Lisa had the coffee ready to turn on. She was a godsend. Such a good help… quiet, efficient, and dependable. I hoped *The Times* wouldn't be a burden for her.

Before I went into my office, I decided to get Ma's work-in-progress. Was I being paranoid, or was something different about her door? I didn't unlock Ma's office very often, but the lock seemed to take an extra turn. Nothing appeared out of place in her office until I opened her desk drawer. The manila envelope was gone.

A chill ran down my spine as I tried to think of whether I had removed it. Had I asked Lisa to do anything with it? How could anyone—and I know who I suspected—get in here? I searched her other drawers, walked to the conference room, and pored through Lisa's work stacks. Nothing. I then went to my office and looked through all of my things. Nothing there, either. How could he have gotten in?

I tried to focus on my own work and get as much done as possible. I feared I might have to cancel the week's edition, but I did not want to appear unable to manage without Ma. Jim Cauley had so much trust in me, asking me to meet with him. Rita and Myrne were being supportive not just with Ma's home plan, but with their comments about my work with *The Times*. Most of all, I just wanted to get the work done and focus on Ma.

Before ten o'clock, I had four calls from ladies in our church who said they would be willing to help with Ma and knew other women would, too. Rita and Myrne both called and advised me that they each had two more volunteers. The friendship and support that poured in warmed me to the core. If I could pay a nurse's aide to come in and bathe her three times a week, I think I could put together a workable plan.

I called Jan Haley and gave her the update. She, in turn, furnished me with a report on Ma, saying she was doing very well this morning. She said she would set the time to meet with Doctor Leary tomorrow. At least this part of my day was going well.

Lisa arrived at eleven. "Good morning, Kate."

"Lisa, as soon as you're settled, could I see you in here for a bit?"

It only took her a minute. "Lisa, did anyone come in yesterday… or go into Ma's office? I know I gave you a key."

"Mr. Ferguson stopped by and headed down the hall, but I told him you weren't here and that no one was to go in either your or Mrs. Hurley's offices. He was very friendly and said he would do anything to help us."

"Aye, I bet," I grumbled. "Hell's bells! Did he leave right away?"

"He asked to use the restroom, and I couldn't turn him down. He left right after. Did I do something wrong?" Lisa asked.

"Of course not, Lisa. You did as I told you, thanks. But Lisa, I have to confide in you that Mr. Ferguson is not who he might appear to be. He used to run this paper his way, and he doesn't like Ma taking over. He'd love to see us fail. He's not to be trusted."

I went to the restroom, and sure enough, the window wasn't locked. We rarely opened the window, and I would bet money that it had been locked until Roger went in there. I looked outside, and there was a milk crate below the window. *The nerve of the old buzzard!*

All I could do now was recreate the stories Ma had been working on, and I would do it if it meant I had to stay up all night. Maybe Lisa could write up my weekly stats. Roger Ferguson be damned!

My first call was to Jim Cauley to set an appointment to see him this afternoon, then to the school committee to get a summary of the fundraiser. Before going to the hospital, I would call Hector to see if I could get a little more time for submission. That proved to be an interesting call. He said Roger Ferguson had dropped off an article for this week's edition.

"He what? When?" Crikey! That proved it—he had broken into our offices. Humph! I knew a call to the sheriff, Roger's good buddy, would do me no good. I was on my own. "Don't print up any of Roger's submissions, Hector, nothing unless it comes directly from me or Lisa."

I decided that the most efficient way to handle today's work was to get the papers from Hector, so I left the office and walked over to his shop. The brisk air chilled my cheeks and nose, but it did nothing to chill my anger. *That man is a no-good scoundrel.*

After retrieving the papers, I returned to the office and went through them, one by one, finding and fixing Roger's changes. He had even added an article about Father Declan and the parish. He said that a new priest was coming to help out with parish and school activities. Nothing slanderous, but totally wrong and inaccurate.

Crikey! A pack of lies! How could anyone take advantage of Ma's misfortune right now? Just in case, I called Father Declan.

"I'd love to have the help, but there is no such plan unless Roger has a direct connection to the bishop." He laughed loudly.

I paced the office for a while, listening to the clap-clap of my own shoes. Finally, I picked up the phone and called Roger.

"Hello." It was Roger's wife. "He's out this morning, Miss Hurley." She sounded very reserved. "I don't know when he'll return."

"Please let him know that I called. I'll try again later."

"As I said, I don't know when he'll return," she repeated. "Goodbye."

"Er... yes. Goodbye," I said, puzzled at her formality.

I spent the rest of the morning looking through Lisa's sorts, the weekly stats, and Ma's writings. Her reports were a bit dated since we'd missed last week's deadlines, but they would still be of interest to the community. All I needed was to add a hospital update, which I couldn't do until I met with Jim Cauley.

On my way to the hospital, I drove past the sheriff's office. Roger's car was parked along the side of the building. I wondered what they might be up to now. Roger and Henry were quite the pair. At least the sheriff's son, Richie, had gotten back in line, as far as I knew.

My meeting with Jim Cauley was a bright spot in my day. Doctor Leary and Kevin joined us. All were elated to share the good news. Doctor Leary was off probation, and the hospital would have another review to confirm the progress and corrections of the past problems. All assured me that everything had been addressed, and the hospital should get its good name back.

My article for now would be brief, assuring everyone of Doctor Leary's return to good standing and letting the town know of the scheduled repeat review. This would allow me time to get a complete edition to Hector in the morning before my meeting with Doctor Leary and the others to finalize a plan for Ma.

Community Hospital Back on Track

After thorough review by the state, Hawthorne Community Hospital has resumed its stellar reputation. The members of our community have never doubted the quality of care or the credibility of the hospital, but the State of Iowa always requires documentation.

The state has been conducting an intensive review process for the last six months, has found everything to be in order, and has released the hospital from the oversight process. The state's review has focused on records and documentation. Never was there a concern about the conditions of the hospital or the delivery of patient care.

Administrator Jim Cauley and Doctor Leary are most pleased with the outcome of the review and are ready to get back to the business of providing the high-quality care that has served our residents for over thirty years.

The state can continue with unannounced surveys throughout the next three years. Mr. Cauley and Doctor Leary welcome the opportunity to demonstrate the hospital's compliance with all regulations. Congratulations to all hospital staff for their efforts and success in responding to the state's report.

Jan called me that evening with a list of names of people who agreed to help and gave me some ideas on how to schedule everyone. She especially stressed that Ma would require assistance at night, at least for a week or so. According to Jan, stroke patients often get confused in the evening and throughout the night. Once daylight breaks, they return to normal—at least to their current state of normal.

Two of the volunteers were nurse's aides and offered to do Ma's baths three times a week. I might have to pay someone to take on the night shifts for a couple weeks. With Jan's input, I wrote up a plan, and we agreed on the details so we would be solid in our meeting.

My mind was so at rest as I drove home that evening. I fixed a toasted sandwich, Ma's simple Irish recipe. I was too tired to do much more, and then I dragged myself to bed.

It seemed so early when the old cardinal crowed. Perhaps it was the comfort of simply having a plan—or maybe the fatigue had caught up with me—but the night had gone by quickly. *Well, up and at 'em. Today is important. Oh, God, please let me be doing the right thing, and please let Doctor Leary agree.*

I fixed myself a boiled egg and a piece of toast, then headed for the office. I could get the final edition organized and drop it off to Hector before my ten o'clock meeting with Doctor Leary.

The office was cold and dark, as usual, but the flip of a couple switches would change everything. I'm so thankful for modern conveniences. I took a quick look into Ma's office and the conference room. Nothing amiss. I stopped in the break room to turn on the coffee and then went to my office. Nothing looked out of place, but I had a strange feeling. Was there a dusty smell, or did I detect men's aftershave? No one was in here yesterday. I went to the bathroom to check the window. It was intact.

I returned to my office and unlocked the desk, finding the manila envelope with today's edition. I opened it and reviewed it, start to finish. Everything was just as I had written it. I was wondering if my imagination was getting the better of me, but I was also curious if Roger was somehow gaining entrance into the office.

For now, I'd get the material to Hector and then stop by the hospital. Maybe on the way back I would change the locks—again.

The hospital was abuzz with activity when I arrived. There were more nurses than usual, and both Doctor Leary and Kevin were down the hall. I heard someone mention Mrs. Ferguson's name. A nurse was talking about a baby coming soon. *Oh dear. I think my meeting will be taking a back seat until lives were taken care of.*

I went into Ma's room. Her breakfast tray was sitting beside the bed. The plate was still covered, and the silverware was still wrapped. "Hi, Ma," I said quietly. She opened her eyes and gave me a slight smile. "I think they've been busy here this morning," I continued.

I peeked under the tray cover. It looked like cream of wheat, and it was still a little warm. I asked Ma if she'd like to try a bite.

I had to laugh at the expression on her face. It was a combination of "Are you kidding?" and "Not again."

"Well, it's better than going hungry, Ma." I unwrapped the silver and stirred a little milk and sugar into the cream of wheat. Ma took a few bites and swallowed without a problem. When it came to the fourth spoonful, she turned away. "I know it's not great, Ma, but we've got to build up your strength. I'm anxious to get you home."

I didn't want to get her hopes up, so I didn't tell her about my plan. Instead, I gave her an update on the hospital and the paper, careful not to mention Roger's efforts to throw me off. She seemed pleased to hear that I got the edition to Hector on time and was glad to learn about the hospital's progress.

It was almost ten thirty when Jan came in to tell me that Doctor Leary was in the conference room down the hall. I picked up my things and hurried to the small room. It had a rectangular, metal table and enough chairs for six people. It was warm and stuffy, very much in need of a window. Jan and Kevin entered at the same time.

"Good morning, Kate," Doctor Leary started as he took a seat at the head of the table. Kevin nodded and smiled. "Hi, Kate."

"Good morning, doctors." I took a deep breath and pulled out my notepad that contained my proposed schedule.

"Well, Kate, your ma continues to make good progress. I think she'll be ready to move on by the first of next week."

"That's great, Doctor Leary. I think I'll be ready for her."

"Taking her home will be a lot of work, Kate, as much as I know you'd like it for her," he replied.

"Well, I have a plan. I've had lots of offers to help, and Jan, here, has given me some suggestions as to what kinds of things we'd need to do for her."

"Yes, Kate, but—"

"Please." I swallowed. "Just let me show you what I have in mind," I pleaded as I began to lay out my papers.

Doctor Leary squirmed in his chair and glanced at his watch.

Kevin, bless him, took a look at my proposed schedule. "Crikey! You really do have a plan, and you've got a lot of volunteers. How did you do all this in such a short time?"

Doctor Leary leaned forward and raised his eyebrows. "Hmm... you do appear to have everything in place. Are these people sincere and committed for a long haul?"

"I really believe so. They came to me. I didn't have to go asking, and there are enough so that no one will be overburdened. I asked Jan to review it with me, and she advised me as to who she would recommend for the different types of work. If you'll order the physical therapy"—I paused as the doctors looked at each other—"I really believe she'll make better progress at home than anywhere else."

"Hmm," Doctor Leary said, "it appears as though you've thought of everything. I suppose we can give it a try." He peered at Kevin for support, and he nodded. Then he glanced back at me and said, "That is, if she continues to make progress throughout the next few days."

I wanted to cry, to hug him, but I knew he wouldn't welcome such an expression. I also wanted to hug Kevin. It was his interest in reviewing the plan that prompted Doctor Leary to look at it. "Do you think I can tell Ma about our plan? Do you think it will encourage her?"

"Of course, Kate." Doctor Leary nodded. "Nice work. Your ma's a lucky woman to have a daughter like you," he said.

Jan and I left the room together as Doctor Leary and Kevin started to discuss another patient. As we ambled down the hall, the orderly pushed a gurney around us. The patient looked like Roger's wife. Her shoulder was wrapped in a sling, and she had bruises on the side of her face. I was quite sure that it was Mrs. Ferguson.

CHAPTER 32

Ma stayed in the hospital another week. I had briefly considered a celebration to welcome her home but then realized how much energy it would take for Ma just to make the move. Two of her Coffee friends, Mary and Maggie, came over to help get ready for her return. We got a hospital bed for the parlor and brought in a card table.

I cleared some of the shelves to make room for the supplies she would need. The physical therapist, who was one of Maggie's cousins, came over to give us some ideas. He was very helpful and made suggestions to make it easier and safer for Ma to get around with a walker. He also arranged for the delivery of a commode. Ma wasn't ready to walk as far as the bathroom.

I gave my list of volunteers to Mary and Maggie, who had offered to coordinate the schedule. I contacted the Visiting Nurses Association to line up the nurses' aides for her bath schedule. I took a deep breath as I reviewed my checklist. *I think we're ready.*

Kevin called and asked me to go to dinner the night before Ma was to come home. I think the dear man wondered if I'd be able to get an evening out after she returned. I was wondering the same thing, so I gladly accepted.

Kevin suggested we go to the little café in Bickford where we might not see as many people from town. It was just what the doctor ordered. I sat with my back to the door and let Kevin order the dinner. I was too exhausted to care.

"I hope I am doing the right thing, Kevin. I didn't think about everything that is involved in taking care of someone at home, but I'm sure Ma will do better at home than anywhere else. Don't you agree?"

"If anyone can do it, you can," he replied, "and your ma has so much support in Hawthorne. Just take it one day at a time."

"Mary and Maggie have been a huge help already. And the physical therapist made some great suggestions. The nurses' aides are all set up, and—"

Kevin interrupted and reached for my hand. "And you know that if there are any medical problems, Doctor Leary or I will be there in a minute. Just take a deep breath and remember we're all here to help you." The touch of his hand warmed my entire being.

Supper arrived, and left, and I was barely aware of what I ate. It was a relief not to see anyone I knew. No questions to answer. Kevin took my hand and suggested a walk around the block. We stopped across from a small field and gazed up at the moon. When he put his arm around my shoulder, I leaned toward him and felt the comfort and warmth of his body. He wrapped both arms around me and lifted my head toward his. "Kate Hurley, I'll always be here for you." He turned me toward him and pulled me close. I didn't want him to ever let go.

*   *   *

Even though my heart was feeling blissful, my mind was still going in a hundred different directions. We had decided to bring Ma home on a Friday so I wouldn't be worried about submission details for *The Times*. Mary and Maggie were there, and Emily had brought a tray of banana bread and blueberry muffins. She also supplied us with enough meals to last through the weekend.

When the nurses' aide wheeled my mother through the front door, Ma's eyes lit up with her old sparkle and a tear ran down her cheek. "Oh my... my home, my home," she managed to say.

The aide veered Ma through the kitchen and to her "room" in the parlor and helped get her into the bed. As she moved Ma about, she talked me and Ma through every step and turn. Ma grimaced and held her breath as she pushed herself back toward the center of the bed. Once she had her feet up and settled, she smiled. "You don't know how good this feels." She sighed.

The aide gave me the few belongings we'd left at the hospital and handed me the bag with Ma's medications, all of which had been reviewed with me at the hospital. By the time we put her things away, she was sleeping quietly. I had hired aides to stay around the clock for the first two days so that I, and any of our volunteers, would get comfortable helping Ma in and out of bed.

By the time I returned to work on Monday, things seemed to be under control. Maggie and Mary showed up together before I started breakfast. We wheeled Ma to the dining room table and ate together, finishing the last of Emily's banana bread. Ma needed help with her egg but otherwise enjoyed her breakfast. She took fluids best with a straw, so she waited for the coffee to cool.

It was almost noon when I left home. Just as I was walking to my car, Father Declan pulled up.

"Good morning, Kate. I just thought I would check on my favorite parishioner. How is she doing?"

I gave him an update and told him he'd better get in there quickly, as his favorite parishioner was likely to doze off soon.

Lisa was busy in the workroom when I arrived. She soon appeared at my office door with a cup of hot coffee. "How's Mrs. Hurley doing? I'll bet she's glad to be home." She placed the cup on my desk.

"Yes, she is, Lisa, and she's doing well. Two of the Monday Coffee ladies are with her this morning, and another friend is coming this afternoon. After she has adjusted to her new routine, I'm sure she'd love to see you, and little Billy, too."

I started to review some of the papers on my desk but

looked at the clock. "Oh dear, I just realized that I had better go to Emily's and see if anyone has stopped in for the Coffee. I forgot all about it."

I put my coat back on, left my coffee on the desk, and headed out the door. "Please call Emily's if Maggie or Mary phone with any questions or problems."

When I entered Emily's, the place was crowded. Emily had seated the ladies at a larger table, and several other people were standing around.

"Kate, how is she?"

"I hear she's home. Is she doing okay?"

"Is she going to get back to the paper?"

I swallowed, and my eyes started to water. I asked Emily for some water. I couldn't get any words out. I scanned the crowd of Ma's dear friends and nodded.

"She's doing quite well," I finally managed to say, "and is very happy to be home." For the next half hour, I answered questions and accepted comments of support. Once assured of Ma's status, many of the folks left.

Myrne stayed and said, "Kate, I'm so glad to hear that Ellie is doing well. Let me know if there's anything I can do. And… I'd like to talk to you when there aren't so many people around. Can I stop by your office later?"

"Of course. You can drop by anytime."

"I'll come over around two o'clock, if that's all right."

"Sure. I'll be there unless something comes up at home."

I went back to the office with no new stories for the paper, just the reassurance that the people of Hawthorne were on our side. They wanted me, Ma, and *The Times* to succeed.

Maybe an update on Ma would be fitting for the next edition. I sat down to write, and my mind was flooded with the memories of so many years. Ma has had quite the life. She is such a strong woman and has always made the best of every situation. Now she is barely able to get out of bed and has trouble eating her breakfast. How do I tell her followers that she has met such a hurdle without making her look weak? What would she want them to read?

Right at two o'clock, Myrne came through the front door. I heard her ask Lisa where she might find me. Lisa walked her to my office and offered us both tea.

Myrne replied first, "No thanks, dear. I won't be here long."

I introduced Myrne to Lisa and explained that she had been with us for a few months and was a valued member of our staff.

Myrne nodded. "It's nice to meet you, Lisa."

After Lisa left, Myrne sat in the straight, wooden chair that backed up to the wall. "Kate, well, I have to let you know about a rumor going around. Not about your ma. It's about Roger Ferguson. Actually, it's about Mrs. Ferguson. She's in the hospital with some injuries. People think that Roger did it. No one has any proof, but that's what everyone is saying. And their son... well, I guess he couldn't stand being around them any longer. He left town."

"Oh, I'd be sad to know Roger could do something like

that. The poor woman," I said as I remembered seeing the patient on the gurney. I didn't want to add to the rumor mill, so I kept that memory to myself. What would I do with that knowledge anyway? I thanked her for bringing me the information and for being discreet. "I do hope it's not true and that she is doing well."

Myrne asked again about Ma and assured me she was available if either of us needed anything.

As she left, I walked her down the hall and showed her around the office. She had been there once before, but it was in the evening. Everything looked brighter today, and Lisa was working in the conference room, proficiently reviewing the teletype printout.

Back at my desk, I hammered away at the typewriter. I finished my article and decided to take it home to Ma to edit and approve before it went to print.

On my way home, thoughts of Roger Ferguson and his wife kept coming to mind. I was sure the woman on the gurney was Mrs. Ferguson, and she was in pretty bad shape. I knew he was a scoundrel, but I'd hoped he wouldn't do something like this. I decided not to tell Ma about seeing her, nor about the rumors, at least until I heard more details.

Ma's day had gone well. She had been home for less than a week but was adjusting to the new routine, though we all hoped her future would bring a return to her usual activities at home as well as in the office. After supper, I told her about my article.

At first, she wanted nothing about her to be written in

The Times, but after she'd read it, she bit her bottom lip and nodded. "You did a great job, Kate, but I really don't like anything personal in the paper."

I smiled at her. "Ma, everyone—and I mean everyone—has been asking about you. They want to know what they can do to help. I went to Emily's for your Coffee this afternoon. There were no empty chairs, and people were standing around. They want to know how you're doing. This town loves you, Ma. They depend on you and are so glad to see credibility return to *The Times*. I'm just sharing the truth."

"Well, hell's bells! I'm just doing my job down there… what Liam would have done." Her eyes clouded as she looked up at Liam's picture and then down at the floor.

I swallowed the lump in my throat. "Well, whatever you think is best. Meanwhile, let me help you into bed. We can talk more in the morning."

I went to the living room and picked up my book, but the words were a blur. I thought about Ma, *The Times*, Liam, and my da. *Would I ever measure up to my brother? Would Ma ever ask what I would do?* I fingered the small, gold knot that hung around my neck and remembered Da's words. I thought about growing up in this house, in this town. I thought about my old job in Omaha and Sister Edward Joan's words, "Don't hide your light…" I thought about Kevin. I also thought about Roger Ferguson and knew someone had to address that scoundrel.

As I sat there, my thoughts were interrupted by the sound of a car slowing down by our drive. I glanced out the window, and sure enough, it was the same black car that I'd seen a few weeks before. I closed my eyes and took a deep breath. I got up and locked the doors, then I went upstairs, grabbed a pillow and blanket, and returned to the living room.

I awoke in the morning with a headache and a crick in my neck. I checked to see Ma sleeping quietly and then went upstairs to get ready for work.

Maggie arrived with some muffins from Emily and immediately began to fix some eggs. I told her that Ma was still sleeping.

"I know, dear," she said. "These are for you."

CHAPTER 33

I arrived at the office a little early that day, long before Lisa. It had been a while since I was the first one there. I had forgotten how cold it was first thing in the morning. The chill was just lifting when I heard the front door open, followed by footsteps rambling down the hall.

"Good morning." No answer. "Is that you, Lisa?" Still no answer. I sat up straighter in my chair and listened. Iciness went down my spine as I heard someone try to open Ma's door and then mumble something unintelligible. I held my breath as my heart started to race. I quietly got out of my chair and moved to the space behind my door.

The mumbling and heavy footsteps continued. I could see through the crack in the door that it was Roger Ferguson—a very disheveled Roger Ferguson. He came into my office and went to my desk. As he rifled through the top papers, he grumbled, "Damn bitches. Not gonna keep doin' this." He stumbled over the wheel of my chair. As he caught himself, he looked up and noticed me behind the door. "What are you doing back there, you sweet, little thing?" He pulled the door toward him and slammed it shut.

"Roger, you need to leave," I said as firmly as I could.

"But I jus' got here, my sweet."

His greasy hair hung over his bloodshot eye, and he was unshaven. His half-buttoned shirt revealed a soiled undershirt and scratches on his chest.

I struggled to control my voice. "Roger, I said you have to leave."

"Ha! Try an' make me, sweetheart. Can't throw me out o' here," he said, holding on to the desk for support.

My hands were sweating as I tried to focus. How to distract him? "Well, then... uh... what have you been doing with your free time?" I prayed.

He stood there, still holding the corner of my desk, swaying back and forth.

"Please, Roger, have a seat," I said, trying again.

"I'd rather do something else, Katie," he mumbled. He took a step toward me but swayed backward. I inched closer to the door handle, but he said, "Oh, no, you're not goin' anywhere. You know, you and your ma think you can run this paper without me, but... but look what happened to her. She's just a weak, old bag and you're just like her. Brother wasn't any different. I taught him the ropes, and he thought he could do it better. Ya... better off without him."

I clenched my jaw but couldn't reply. Just then, I heard the front door again. "It's nice and warm in here today, my little one," Lisa said. "Miss Kate must be here already."

"Another bitch you're raisin', huh,?" Roger slurred as he continued to grasp the corner of my desk. "You women think you can get along without a man in this business. Well, you'd better... you'd better think more about that."

I heard Lisa walk past my door, talking softly to Billy, "Miss Kate must have a visitor, little one. We'll see her later."

My heart raced as I tried to think. "So, Roger, how is your wife doing? I heard she had an accident."

Roger's face froze as he glared at me. "She's jus' fine, yeah, right where she belongs."

I was afraid to ask any more about her.

He let go of the desk and approached me. Swinging his left arm, he grabbed the sleeve of my blouse but lost his balance and moved back toward the desk.

I caught my breath and inched closer to the door handle. I could feel the sweat trickle down my back.

"So, uh... how's your son, Roger?" I asked, still trying to distract him. "Does he still live here with you? I haven't seen him around."

"Naw, he moved to... hiccup... Des Moines. Guess this town's too small for him."

Roger's eyes started to droop, and he moved back to my chair and plopped down. "Yeah, Hawthorne's too small, too small." I inched toward the door again as his head nodded.

I opened the door and scurried to the workroom where Lisa was starting to pull up the day's printouts. "Good morning..."

"Shh, Lisa. Pack Billy up and get out of here. Roger

Ferguson is here in my office. Drunk and belligerent, but fortunately, very sleepy. I have to call the sheriff."

Lisa's eyes widened. "But Kate, you come with me."

"No, Lisa. I need to get the sheriff over here and get Roger out of this office." As she gathered Billy, I dialed the sheriff. Henry Richardson answered the phone.

"Ha!" he roared. "Ol' Roger's probably had a little too much to drink and forgot to go home. I'll come over myself and give him a ride."

The sheriff arrived ten minutes later with a grin on his face. "Yeah, he's been having a hard time, needs some rest. He just has to sleep it off."

"Sheriff, I want him to stay away from this office," I said. "I don't want him in here again."

"Why, Miss Hurley, Roger wouldn't harm a flea," replied the sheriff with a smirk. "Isn't your office open to the public? Isn't anyone welcome to come in here and offer information or tips for the news? Besides, he's still on the board of directors, right? He might be very helpful to you," he continued with the same sneer on his face, "if you'd let him."

The sheriff went into my office where Roger was out cold, slumped over my desk. "Hey, Roger, my boy, it's time to get you home." Roger didn't budge. The sheriff finally had to call one of his deputies, and they eventually got him out of the office and into the patrol car.

It was several days before I saw Roger again. He came to the board meeting looking sleek and professional, as usual, and acting toward me as if nothing had happened. I was filling in for Ma. Tom Burton and Bob Burger had okayed my being there. There wasn't much Roger could do. Tom brought up the issue of an additional board member. Bob readily agreed, and Roger did so without any comment. Jim Cauley was their first choice.

Meanwhile, Ma was making good progress at home. She was able to eat and feed herself with minimal assistance. She was walking from the parlor to the kitchen with a walker, though never alone. Her speech was improving. Either that or I was getting better at listening. She would read the weekly edition but didn't ask questions about the paper or how things were going at the office. She would get emotional over small things, a change so unlike Ma.

Both Kevin and Doctor Leary came and checked on her a couple times a week. Kevin was especially reassuring. The physical therapist said it was time to reduce her schedule to three times a week. Her group of volunteers continued their routine without fail. Some days, I was so optimistic. Other days, it was such a struggle to believe that we'd get through this change in our lives.

Mary, Maggie, and Myrne were my inspiration, but Kevin was my main source of emotional support. He would schedule his stop at our house to be the last of his day, and then we'd sit and talk. He'd stay for supper if I had something ready. I made it a point to keep my menu flexible.

This particular Thursday evening, I had stopped in at Emily's after dropping off the latest edition with Hector. She had made her famous beef stew and had plenty. I brought home an extra portion... enough for myself, some for Ma— what little she would eat—and plenty for a guest.

Kevin knocked on the door at four thirty. He checked on Ma and helped me get her to the table. He offered to assist me with the food.

"I made it easy for us tonight. I picked up some of Emily's beef stew. There's more than enough if you'd care to join us." I didn't need to twist his arm, as I knew it was one of his favorites. After supper, we got Ma back into bed and returned to the dining room.

Kevin picked up the dishes and began washing them as I made some coffee.

"How are things going for you, Kate?" he asked.

I let out a sigh, bit my lip, and turned to him. Without drying his hands, he pulled me to him. I put my head on his chest and stifled a sob. "I... I never knew it could be so difficult. I'm doing what I love, whether I'm at work or at home, but it's so hard."

He placed his big hand on the back of my head. "You're doing great, Kate, and things will get better every day. It's hard to see progress when you're in the midst of everything. Think back a couple weeks and you'll realize just how far you've come. You're going to make it."

With that, I gazed up at him and leaned toward him. He

wiped a tear from my eye, and his lips brushed mine. Once, then again. Then I never wanted to let go.

It was true. When I looked back on the days since she had come home, I could see her progress, thanks to her many friends and supporters. From that moment forward, things did change. Ma did a little more for herself every day. Her progress was rapid and visible. Her friends visited every day, but it seemed more like a social call than a time for help.

Doctor Leary and Kevin dropped by less frequently... that is, unless Kevin came for a social visit. On two occasions, I got some of the ladies to stay for an evening so I could go out with Kevin. I'm sure the rumors were starting, but neither Kevin nor I cared about rumors anymore.

One evening, we went to Bickford for dinner. On another evening, we went to Emily's, just before closing time. She was glad to have Kevin's favorite stew left and told us to take our time. I cherished our evenings and began to long for our hours together.

Father Declan's visits were the only ones that maintained their frequency. He came by at least twice a week. Ma had asked one of the aides to wash and iron the altar cloths, and Father Declan dropped by and picked them up. He always stopped in to give Ma his blessing. If she was up in the chair, he would sit and chat a bit.

"Ah, my Ellie, it's good to see you doing so well. May the Lord bless and keep you." A look of peace would come over Ma's face, and she would take his hand.

Things went well at the office, too. Lisa was learning more about the business and taking on additional responsibility. Little Billy came along frequently but was wakeful more of the day. We finally had to set up a playpen for him so we wouldn't lose the daily printouts to his busy, teeny hands.

The only time I saw Roger Ferguson was at the board meetings. He was cordial and quieter than before. Jim Cauley had agreed to accept a board position, and I became Ma's official designee.

Even the hospital activity was back to normal. Doctor Leary, Jim Cauley, and Kevin included me in the monthly meetings. The Monday Coffees were well attended, and Ma was getting ready to get back to the office, or maybe to Emily's, for a few hours.

I invited Kevin to come for supper every Thursday, since that was his evening off. Once Ma was in bed, we'd relax in the living room with a cup of tea or a spot of brandy.

On this particular evening, we talked business—the business of Ma and when she might actually be able to get out of the house, maybe even back to the office. I knew she wanted desperately to return to *her paper*. She often spoke about it in just those terms, *her paper*. As much as I could, I brought the essential parts of the paper home for her to edit before I took it to Hector. She didn't care so much about the routine stats or the society articles, but she read through the front-page articles with a fine-tooth comb in one hand and a red pen in the other.

This past week, she had been saying that she'd like to sit in on the meetings with Jim Cauley and maybe get into the office to straighten her desk. She also asked about Roger. I replied vaguely with regard to him, but I wasn't going to be able to keep her in the dark much longer.

I wasn't sure if Kevin was trying to keep me in the dark as well. This evening, he took both of my hands and looked me in the eye. "Kate, many people survive strokes but don't truly return to their usual state. Your ma is a strong woman, but we can't make any assurances that she will return to her full capacity."

I understood his reasoning, but I didn't totally agree with it. "Ma has made such good and rapid progress, and she is very sharp, to the core," I pleaded. "And she is so motivated. I'm sure she'll be back to her normal self."

"It won't hurt to try," Kevin warned, "but I don't want to get her hopes up—or yours, either."

"Thanks for your support and your honesty. I'll let you know when we have a plan."

After Kevin left that evening, I tiptoed into Ma's room and watched her sleeping. Her face was relaxed, and her breathing was slow and regular. Her dark hair, now streaked with gray, fell over her eyes. I saw her body aging, but she was still a picture of stubborn strength. At that moment, I felt confident she'd return to the paper and resume her active role in the community. Her friends were keeping her spirit alive and her mind active.

I went to bed and enjoyed a peaceful sleep. My old friend

woke me at first light. I asked myself, "Is that the same bird I heard as a child, or has a new generation taken over?"

I fixed coffee and breakfast for Ma and myself. I had to leave early, but the aide would arrive between nine and ten to help Ma with her morning bath and getting dressed. I left Ma comfortably seated in the parlor with her walker and a cup of coffee within reach.

Lisa had arrived before me, so the office greeted me with warmth and the smell of fresh coffee.

"Good morning, Kate," she called from the workroom. She was already doing her sorts. Little Billy was home with Lisa's dad, and she had most of the day to get caught up.

As part of my new routine, I checked Ma's office as I walked by. The door was secure. I unlocked the door and went in. Nothing appeared out of place on her desk. Liam's picture was looking a little dusty, so I brushed it off with my sleeve and vowed to spend some weekend time cleaning the rest of the office.

I went to my own desk and started to edit and revise the front-page stories. Not much had happened in Hawthorne the previous week, so I had to scrounge the AP for new stories of interest.

Just as I was finished with the second article, the phone rang. It was Ma's aide. "Please, Kate, hurry home. Your ma was on the floor when I arrived."

"Oh my God!" I screamed. "Is she all right? Is she conscious? What happened? Have you called the ambulance?" Lisa came rushing in when she heard me. "I'll be right there."

"Lisa, just take care of things as usual. Ma fell. I have to go. I'll call you later."

The ambulance was in the driveway when I arrived, and Ma was being carried from the house on a gurney. I ran to her and took her hand. She gave me a weak smile. "I'm sorry. It was my own damn fault. I tried to walk to the kitchen. And... oh God, it hurts. I think I broke my hip."

I was glad that she was conscious. "You'll be okay, Ma. Just take it easy. I'll follow the ambulance to the hospital, and you'll be taken care of soon."

Kevin and Doctor Leary were in the ER waiting for Ma. The look on Kevin's face told me this was going to be a real setback. To Ma, he said, "We'll get you fixed up real soon, Mrs. Hurley. Your hip looks like it might be broken. We don't need an X-ray to tell us that, but we do need it to let us know exactly where the break is and how bad it is. Have you eaten today?"

Ma described her breakfast.

"Okay. We'll stabilize your hip and give you something for the pain. If we have to do surgery, it might be tomorrow or the next day."

Doctor Leary nodded in agreement. "You're a tough woman, Ellie, you'll do okay. A little setback is all."

Ma nodded and gritted her teeth. I took her hand but had no words to comfort her. I went out into the hall as they got

Ma settled. They gave her some pain medication and positioned her leg.

"I'm sorry, Kate," I heard Kevin say behind me.

I wanted to put my head on his chest but knew this wasn't the place. "If I'd only waited until the aide came. It would only have been a half hour. The office could have waited."

"Kate, don't. It wasn't your fault," he said.

"She was making such good progress. Maybe I encouraged her too much. She probably thought she could do more than she was really ready for," I said.

"You've got to admit, she has a mind of her own, and I don't think she would have slowed down for anyone."

I knew Kevin was right, but it didn't make it any easier to look down the road and see how this would set her back.

They took the X-ray, got Ma settled into a room on the ward, and scheduled surgery for the next morning.

Once she was situated and fairly comfortable, I went back to the office and gave Lisa an update. I sorted the work on my desk so I knew what I needed to do to meet the Thursday deadline. I talked with Lisa about her schedule and reminded her not to let Mr. Ferguson into the office. She was a godsend to me.

I ate alone that evening, straightened the parlor, and made Ma's bed, placing her blue afghan at the foot. Aunt Nell had crocheted that afghan. A bit worn but still soft, it was a granny square pattern and had been on the foot of Ma's bed for many years. Ma still uses it if she naps and wraps it around her shoulders when sitting in the living room on a cool evening. I paused for a minute before I picked it up, took it to the living room, and wrapped it around my shoulders. I was too tired to build a fire that evening and knew I'd only be up for another hour or so.

One of Fulton Sheen's books was on the end table, closely aligned with a picture of me, Da, and Liam. The photo had been taken just before Liam left for basic training and shortly before Da had passed. So much had changed in the few years since she captured those familiar smiles. Sometimes I wondered if Ma would have suffered the stroke if her life had gone differently, if she hadn't had so much happen in such a short time.

Without further thought, I trudged upstairs and got ready for bed. Who knew what the morrow would bring?

CHAPTER 34

I arrived at the hospital as they were prepping Ma for surgery. She was smiling weakly, and her speech was a little slurred. I asked the nurse if Ma was doing okay. She said that she was fine and had just been given some pain medication. I kissed Ma on the cheek and told her she was in good hands.

Doctor Leary came in and advised her that she would be going to surgery shortly. He took her hand and assured her she would soon be as good as new. Ma gave a little laugh but was too groggy to offer any conversation.

Then he turned to me and said, "Surgery will take a few hours, and then she'll go to the recovery room for a few more hours until she's awake and her vital signs are stable. You won't need to wait around here all that time. I can call you when we're finished, if you'd like."

"That would be…" I started to reply, "but are you sure she'll be all right?"

Doctor Leary expressed confidence that he expected her to do well and that the surgery should not be complicated.

"Okay." I took a deep breath. "I do have a few things to do."

Just as Doctor Leary was leaving, Father Declan walked in.

"You'd better talk to her quickly, Father. She's about to drop off to sleep," advised Doctor Leary.

I went to the nurse's desk to give them my office phone number.

When I returned, Father Declan was holding Ma's hand. "I love you, dear Ellie. You know how much you mean to me. We'll pull through this." He quickly moved his hand as I stepped into the room.

I hesitated for a moment. "Good morning, Father."

His face flushed as he muttered, "I just heard, and I wanted to give her my blessing before she went to surgery. Er... how did this happen?"

I looked at him and then at Ma. "Well, it was yesterday, and I... I had gone into the office and... and how did you hear, Father Declan?"

"One of the nurses called me before she went home from the night shift. I came over right after Mass." He glanced down at the floor.

The orderly interrupted and told us it was time for Ma to go. Father Declan gave her his blessing, and I kissed her on the cheek.

"I'll pray for you, Ma. I'm sure you'll do all right."

Kevin came in just as they wheeled Ma down the hall. He put his hand on my shoulder as he reassured Ma, then he followed the gurney to surgery.

After they wheeled her away, Father Declan asked if I'd had breakfast.

"I had a quick bite before I left home, and I need to get to the office." I turned and left quickly.

As I drove to the office, Father Declan's words rolled through my mind, "I love you, dear Ellie." I hadn't heard such affection from him before. I thought back on all the times he was there for our family, for Ma. He was there throughout Da's illness and when he died. He was there with the soldier when they'd told Ma about Liam. He was there every morning afterward for a long time. I remember his tears at Liam's funeral.

"No," I told myself. "You're reading too much into a few words. He's like family. He's known Ma since they were kids. Of course he loves her."

Lisa was at the office when I arrived, doing her sorts. I gave her the update on Ma, then we both got to work. We had everything organized and print ready when Doctor Leary called.

"She did just fine, Kate. She's in the recovery room now, and they'll take her back to the ward in a couple hours."

I turned everything over to Lisa and went back to the hospital. The place was beginning to feel like a second home these days. I knew all the nurses and the orderlies. I knew where the ward refrigerator was and helped myself to some orange juice. The day nurse asked if I'd had lunch. She said that a tray was delivered for a patient who had already gone home, so she gave me a sandwich and a dish of Jell-O. It wasn't very tasty, but it stopped the growling in my stomach.

I dozed for a minute, sitting in the chair in Ma's room, and was awakened as they rolled the gurney into the room. She mumbled a bit but barely moved as they lifted her onto the bed.

The nurse checked her vital signs and examined the bandages on her hip. "Everything looks good, Mrs. Hurley. Here's the buzzer if you need anything. I'll be back to check on you soon." Then she went on her way.

As I sat there, Father Declan's words came back to me. "I love you, dear Ellie." I could hear a love and concern in his voice that I hadn't noticed before.

Ma was flushed and her skin was warm. As I took her hand, she responded, "Hi, honey."

She drifted on and off for the next couple hours, mumbling from time to time. "Where's our Liam?" and "Is that you, Declan?"

I placed my hand in hers and reminded her, "It's me, Ma. It's Kate. You've had your surgery and you're doing well."

She denied any pain and gave a slight smile. Her breath smelled like ether.

The nurse had instructed, "Nothing to eat or drink, not until tomorrow."

I looked at Ma and brushed the hair off her face. *There's so little I know.*

I stayed with Ma until after the evening nurse arrived and

checked her out. She assured me that Ma was doing fine. It was about five o'clock as I was leaving, and Kevin came by.

"How's she doing, Kate? I've been tied up in the ER most of the day." I gave him an update as he inspected her dressings and listened to her chest. "She appears to be doing well. How about you? Would you like to join me for a little supper?"

I hesitated only a minute. "That would be great. I guess I am hungry."

We made it to Emily's just before it closed and the place was empty, except for Emily. "Come in, dear ones," she said. "The special today was chicken and dumplings, and I have two servings left."

"Are you sure we're not too late?" I asked, hoping and knowing she would let us stay.

"Not at all. You're family, Kate. Now tell me, how is Ellie doing? I heard she was having surgery today."

"She's doing okay. The break was pretty clean, so the surgery went smoothly, right Kevin?" I looked at him for reassurance.

Kevin replied, "Yes, she's doing well, but still pretty sleepy."

My shoulders sank as I sighed. "She was making such good progress. This will set her back a while."

"She's a strong woman, but I'm so sorry this happened. It's a good thing you're here with her, Kate." Emily paused and wiped her hands on her apron. "But you two just sit down, and I'll bring you some dinner. I have a little wine in back if you'd like some. It's on the house, you know. I can't sell it."

She turned the "Open" sign around and went to the kitchen. Kevin took my coat and hung it on the rack beside his. We sat at our usual table in the corner, out of view from the window.

Emily returned with two steaming-hot dinners and two glasses of wine. "Just let me know if you need anything. I'll be cleaning up."

The chicken and dumplings were perfect, but my appetite was gone. The wine, however, went down easily. I rattled on to Kevin about anything and everything. I was telling him about growing up in Hawthorne and about my parents always advising me that I could do anything or be anything. "Da would tell me I could do anything, but he always steered me toward the usual feminine things. But Liam... my parents helped him do whatever he wanted." I reached for my gold knot as I thought of my father. "Da often said that I would make someone a good wife."

Kevin looked at me with a silly grin on his face. He reached over and put his hand on mine. "I think your da was right, Kate, but there's a lot more to the Kate I know. *The Times* is more a part of you than you even realize. And you'll always be there to support your ma. You're quite the woman... a woman of many talents and abilities. And right now, I think it's time to get this woman home."

I felt a little dizzy as I stood up. Kevin put my coat around me and held me firmly as we headed to the car.

When I awoke the next morning, it was bright and sunny, more so than most mornings. Then I realized that it was eight thirty. I rushed to the closet and picked out my old, gray sweater and tweed slacks. It was then I noticed that my nightie was on backward. And my coat was draped over the bedroom chair. *Oh dear.* I tried to recall the evening before, step by step. Emily's. Chicken and dumplings. Kevin. Wine... Kevin. He brought me home. Did he help me into bed? Oh my, I must have been so tired. Surely, we didn't... no, no, I would remember.

Downstairs, I shook my head and poured a little more coffee. After gulping down a piece of toast, I went to the hospital.

Kevin was at Ma's bedside, wearing his white coat with his stethoscope around his neck. His soft-blue eyes gazed at me. "How are you this morning, Kate? Your ma is doing well."

I knew my face was turning red. I shook my head and stared at the floor. "I'm... well, I'm doing fine. I overslept this morning."

Kevin straightened Ma's covers before we walked out of the room. "Not to worry, Kate. You've had so much to tend to these last few weeks, you earned a little extra sleep."

CHAPTER 35

Ma's recovery progressed ahead of schedule. Doctor Leary was impressed, but we all agreed on a more cautious approach to recovery this time. Ma stayed in the nursing home for two months.

Lisa and I fell into a regular routine at the office. She added on a few more hours and assumed the role of confirming the details of the daily statistics.

Kevin and I were developing a regular routine as well. At first, he came over on Thursdays after work and we shared dinner, either something I prepared or something he picked up from Emily's. Sometimes we drove to the little place in Bickford. We always ended up back home for coffee.

"Back home" was the part I began to cherish. It was so easy to talk to Kevin. I shared my deepest thoughts with him. I trusted my heart with him. Kevin would never discuss his patients by name, but he shared the aches in his heart as he saw them through their sufferings. He shared, too, the joys of bringing a new life into the world or making a life more comfortable. He was the kindest, most caring man I had ever known.

Since Friday was his day off, he would stay late on

Thursday evening. I always had dinner ready so we could eat early and afterward enjoy some music on the record player in the living room. We were both delighted with classical music, but this one evening, I put on a record by Perry Como. When he started to croon "Sentimental Journey," Kevin looked at me.

"This reminds me of New Year's Eve," he said, as he reached for my hand. "Shall we?"

The carpet was not a smooth dance surface, but I melted in his arms as we swayed to the soothing sounds of my favorite music. As the song ended, Kevin placed his fingers under my chin and said, "You have brought so much pleasure to my journey, Miss Hurley." Then he pulled me closer and his lips met mine, softly at first, then more firmly and deeply. My lips parted as his body warmed my entire being. We walked back to the couch. His hands slipped down toward my hips, and his lips moved to my neck and below. My body so easily responded to his, and we fit together perfectly.

"Oh, Kate," he groaned.

I could barely breathe a reply. "Yes."

* * *

Once she could walk without any devices, Ma was ready to come home. The nursing home director was ready to let her go, too. They had their confrontations as my stubborn,

Irish mother was giving suggestions on how to run the facility.

Her friends who had come over after her stroke were right back in line to help her at home, though she didn't require much assistance. Her time in the nursing home allowed her to receive regular, post-stroke therapy as well as daily walking exercises. She came home better able to perform her usual household activities.

Lisa visited on a regular basis, bringing little Billy with her. These visits were the highlight of Ma's week, even though Billy was getting active and loved to investigate every corner of the house. Lisa was careful to keep him away from anything breakable.

Ma allowed him to explore the cupboards in the parlor, where he found some of my and Liam's old toys. Liam had some little, plastic soldiers in the back of a lower cupboard. Billy brought them out and asked Ma to look at them. Understandably, it brought a tear to her eye, but I also detected a tear in Lisa's eye. Lisa seemed so touched by the connection. At the end of their visit, Ma usually let Billy take something home, and the soldiers were his favorite prize. Billy was not interested in anything from my cupboard, where I housed my old, plastic horses and some small books. Or was it that Ma had directed him to Liam's old shelves?

When Billy's birthday came around, Ma ordered some things from the Sears Catalog and asked me to make a cake for his big day. We had a party on Saturday afternoon two days after the actual date. He didn't have much celebration at his own home since Lisa's mum wasn't really up to it. Lisa's mum and dad came to our house for the party. I made a chocolate cake and got some ice cream and candles. We had a fun afternoon, especially Ma and Billy. Lisa was rather quiet and stood off to the side for much of the party. She was smiling, but occasionally, her lower lip trembled and she would turn and walk into the living room.

Ma seemed to notice it, too. At one point, she took Lisa's hand and said, "You are a good ma for your little guy. He's such a happy child. I'm sure his daddy would be proud."

"Thank you, Mrs. Hurley. I do wish his daddy could be here, be a part of his life. Someday, Billy will be a proud, young man and know who his daddy was and what he did for our country."

Ma's eyes softened as she looked at Lisa. "You know, my Liam would have made a good daddy if he hadn't given his life over there, too."

Lisa glanced at Ma and swallowed. She opened her mouth as if to speak, but no words came out. After a few seconds, she said, "I'm sure he would have, Mrs. Hurley." The two of them seemed to have bonded as they shared the pain of their losses.

Ma surveyed the room and settled her eyes on Lisa's parents. "Mrs. Ward, would you like more tea? Kate will get it for you."

At the sound of my name, I turned to see Ma holding Lisa's hand and smiling at her mother.

"Of course, Mrs. Ward, I'll get you another cup. More cake, too?" I heard myself ask.

As I walked to the kitchen, my jaws were feeling tense. I boiled more water and cut two pieces of cake, one for Mr. Ward, too. I peered out the kitchen window and wondered how Kevin was doing today. Saturdays were unpredictable at the hospital. No scheduled procedures, but accidents or sudden illnesses filled the day.

"Kate? I hear the kettle boiling. Are you out there?"

"Oh, yes, Ma, sorry. I was thinking about something else."

I steeped a cup of Earl Grey and placed everything on a tray. "At your service," I muttered under my breath.

Lisa helped Billy open his presents, and he responded by running around the room, showing each person his new treasure. His excitement was infectious. I couldn't help but smile.

By the end of the afternoon, everyone, except Billy, was worn out.

"We really must go, Mrs. Hurley. My mum is looking pretty tired, and so is Dad. Thank you so much for doing this for us." She turned to me. "And thank you, too, Kate. Everything was so good and so much fun."

I helped Lisa carry Billy's gifts to the car, and then she and I pushed her mum in the wheelchair.

When I returned, Ma was dozing in her chair, snoring lightly. I went to the kitchen to clean up the cake plates and teacups. After everything was cleaned and put away, I returned to the living room and picked up my book.

Just as I did, Ma awoke with a smile. "Ah, that was such a good party. That little Billy is a darling boy. He reminds me of Liam at that age. So full of life and bursting with energy."

Ma rose from her chair and walked around the room, pausing in front of Liam's picture and stopping at the window. She stood there, silently, for at least ten minutes, then returned to her chair and resumed reading her book. Two hours went by in silence, with Ma turning only three pages.

"Did the party tire you, Ma? You're rather quiet this afternoon."

"Oh no. Well, yes, I guess it did, but the joy it brought Billy and Lisa made it worthwhile. That girl has done so much for us, it's nice to do something for her. Yes, she was a good addition to the office. Father Declan knew she'd fit in well with us."

I had forgotten that he was the one who found her for us.

"Well, Kate, I didn't think I'd be hungry after eating that cake, but I'm wondering what we're having for dinner."

I looked at Ma and couldn't answer. I stared at her for a minute, swallowed, and took a deep breath. "I didn't plan anything for tonight, but we have some leftover roast. Maybe we can each make a sandwich or something." I ambled to the kitchen, waiting for Ma to follow.

As I started to slice some beef, Ma called out, "What are

you fixing, Kate? I'm really too tired to be of much help tonight."

"How about a roast beef sandwich, with gravy?"

"Sure, hon, that sounds good," she replied.

CHAPTER 36

Ma was planning to come into the office on Monday. I hoped she wasn't being unrealistic, but I felt setting a goal was good motivation for her. Lisa had agreed to come in for the whole day so that together we could tend to Ma, if needed, and get the work done.

A loud spring rain greeted us that morning. There was thunder and lightning and it poured down rain, but Ma was not deterred from her plan.

"What a way to go back, eh, Kate?"

"Ma, you can wait a day. I'll go in and Lisa and I can get a jump on the work for the week, then you can come in tomorrow."

"Oh, hell's bells! What's a little rain?"

"Ma, this is more than a little rain. It's slippery out there and cold this morning," I pleaded. "Please think this through, Ma."

"Oh, I've thought about this day for a long time. A little rain is not going to stop me."

There were no words that were going to change her mind.

I fixed breakfast, did the dishes, and made some lunch for us to eat at the office.

"I'll pull the car around to the front, Ma. It will be safer to walk from there."

I took Ma's things to the car. She had packed her old, flowered satchel with papers, a new picture, and several odds and ends for her office. As I carried it out, the wind ripped my coat open and wrapped my hair around my face. The water on the sidewalk seeped up around my shoes and threatened my balance. I threw Ma's bag in the back seat and went back to help her.

When I went in for Ma, she was waiting at the door. Her walker was still in the parlor.

"Where's your walker, Ma?"

"I'm not going to need that thing at the office."

"Well, maybe not once you're inside, but you'll need it getting to and from."

"I'm not going to need it," she said as she glared at me.

"Ma, you're not leaving this house without it! If the walker doesn't go, neither do you."

She started to walk by me toward the door. I jangled the keys at her as I went to the parlor to retrieve her walker.

"You are not stepping out that door without your walker. That's insane to think we can take the risk of you falling before you've had one day back at work."

Ma let out a groan and turned to wait for me. "Hell's bells, Kate! You're treating me like a child."

"Well, Ma, right now, you're acting like one."

By the time we arrived at the office, we were both dripping wet. My hands were cold and stiff, and I had trouble getting the key in the door. Once open, the office greeted us with warmth and the aroma of fresh coffee.

We shed our wet coats at the door, and I walked with Ma to her office. The door was open and the light was on. Lisa had dusted and polished her desk and bookcase and placed a small plant on the corner of the bookcase next to Liam's picture.

"Oh my, Lisa, you're so thoughtful. It's so good to see this place."

"Do you want coffee or tea this morning, Mrs. Hurley?"

"Tea would be lovely, dear. Thank you."

As Lisa went to brew the Earl Grey, I got Ma settled and then proceeded to my own office. My shoes were soaked, and I wished for something warm to change into. Perhaps it would be a good idea to keep a change of clothes and shoes in the closet for days like this.

"Can I get you some coffee, Kate?"

"That sounds wonderful, Lisa, thank you."

When she returned, I asked about Billy. Lisa's mum and dad were home today, and her mum was doing much better. "I told them I'd call at lunchtime and see how things were going. I think they can handle him all day. He's so tired after yesterday, he should take a long nap."

Lisa went back to the workroom and started her sorts. The teletype was printing out the latest news.

I could hear Ma talking on the phone. "Hello, Jim. How

are things going at the hospital? I wanted to let you know that I'm back at work and look forward to seeing you. If you have the time, could you stop over here sometime this week? I'd like to catch up on your progress. Sure, and if Doctor Leary has time, bring him along."

I closed my eyes as I felt my chest tighten. I had kept her informed every step of the way. I wondered if she planned to include me in the meeting. I looked at the notes I'd left on my desk and tried to remember what I needed to do to follow up. Then I recalled that it was Monday, and the Coffee group would be at Emily's. I squeezed back into the wet shoes and shivered as I donned my coat.

"I'm going down to Emily's, Ma. Is there anything you'd like me to tell the ladies?"

"Oh, I wish I was up to getting down there myself, but with this rain, I think I'll stay put today. Tell them all 'hello' for me and that I'll be back to see them as soon as possible."

"Sure, Ma. I know they will be happy for you to be back at work."

I told Lisa to call me if she needed anything or if Ma required help.

The table at Emily's was full. I guessed that they knew Ma was coming back and thought they'd either see her or get the latest news. The blueberry scones were heavenly, just what was needed on this dreary day.

"Good afternoon, ladies. How nice of you to come out in this rain."

Mary and Maggie were asking about Ma. "How did she

do, Kate? Do you think she'll last all day? We can help her get home if you need us to."

"Thank you both. I planned a flexible day so I can take her home early if necessary, but you never know what might come up in this business."

Myrne was there, too.

"Welcome, Myrne. It's so good to see you."

"Hi, Kate. The store was kind of slow this afternoon, so I thought I would drop by."

I gave them an update on Ma's progress. None of them had much news for me, but it was a heartwarming meeting.

"Are you going to keep coming to our Coffee meetings, Kate? It's been great to get to know you better. You've got so much energy."

I felt my face warm and my shoulders relax. I didn't even know that I was tense, but Mary's comments put me at ease.

"Thank you, Mary, I hope so. And Ma is anxious to get back here and see you, too."

"I hope you'll keep coming, too, Kate. You shed a little different light on things," said Maggie.

"I'll talk to Ma about it. I'm sure she has plans."

As we got up to leave, Myrne stopped me. "Kate, I've been meaning to ask if you are still having your After-Five meetings. Rita and I would both like to see you sometime."

"I haven't had a meeting in a while. With Ma's problems, I've had to be home most evenings."

"Well, Rita and I get together for supper every now and then. Maybe some evening, you could join us… that is, if you'd like to. We really didn't give you a fair chance, and we wanted to try again."

I swallowed the lump in my throat and smiled. "Myrne, I would love to. Right now, I have to plan around Ma, but if I know a few days ahead, I can make arrangements."

"Would this Thursday work for you? I'm pretty sure that Rita is available. We could come to my house. I'll put something together."

"I'll see what I can do. I would really love to see you both. Thank you."

There was a break in the rain as I returned to the office. I had wanted to drop by the hospital and catch Jim Cauley, but I had no reason to be at the hospital. When I arrived at the office, I recognized Roger's car parked on the side street. He's the last person either Ma or I needed to see today.

Ma's door was open, and she motioned for me to come in. Roger was seated in a chair with his back to me. Ma's face was strained and a bit pale.

"Hello, Roger," I offered.

"I think he was about to leave," said Ma.

"Drive carefully out there. The roads are slick with all this rain," I said through clenched teeth.

"I just stopped by to welcome your ma back to work. It's been a long time. I'll bet you're glad to have her back." He was making no move to leave.

"How's Mrs. Ferguson doing?" I asked.

Roger jerked his head and moved himself back in the

chair. "M-m-much better, now. She needs to watch where she's walking. She's getting a little clumsy."

"Really, Roger? I guess I haven't seen her out lately," I replied.

"Thank you for stopping by, Roger. I'll see you at the next board meeting," said Ma.

He took the hint but stopped by the workroom and said hello to Lisa. Lisa nodded but offered no conversation. I finally heard the door close behind him.

Ma shook her head. "That man is still up to no good. What happened to Mrs. Ferguson?" she asked.

"I guess I didn't tell you, but I saw her at the hospital when I went to visit you one evening. She had some bandages on her head and maybe a broken arm. Everyone was hush-hush, but there were rumors. She doesn't have many friends that I know of, and you rarely see her without Roger. People were asking questions." I thought about telling Ma about the incident here in the office, but she didn't need any new worries right now.

The day went by quickly, that is, until about three o'clock. Ma called me into her office and, with droopy eyes, asked me to take her home.

"Are you all right, Ma?" I asked.

"Yes, yes. It's just been too long of a day. I really need to get home and rest."

"Of course, Ma, of course," I said without adding 'I told you so.'

Lisa agreed to tidy up Ma's desk and lock up her office. I

told her I'd return unless Ma required my assistance at home. On the way home, Ma didn't hesitate to use the walker. The rain had let up, and we both remained a little drier.

I got her settled in the parlor, then I changed into drier clothes and shoes and went back to the office.

Lisa had everything in place, ready for another day.

"You can go home if you need to, Lisa."

"Thank you, Kate. My mum is probably getting worn out today. Would you like me to try to stay most of tomorrow?"

"That would be great. Thank you again for all your help."

After Lisa left, I locked the door and headed to my office to finish up the day's stats and made some notes about the Monday Coffee. As I passed Ma's office, I noticed that the light was still on, so I opened her door. Her calendar was open on her desk. I saw that she had scheduled something for Thursday—a meeting with Jim Cauley and Doctor Leary. I sighed, turned off the light, and moseyed back to my office.

The stats seemed extra boring today, and I had trouble concentrating on my summary of the Coffee. I rewrote the first paragraph three times. I began thinking about my future. *What is it going to take to hold my own here in the office? Will my work ever have validity in Ma's eyes? Will I ever measure up to Liam?*

I thought about my work in Omaha, my friends, and the school newspaper. I thought about the fun we had after work. Then, too, I thought about Kevin… and the comments from Myrne this morning. "One day at a time," I said aloud.

When I arrived home, Ma was asleep on her bed with her afghan wrapped around her.

I made a cup of tea and curled up in Da's chair in the living room. Something about Da's chair always assured me that everything would work out in time.

After a few minutes, I heard Ma getting up in the parlor. "Do you need anything, Ma? Looks like you had a good rest. Are you about ready for supper?"

"Oh, yes. Crikey! What a day. I didn't know it would take so much out of me. A light supper would be fine."

I warmed the leftover stew. Its aroma filled the kitchen… the perfect cure for a long, chilly day.

Ma didn't eat a lot, but she seemed to enjoy it. "That hit the spot, Kate, thank you."

"Other than wearing you out a bit, how was your day, Ma?"

"For the first couple hours, it was great. I could have done without the visit from Roger. The old devil hasn't changed." She shook her head and gave a wry laugh. "But it felt good to be back among the living."

"I heard you talking to Jim Cauley. Anything new?"

"He didn't have much time to talk today, but he agreed to stop over later in the week to bring me up to date."

"I'd like to join you, Ma. I've been working pretty closely with him and Doctor Leary in your absence. It actually afforded me the chance to be a real part of the paper."

Ma smoothed down her napkin and stared at the table. "I don't know that it's necessary."

"I've been involved, and I'd like to hear if there are any new developments. I may be able to give some insight. Besides, until you're more mobile, I might continue to sit in on hospital meetings."

"We'll see." She cleared her throat and nodded her head. "I'll look at my agenda."

"Sure, Ma." I removed the dirty dishes from the table and started to clean the kitchen.

Ma decided to work only mornings the rest of the week. As I drove her in on Wednesday, I inquired about her meeting with Jim.

She peered out the window. "It's tomorrow morning." She made no other comments, so I concluded that I wasn't invited.

Thursday morning was crisp and, thankfully, sunny. Ma dressed in her gray suit. I wore my maroon skirt and gray blazer. Ma used the walker to get to and from the car, but once inside the office, she put it in the back room. She grimaced as she stood tall and walked gingerly back to her office.

Jim Cauley and Doctor Leary arrived a little after ten.

Just as they got seated, I walked by Ma's office. "Good morning, gentlemen," I said.

"Hello, Kate. Nice to see you," said Jim. Doctor Leary nodded.

"Will you be joining us?" Jim asked.

"Well, if you need me, I'd be pleased to do so."

Jim looked at Ma as she flushed.

"I don't—"

Jim interrupted, "Kate has had some good ideas and been quite helpful to us."

Ma's jaw tightened as she swallowed. "Sure, that would be fine, unless you're busy with your stats, Kate."

"Lisa has been doing the stats. I can take a few minutes to join you. Let me get a couple things." I smiled as I returned to my office for some notes I had prepared, and I made a mental note to repay Jim Cauley.

I asked Lisa to sit in my office and work on my stats so we could meet in the workroom. As we were seated, Lisa peeked in and offered tea or coffee. I commented to Ma and the men that Lisa had been so helpful and learned to take on more responsibility, freeing me up to take care of other things.

Jim stated that it had been very helpful to have me at hospital meetings, especially as the restrictions had been lifted.

Ma leaned forward and looked at me as she added, "Yes, she brought me up to date at home, and we discussed several ideas."

Jim glanced back and forth from me to Ma. "I appreciated her summaries in *The Times*. Kate really stepped up to the plate."

Doctor Leary chimed in, "She let the community know that I had resolved my issues with the state and was back into full practice. Her articles were sensitive yet thorough."

I bit my lower lip and nodded. "Thank you, thank you. I enjoyed the opportunity to be more involved."

"I hope you'll stay involved, Kate," said Jim as he and Doctor Leary both nodded. He turned toward Ma. "You are lucky to have such a capable and talented partner, Ellie."

Ma smiled weakly and nodded. "Yes, I know, Jim. And she's been so helpful at home."

The meeting went smoothly and efficiently. I was able to apprise everyone with updates and offer suggestions for future planning. I walked Jim and Doctor Leary to the door and thanked them for coming.

Jim extended his hand, nodded, and said, "Thanks for all you have done, Kate." I accepted the handshake and smiled.

As I sauntered past Ma's office, she had her head bowed over some papers on her desk. I paused and asked, "Do you want to discuss the follow-up, Ma?"

She looked at me and shook her head slightly. "Maybe later." I wasn't sure if she was tired or just thinking about the meeting.

"Sure. Let me know," I said, then returned to my usual daily work.

CHAPTER 37

The next few weeks progressed in a similar manner. Ma stayed at the office a little longer every day but hadn't yet driven the car. I continued with the Monday Coffees, and I attended a couple meetings at the hospital. All in all, I guess I was doing all of the outside activities.

Ma and Lisa stayed in the office. Lisa managed her own schedule, coming and going as she felt needed and as her home schedule would allow. One Friday, I asked Lisa if she would stop by the church and collect the altar cloths for me. She had to pick up Billy, so the church would be an easy stop on her way.

*   *   *

Lisa was gone longer than we had expected. She had run into Father Declan at the church.

"Lisa, how nice to see you. This is your little fellow, huh? I've heard a lot about him from the Hurleys."

"Yes, Father. He just turned one last month."

"He's a cute, little lad, Lisa, but I have to ask, has he been baptized?"

"Well, no, Father. I just… uh… haven't gotten around to it."

"Ah, Lisa, that's a poor excuse. He should have been here a long time ago."

"Do you have a minute, Father? I have some questions."

Lisa and Father Declan went into the rectory office.

At the conclusion of their meeting, Father Declan was pale and distracted. He put his hand on Billy's head and said, "Bless you, little man."

Before she turned to leave, Lisa asked him, "Do you think I should tell Mrs. Hurley? My parents know, but no one else does."

Father Declan shook his head. "Not just yet, Lisa. Let me think about it, and we can talk again."

"Thank you, Father." Lisa sighed as she carried her son back to the car.

Father Declan gazed fondly at the child, searching for a family resemblance. It was easy to see he was a smacking image. Father Declan wondered if Ellie had seen it. Surely she would have told him. It's funny how blind we can be when the truth is staring us in the face.

Lisa returned to the office with Billy and the altar cloths in hand. She said hello to Ma and then settled Billy in the workroom. She dropped the altar cloths in my office, then fixed Ma some tea as usual and put it on her desk without a word.

Ma had moved Liam's picture to the other side of the table behind her chair. Lisa looked at it before leaving Ma's office. Ma asked how Billy was doing.

"Oh, he's just fine, Mrs. Hurley. I think he'll be asleep in the playpen in no time." Lisa hesitated and then quickly returned to the workroom.

The mild weekend allowed Ma and me to take a short walk, with Ma using her walker. She was slow but took every step without help from me. She caught several catnaps throughout the day as well.

On Monday morning, she got up, dressed, and made the coffee before I came downstairs. "It's a beautiful morning, Kate."

I smiled and nodded. "It sure is. I think it's going to be a good day."

We dropped the altar cloths at the church as usual.

Father Declan was just coming back from Mass and stopped to say hello. "How's your new help at the office?"

"Aye, she's a great girl, Father. We're so lucky to have her," Ma replied.

"I met her and the wee one the other day. He's a handsome lad, he is, don't you think?"

"Yes, and a good little boy, too," Ma said.

"How old is he, Ellie?"

"About thirteen months old. We had a party for him last month. His grandparents came along, and we all had a great time, even though little Billy didn't know he was the center of all the fuss."

"I understand his father was killed in the war, right?"

"Yes, and Lisa doesn't talk about him much," Ma continued.

"I also understand the lad hasn't been baptized yet."

"I'm not sure why, Father. I've asked her about it, but she doesn't share much. Don't judge the poor girl, Father Declan. She carries a heavy burden."

"Oh, I don't mean to judge her. I'm just wondering… well, just wondering, I guess."

We went on to the office. Lisa was already there. The aroma of the coffee and the flow of heat warmed my bones. While Lisa fixed tea for Ma, I poured a cup of coffee.

"How was your weekend, Lisa?" I asked.

"It was so nice. I took Billy out for a stroll. On days like this past weekend, I sure miss his daddy. He would have had so much fun with him."

It was one of the few times I heard Lisa mention Billy's da. "I'm sorry, Lisa, it must be so painful for you."

"Yes, it is. At least he has a lot of family around him."

"Do you have brothers and sisters, Lisa?" I probed.

"I have one brother, but he lives in Missouri. I don't see much of him."

"So family is your ma and da, then?"

"Oh, well… uh… I guess I think of you and Mrs. Hurley almost like family." She looked at the floor and swayed her foot back and forth across the wood.

Lisa took the tea to Ma and then went to the workroom.

That evening, I told Ma about Lisa's comments about thinking of us as family.

Ma's eyes lit up. "I take that as a compliment. I'm quite fond of her, and I adore that little Billy."

I bit my lip as I tried to let go of my questions.

After a busy week, I went out with Kevin on Friday evening and decided to share my curiosity with him. "Do you know Lisa, who works in our office?"

"I've met her once or twice. Why?"

"She has this little boy, Billy. He's adorable, and his father was killed in the war. She never says much about him, but today she mentioned how much she misses him. She also said that she considers me and Ma as almost family. I had the feeling she wanted to say more."

"It sounds like she's a pretty lonely girl."

"I suppose that's all there is to it," I said, just as our food arrived. "But sometimes I wonder what she expects from us. Perhaps there is something we could do for her."

Kevin reached across the table and took my hand. "She's lucky to have you in her life. And Kate, so am I."

I gazed into Kevin's warm, gentle eyes. I knew he was someone I wanted to be with for a long time.

After dinner, we went for a walk. Kevin took my hand in his, and we laughed about silly things.

"Do you look forward to children someday?" He brought my hand up to his lips.

"Of course I do, when the time is right," I replied. "I've never thought too much about it. Being a mom is an important job."

"You'll make a great mom." He pulled me toward him, and we both laughed.

The next morning at breakfast, Ma suggested we invite Lisa over for lunch on Saturday. "Her parents could use a break, and I love watching that little Billy."

"Sure, Ma, why not."

"It wouldn't have to be fancy, just sandwiches or maybe some soup."

My shoulders tensed as I started putting together a grocery list.

Lisa arrived at eleven o'clock sharp. Little Billy went directly to the cupboard in the parlor, knowing exactly where to find Liam's old cars that Ma had brought out for him. He sure brightened Ma's day.

As he played, we ladies enjoyed a cup of tea and talked. It was Lisa who brought up the subject of Billy's baptism. "My folks keep suggesting it, and I know it's about time. I guess most babies are baptized much earlier than this. Father Murphy asked me about it, too."

Ma smiled and nodded. "Well, it's not a bad idea, Lisa. What's keeping you back?"

Lisa looked down. "Well, nothing really. I guess I just…

um… haven't gotten around to it." She peered out the window and adjusted her skirt.

It seemed to me that there was something she wasn't telling us. It's really none of our business, but she brought it up.

"Do you need help planning it?" Ma asked.

"No. There's not much to plan, is there?"

"Well, you need to select godparents. Some people have a little celebration afterward. You know, a little lunch or something. We could help with that if you need."

Lisa looked at Ma, then at me. She rose and walked to the window. "Thank you. I'll let you know."

While we ate lunch, Billy fell asleep on the carpet. Lisa got up and slipped a blanket around him. We topped off the meal with a little lemon cake.

Ma and I went to early Mass on Sunday. Afterward, we talked with Father Declan.

Ma smiled at him. "Lisa and Billy were over yesterday, and she brought up the subject of Billy's baptism. Don't be surprised if you hear from her soon."

Father Declan raised his eyebrows and rubbed his chin. "Ah, maybe we'll finally bring him into the fold."

Later that day, Father Declan called Lisa. "I saw Mrs. Hurley after Mass this morning, and she mentioned that you might be considering a baptism in the near future. Perhaps we should get together with her."

"I don't know if I'm ready, Father Murphy. How do you think she'll take it?"

"She'll be shocked at first, but I believe in the end, she will be quite thrilled."

"How do I tell her? What should I say?"

"Let's get together this week and discuss it."

They set an appointment for Friday morning, as that was a day when the week's work was done and Lisa could easily come in late. On Wednesday, she told us that she would be arriving late on Friday. "Nothing to worry about. I just have an appointment." Lisa looked toward the door as she spoke.

"Not a problem, my dear. You can take the time any time you need it," said Ma, nodding her head.

Lisa came in a little before noon on Friday. "I thought you might like to know I talked to Father Murphy about scheduling Billy's baptism. He was quite pleased and helpful with planning ideas. We have a couple dates in mind, but I'd like to check with you. You must be there. I would also like Kate to be his godmother." Lisa's eyes sparkled as she spoke.

Ma hesitated for a minute. "Well, sure, and I know Kate would be proud to be Billy's godmother. Let me know what I can do to help."

Lisa's next stop was my office.

"Kate, I did it! I made plans for Billy's baptism, and I'd like you to be the godmother. Would you do that for me, please?"

"Of course, Lisa. I'd be honored to be Billy's godmother. When is the big day?"

"I need to talk to you and Mrs. Hurley to see what works best."

"How about the three of us go to Emily's for lunch and set a date," I suggested. "I'll check with Ma."

We arrived at Emily's at one thirty, just as the usual Friday crowd was thinning out. My mouth was watering at the thought of Emily's salmon patties. Luckily, she had enough left for the three of us. As we sat, we decided on a date and talked about a celebration. It would be at our house as Lisa's parents didn't have room.

"I haven't selected a godfather yet. I'm not really close to anyone. I have an uncle in Des Moines, but he doesn't get around much. Father Declan said I could ask him and then have someone stand in for him."

"I'll bet Doctor Kevin would do that, if you'd like," I offered.

Lisa raised her head and smiled. "Do you think he would? That would be grand."

Lisa wrung her napkin and stared at the table. "I will make an appointment with Father Declan. Would you come with me, Mrs. Hurley?"

Ma tried to catch her eye, but Lisa continued to look down at the table. "Well, sure. Do you want Kate to join us, too?"

"Not this time."

Ma furrowed her brow and glanced at me, then back at

Lisa, who continued to stare at the table.

The following Wednesday, around four o'clock, Lisa drove Ma to the parish office. She got her settled in the chair next to Father Declan's desk and then went to find Father Declan.

On the desk was a stack of papers, the top one being "Certificate of Baptism." Ma smiled as she took a casual glance at it. "It's about time," she whispered as she picked it up. Then her head started to swim, and her hands shook as she read the details—William Michael Hurley, son of Lisa Ann Ward and Liam Joseph Hurley. Her heart skipped a beat. She read again, Liam Joseph Hurley. Was she reading this correctly? Is Billy Liam's son? She tried to envision Liam's face, Billy's face. She tried to count the months. Her head just wouldn't let her conclude anything.

She didn't hear Lisa and Father Declan enter the room.

"Oh, Ellie," said Father Declan as he placed his hand on Ma's shoulder. "I… I am sorry. I mean, we didn't mean for you to read it on a piece of paper. That was the reason we asked you to meet with us. Lisa wanted to tell you."

Ma's face drained, and she was unable to utter a word as she looked from Lisa to Father Declan. The baptismal certificate trembled in her hands.

"Mrs. Hurley, I am sorry. I wanted to tell you so many times. It's why I waited to get Billy baptized. I was afraid to tell his name."

"I don't know what to say. I... Little Billy, that darling, precious boy is my grandson? Liam is Billy's father?"

She locked eyes with Father Declan.

"Yes, a grandson, Ellie." His eyes moistened as he said the words.

Ma shook her head and stuttered. "I... I can't believe I'm hearing this, but oh my God."

Lisa looked at Ma, then at Father Declan. Then she stared back at the floor. "I hope you'll forgive us. We had talked about getting married someday, but then the war came. I didn't know before he left... and, well, Liam never knew. I didn't know how to tell him. I started a letter at least four times, but I could never find the right words. I loved Liam, Mrs. Hurley, and I miss him every day."

Ma thought about the times Lisa had stared at Liam's picture. She'd often got tears in her eyes, but Ma thought it was just a reminder of the soldier she had lost. "Oh, Lisa, my dear girl, shame be gone. You have brought Liam's life back to me."

The three of them sat in silence for a while, then Father Declan spoke, "Perhaps we should give this a while to settle in. I do think we should get little Billy baptized soon, but let's say we get back together again in a week or so."

Ma and Lisa agreed.

As Lisa rose to leave, Father Declan offered to take Ma home after they had a chance to talk things over. Lisa thanked him and left by herself.

"A cup of tea, Ellie?" Ma did not reply. "Perhaps you'd prefer a little brandy?"

She still didn't respond, but Father Declan went to the other room and returned with two small glasses.

"God acts in mysterious ways, doesn't He, Ellie?"

"Oh my, yes," Ma said as the brandy warmed her throat. "I just don't know what to think. Who needs to know? How much does Lisa have to know? If truth be told, this little boy's last name would be Murphy. Does Billy need to know some day? Don't they both have to know, Declan? Would innocent little Billy become an outcast?"

They stared at each other in silence, but for the clock ticking in the background. It would ruin both of them for the community to know their secret. Like some stories that might sell newspapers, this truth would hurt too many innocent people.

"Aye, but the Lord does indeed work in strange ways. As He has forgiven us, so we should forgive Lisa and Liam. We sinned out of love as did they. Surely, the Lord has forgiven us."

Ellie thought back to that night, shortly before she married Sean. Declan was home from the seminary, and the two had been together at a wedding of friends. Declan confided that he sometimes regretted not choosing to have a family or the love of a woman—her love. One thing led to another. Ellie didn't know until after her own wedding, but she was sure it was Declan who fathered her first child, her only son. She told Declan when Liam was a toddler, but

Sean never knew. Now she wondered if Billy ever needed to know.

When Ma arrived home, I had dinner warming in the oven. Ma had a faraway look in her eyes as she sat at the table.

"It's been a long day, hasn't it, Ma? How was your meeting with Father Declan?"

"Fine, fine. Yes, it was fine." Ma didn't look at me and didn't offer further comments.

"Did you set a date?"

"No, not yet." She paused. "There are details to take care of." She shook her head and picked at the food on her plate.

Shortly after dinner, Ma said she was tired and went into the parlor, her new bedroom, and closed the door.

I did the dishes and tidied the kitchen, then retired to the living room with my book. After an hour, I checked on Ma. She was still sitting in her chair. "Are you all right, Ma?"

"Oh yes, yes, I'm fine."

"Let me help you get ready for bed."

Ma was a little slow going the next morning, and Lisa was in the office with the coffee brewing when we arrived. Billy stayed home with Lisa's dad that day.

I got my coffee before I went to my office. Lisa took cup to Ma. I heard Ma mention Liam's name before Lisa closed the door. Lisa and Ma set another date to meet with Father Declan. I wasn't invited but was quite certain that I would be included when they got down to the specifics of the ceremony. They would probably include Kevin as well. I wondered what the need for extra meetings could be. *Weren't baptisms pretty simple?*

When Lisa returned after lunch, she brought Billy with her.

Ma paled as she said to Lisa, "Let me hold that little boy." Tears came to her eyes as she hugged him tightly. Ma had developed such a fondness for him. After Lisa took him back to his playpen in the workroom, Ma closed her door, turned in her chair, and stared at her picture of Liam. Her shoulders shook and tears flowed.

Two weeks went by before the subject of Billy's baptism came up again. They had set a date, and Lisa had spoken to her uncle. He gladly agreed, but as expected, he could not come for the ceremony. Kevin made sure he could be off for the day. We planned a small party at our house.

On Friday after work, Ma suggested we sit in the living room to relax a while before supper. She was rubbing her hands and looking up and down as she sat on the sofa.

"Kate, there is something you should know." She told me about reading Billy's baptismal certificate. "While I was waiting for Lisa and Father Declan, the certificate was just sitting there on the desk and I couldn't believe my eyes— William Michael Hurley. Kate, that beautiful, little boy is my grandson and your nephew. He's a gift to us… Liam's son."

I was immobilized. I didn't know what to say, what to think. Liam and Lisa have a son.

Ma went on, "Lisa didn't know she was pregnant when Liam left, and she didn't want to write it in a letter to him. Liam never knew. Her parents know, but no one else does."

"She knew this when she came to work for *The Times*. No wonder she considers us part of their family. Are you okay, Ma?"

"At first, I didn't know what to think, but I admire that girl. She is a good, little mother and has borne this secret every day. What I really feel is that a part of Liam has been brought back to us. He's a beautiful, little boy and has a special place in my heart. I hope you will accept him—them—too, Kate."

"It's a shock, Ma, but… but…"

The big day arrived with bright sunshine and a warm, mild breeze.

Knowing that Kevin would learn Billy's name during the ceremony, I told him ahead of time.

"Crikey! I never suspected," he said, shaking his head, "but it's a good surprise." He assured me that he had cared for many unwed mothers, and that Lisa's decision to raise her son was a decision of sacrifice, generosity, and love.

The ceremony and the party all went well as we welcomed little William to the fold of our church. Lisa's parents and Father Declan were the only other guests. Everyone was in great spirits, especially Ma, who couldn't take her eyes off the new, little Christian.

Kevin assisted me in the kitchen and in serving the food. When the day came to a close, he carried Billy to the car. He stayed for a light supper of leftovers and a sip of brandy with me and Ma before she retired to her room. He sat next to me on the sofa and pulled me close to him, gently kissing the back of my head.

"Kate, how do you do it all?"

I shook my head and laughed gently. "I just do what I have to do, Kevin."

"But you do it so well and with such ease. I just watch you and wonder. I watch you with Billy, too. It seems to be second nature to you to interpret his needs and have the right answer for him."

I closed my eyes and let my head rest on the crook of his shoulder.

"What I'm trying to say, Kate, is that I love you, and I want to be a part of your life."

I sat up and turned toward him.

"Kate Hurley, will you make my life complete? Will you marry me?"

My entire body warmed, and my lips trembled. There was only one answer. "Yes! Yes!"

He drew me closer, and we fell back toward the sofa. He put his arms around me, and his lips met mine. I felt warmth in places I never knew existed.

"Whoa, Kevin." My mind wanted to resist, but my heart

and body could not. We wrapped in a full embrace, and his hands slid down my body.

"Kate, I love you, I love you. I've waited for the moment when I could say those words." He pulled away gently, and we both sighed. "Let's not complicate things," he whispered.

We sat up and sipped the rest of our brandy before he said he'd better get home. I didn't want him to leave, but the thought of our future together promised sweet dreams.

The following Wednesday, Kevin and I had supper at Emily's and then took a walk around town. We decided to tell Ma about our plans. We weren't sure how she would take it, as it would disrupt her current setting. Would she agree to live with us? Would she be willing to leave her home and move into ours? Would she want us to live in her house? Kevin and I both wanted her with us but didn't know where. We decided to tell her on Sunday afternoon.

CHAPTER 38

The next morning, Ma and I arrived to a cold, dark office. It was strangely quiet.

"Did Lisa say anything about not coming in today?" Ma asked.

"No, not at all. I thought she would be here all day."

At that moment, the phone rang. A teary Lisa was calling. "Kate, I can't be there today."

"What's wrong, Lisa?"

"It's my dad." She swallowed. "He... he... oh Kate, he's gone."

"I'll be right over, Lisa."

Ma gathered her things and followed me to the car.

Lisa was wearing a pair of old, wool slacks and a baggy sweater. Her hair was uncombed, and her eyes were red. Billy was pulling on her pant leg.

"I heard him moan during the night, but it didn't seem unusual. Then when my mum cried out for some help, he didn't answer. I went to check on him, and he was cold. If only... if only I had gotten up when he moaned."

Ma went to Lisa and hugged her. "No, no, Lisa, my dear. Don't say that. There was nothing you could have done."

I picked up Billy and realized that Lisa's mum was not around. I walked to her room and peeked in. She was awake but appeared to be in a daze.

"Is that you, Paul?"

"No, Mrs. Ward. It's me, Kate Hurley."

"Where's Paul?"

I hesitated, not sure what to say. "He's not here right now, Mrs. Ward. Is there something I can get for you?"

"Well, no, I guess not." She closed her eyes.

I went back to the living room where Lisa sat on the couch. Ma was in the kitchen fixing tea.

I sat by Lisa and took her hand. "Lisa, have you called your brother or your uncle?"

"Yes, and they're both coming over this afternoon."

As we relaxed with our tea, two neighbors stopped in and Father Declan arrived. One of the neighbors helped get Mrs. Ward up and into a chair and fix her something to eat. Father Declan offered his condolences and gave a blessing to Lisa and to her mum.

I hadn't realized how ill Lisa's mother was. Lisa had not shared the details with us, but it appeared that her mum had significant dementia. Lisa's dad must have had a full-time job caring for her. Ma and I stayed until her brother and uncle arrived.

On our way back to the office, I said to Ma, "Poor girl. She is going to need a lot of help."

"Yes," said Ma, "and I don't see how she'll be able to stay

on with the paper and care for her mum. I didn't realize how bad things were for her, but we are her family now."

I swallowed and nodded my head.

Over the next few days, Ma and I were up to our earlobes with work at the office and helping with Mr. Ward's funeral. Mrs. Ward was unable to attend, and a neighbor stayed with her and Billy. The church was cold and dreary with only a small crowd at the funeral. Afterward, Ma and I and a couple neighbors assisted Lisa while visitors came to her house.

The next morning, her uncle went back to Des Moines, but her brother stayed a couple days. We went over just as her uncle was leaving. We sat in the Wards' living room. Lisa's face was pale, as she stared across the room and absently rubbed her arms saying, "I don't know how I'll be able to come back to *The Times*. I'm the only one to take care of my mum and Billy, and I can't leave them alone."

Ma put her arm around Lisa. "We're your family now, too. We'll help you make it."

"Yes, Lisa. We'll be here for you," I added, although I wondered what we could do.

For the next couple weeks, Ma called Lisa daily, and I went to the Wards' home after supper and helped Lisa get her mum and Billy settled for the night. Mrs. Ward's room had an odor of urine, and Lisa confided that her mum called out during the night several times and she couldn't always get to her in time.

"I don't know how my dad did it all the time. He always kept everything nice and clean for her. I think she knew who he was, but now I'm not sure. Sometimes she calls me by her sister's name. Her sister died when she was young."

"Lisa, you're doing the best you can."

"No, Kate," she said wiping a tear, "I'm not, but I don't know what else to do." Lisa talked for a long time about her mum and her dad. She talked about how they always put Lisa first and how much they loved Billy. "I have to take good care of her."

As I went to leave, I gave her a hug. "You're doing everything you possibly can, dear. You have a big load on those shoulders. Don't be too hard on yourself."

At home, Ma and I discussed Lisa's straits.

"She needs help, Ma. It's not working well for any of them right now. Lisa is worn out and is doing all she can for her mum and for Billy, but she can't do it alone and I don't think she can afford to hire someone. And Ma, you and I can't be there as much as she needs us."

Ma shook her head. "I don't usually think a nursing home is a good idea, but it might be for Mrs. Ward if there is any way Lisa can afford it. Maybe I'll broach the subject with her. The home next to the hospital is a pretty nice place."

I closed my eyes and bit my lower lip. "It might be the right thing. Be gentle with her, Ma. She probably won't take to the idea, but if it's coming from you…"

"Maybe Father Declan would help," Ma pondered aloud.

"I'll talk to Kevin, too. I'm sure he sees things like this once in a while. Maybe he'll have some ideas."

The following Sunday, Kevin came for lunch. We broke our news to Ma, as planned.

"We'd like to start with some good news first," Kevin said, opening the conversation. "Mrs. Hurley, I would like to marry your daughter. She is the love of my life, and I want her to be part of my life until death do us part."

Ma's eyes lit up, and a big smile spread across her face. "Well, faith and begorrah, this is good news! I am delighted to accept you into our family. God bless you both. This calls for a little celebration!"

"I just happen to have some sparkling wine with me," said Kevin as he sauntered to the kitchen.

We laughed and smiled as we talked about the details that we were working out—the church, the wedding party, the reception, and, of course, a honeymoon as soon as we could work it in. "We need to discuss where to live, Ma. We'd like to have you with us."

"Oh, I don't know if that's a good way to start out your married life. I can get by on my own."

"Let's think about it, Ma."

"Yes, Mrs. Hurley. Think on it a bit. I am very comfortable with that plan." We chatted about several ideas and then returned to the subject of Lisa.

Ma furrowed her brow and shook her head. "Well, for

now, let's get back to Lisa. Do you think a nursing home would be a good solution for her mum?"

"Mary's Help has a great reputation with the families of our patients, even though most were reluctant to go that route at first. If Lisa would give it a try, I think it might work for her and her mum," suggested Kevin.

"Then she could take care of Billy and maybe get back to *The Times*. Her wages at *The Times* certainly won't pay a nursing home bill, let alone support her and Billy," said Ma.

"Some families have sold their homes and rented. It's a hard decision, but it might be the only solution."

"Let's discuss this a little more and maybe ask Father Declan for his ideas," said Ma. "We can put our heads together again later in the week. We can't wait too long. Lisa is at her wit's end trying to do it all."

Father Declan and Kevin came for supper on Thursday evening.

With a broad smile, Father Declan shook Kevin's hand. "I hear congratulations are in order for the two of you."

"Thank you, Father. I am the luckiest man in the world."

"Lucky, indeed, son. I'm sure you two will be a very happy couple," said Father Declan.

Once I served dessert and poured coffee, Ma sighed and spoke up. "I guess we'd better get to our topic. What about Lisa? Father and I have a couple ideas. First, Lisa would have to accept the idea of the nursing home. We could give her a tour and maybe let her meet one or two families who have placed their parents there."

"Have you thought about the cost, Ma?" I asked.

"Yes, I have." Ma looked at Father Declan, then at me and Kevin.

"If she sold their house," she started, "she and Billy could move in here with me."

I leaned back in my chair and stared at Ma, trying to digest what she just said.

Kevin glanced at me but made no comment.

I leaned forward. "Really, Ma? Have you thought this through? Here in our home?"

"Yes. Then you and Kevin could start your marriage in a home of your own, and I would have the help I need."

"Hmm." I looked at Kevin, whose mouth was moving without words. "Well, maybe you have something there, Ma, but one step at a time. First, Lisa has to agree on the nursing home. I don't want her to think she's not doing a good job, but we can all see that she really can't keep going the way things are."

We agreed that I would bring it up to her that evening when I went to help with her bedtime routine. Kevin offered to come along.

CHAPTER 39

When we arrived, Lisa was getting Billy into his pajamas. Billy's room was painted a light blue, and curtains with a train print adorned a small window. Toys were scattered about the floor, and wet diapers were overflowing in a bucket in the corner. Billy was fussing and squirming while Lisa struggled to keep him still.

From the other room, her mum called out, "Paul, can you come in here?"

"I'll finish with Billy so you can go to your mum."

Lisa sighed and her shoulders sagged as she stood up and brushed her hair away from her red-rimmed eyes. "Thank you, Kate."

Kevin looked from Lisa to me and then to Billy. He bent down to calm the squirming boy so that I could finish dressing him. He offered to read Billy a story while I assisted Lisa with her mum.

Mrs. Ward called me Gladys, the name of her sister who had died years before. She also asked about Paul, seemingly not remembering that he had died. At least she knew Lisa and, I'm sure, Billy.

Once Lisa's charges were settled, she sat in the living room with me and Kevin.

Kevin started, "Lisa, you really have your hands full. I don't think you're going to be able to keep this up by yourself."

She opened up without much coaxing. "I'm really trying," she said between soft sobs. "If I could just afford some help."

"Lisa," I offered, "I know you're giving it all you have, but I don't know if it's possible to meet all of your mum's needs here in your house."

She furrowed her brow and looked at me. "There's no place else for her. I would never put her in a home. Even if I could afford it, I couldn't do it. I just need someone to come here and help us."

"Have you ever visited Mary's Help?" asked Kevin. "It's right next to the hospital. I visit patients over there. They seem well cared for, and their families are pleased. You might give it a look."

"Thanks, Doctor Kevin, but even if I liked it, I don't know how I could afford it. I could go back to work, but that wouldn't cover the expenses of this house, everything Billy needs, and a nursing home. No, there's no reason for me to check into it."

"Lisa, Ma and I have talked about it, and she may have some ideas. Why don't you think about it and just take a look at Mary's Help. Then we'll put our heads together."

"I don't know, Kate, I just don't know." She bowed her head and shook it from side to side.

Over the next three evenings, I assisted Lisa by myself. A neighbor had come in during the daytime and helped catch up with laundry and cleaning, but the job was never-ending.

When Mrs. Ward and Billy were settled, Lisa asked if I could stay for a bit. She had visited Mary's Help and thought maybe her mum would do okay there, at least for a while. She said that her parents had a small savings account that would cover it for a few months. "Then I could get back to work and save some more. I'm not sure what to do after the savings run out."

"Ma has an idea, Lisa. If you can get someone to stay with your mum for a few hours, why don't you come and talk to her. She would love to help you."

I think Lisa was recognizing the urgency of her situation as she called Ma early the next morning and made plans to see her that afternoon. She brought Billy along, and he tottered directly to his cupboard in the parlor. He grabbed an armful of toy soldiers and handed them to Ma, one at a time.

"Do these soldiers have names?" she asked him.

Billy called every soldier "Dada," much to the delight of Ma and Lisa.

"Let's get down to business," Ma started as she ruffled Billy's hair.

Ma presented her plan to Lisa and emphasized how it would work for everyone.

"Gosh, Mrs. Hurley, that is a generous offer, but I don't

know. I mean, I suppose I could sell the house, and that way I could pay you some rent."

"Well, I did say I would need a little help here, so I'd want to pay you. All in all, I think we would come out even." Ma paused and smiled. "Crikey! I would come out ahead," she beamed. "I would have my grandson right here every day. That would be such a joy."

Lisa smiled like she hadn't done in days. "It sounds like a good idea, but I need to think about it."

"What's there to think about," Ma started, but then she nodded and said, "of course."

By the end of the week, Lisa had talked to the realtor and the manager at her bank. She got more information from Mary's Help and returned to Ma with a plan. Every time she and Billy came to the door, Ma's eyes lit up and her face came to life.

I took Ma to Lisa's on Saturday morning, and I entertained Billy while they discussed their ideas.

"Mrs. Hurley, I insist that I contribute to your household."

"Lisa, you will have plenty to do to help me with the house, and you will continue to work at *The Times* because, after all, you know that someday, our Billy will have a place in his daddy's dream."

Ma's words sparked a nerve with me as I recalled so many comments about Liam's dream.

During the following week, Lisa hired a handyman to

make a couple repairs on the house, and she made a down payment at Mary's Help to hold a bed for her mum.

Meanwhile, at our house, I started to prepare Liam's old room to make room for Lisa and Billy. As I dusted and vacuumed, I thought of how Liam used to keep this room. I didn't think he knew where we stored the vacuum, and he rarely kept his clothes on hangers. Knowing Lisa, I thought the room would be spotless, even with a toddler around.

Then I looked at my room. Weekly vacuuming and dusting were part of my routine as far back as I could remember. I made myself a promise, then and there, that I would raise my children—*all of them*—to take care of themselves and do their part to keep the house in good order.

CHAPTER 40

Kevin and I had chosen a date and talked to Father Declan. I had suggested a simple, quiet affair, but Kevin insisted on something much bigger.

"This will be your day, my darling. I want to make it a true celebration for all the town to see the wonderful woman I marry! I want it to be a day to cherish and remember."

Ma had her ideas, too. "Billy can be the ring bearer, and, of course, Lisa will be in the wedding party and you can wear my veil."

I looked at my ma through different eyes that day. "No, Ma. First of all, Billy is too young. He would not be able to follow directions. I'll find a role for Lisa, but the wedding party will be small."

Ma bit her lip and glanced down at her hands. "They are family, you know."

"Yes, I know, Ma, and I will include them in my wedding festivities in my own way."

"Sure, Kate, I... I understand." Her eyes were steely, but they didn't look into mine. Ma was peering over my shoulder.

"We'll talk about the details later. But I was wondering, too, Kate, if you were planning to continue working at *The Times* once you're the wife of the town doctor?"

"Of course, Ma. I wouldn't think of not being a part of it."

"Well, Lisa could take on a bigger role… that is, if you want to spend more time in your new home."

My heart started to pound, and my jaws tightened. There was a knot turning in my stomach. I looked at Ma, nodded my head, and left the room.

Reflecting on the previous day's conversation about Billy's future with *The Times* made me realize that I was on my own when it came to my role here in Hawthorne, or anywhere else. Things hadn't changed since I was a girl growing up in this house. Somehow, being male was a ticket to a substantial future. Sister Edward Joan's words rang in my ears, "Stand up for yourself… live your own life." If I wanted to assure a place with *The Times*, it was up to me.

It was about a week later before a plan started to unfold in my mind. It was triggered by one of the daily stats—a divorce notice on file with the county—Judith Ferguson vs. Roger Ferguson for cruel and inhumane treatment. My suspicions were correct, and I pitied them both. At lunch, I drove past their house and saw the "For Sale" sign, wondering what that meant for each of them.

I circled back to Emily's for lunch and a helping of whatever gossip was being served. I got my fill of both. As always, Emily's pot pie was divine, and I overheard some interesting conversations. The Fergusons' house was being foreclosed on, and Mrs. Ferguson was moving in with her sister. Roger was headed for the streets unless something new happened.

I hated hearing about anyone's poor fortune, but in this case, the poor fortune was earned. This news brought several questions to mind, especially about Roger's interest in *The Times*. Perhaps this was the opportunity I had waited for. I made an appointment to talk to our family attorney, Tom Cunningham. He agreed to do some research and meet again. In the meantime, I talked to Da's cattle broker to see what price I could get for my lot.

I also discussed this with Kevin to get his thoughts on being married to an owner of the town newspaper.

"I would be so proud of you, Kate. And as our life together grows, we'll take it one day, one change, at a time. I have complete confidence in you, darling."

I talked to Ma, too. She was hesitant at first. "How will you be able to do everything?" You'll be a new wife, and someday you'll have a family. I don't know if you're up to the task."

"Ma, you've doubted me all my life." I tried to control my voice. "You put more faith in Liam, even when he's not alive. I've been running the paper myself for the last several months, and I've been doing it well. What more do I have to do?"

I rubbed the gold knot that hung around my neck, and in

as calm a voice as I could muster, I continued, "Ma, you and Da always told me that I could do and become whatever I wanted. I wanted to be a journalist, and I can do it. And I can manage a home at the same time. I don't intend to turn my place at *The Times* over to Lisa or anyone else, even when I become Mrs. Kevin Hagerty."

Ma closed her eyes in silence.

I wanted her support, but in the end, the decision was mine.

CHAPTER 41

Tom Cunningham had called, and we set an appointment for Friday morning. I wore my maroon blazer and gray skirt and topped off my outfit with a favorite gray tam. I put my shoulders back and held my head high as I walked into Tom's office. We went over the details and discussed my finances, and Tom agreed to draw up an offer.

Ma had softened and eventually offered her encouragement, but I kept the specifics to myself as the week dragged on. When the meeting day finally arrived, I wore the same maroon jacket and gray skirt with a new pair of black, leather pumps.

I reached Tom's office about ten minutes early. Roger was ten minutes late. He was unshaven, and his suit was wrinkled and his shoes unpolished.

He looked at me with a scowl. "How could you? You know what this means to me, and you know I'm over a barrel."

Before he could go further, Tom cut in. "Let's get down to business and review the details of Miss Hurley's offer."

1. Roger will receive $500 for his share of *The Hawthorne Times*.
2. Roger will receive $2,500 for his share of the building.
3. Agreement that Roger will resign from the board of directors.
4. Agreement that Roger will stay off the property of *The Times*.
5. Agreement that Roger will obey any restraining order from Judith Ferguson.

Roger's hands trembled as he held the papers. He muttered to himself, "Only $500 plus $2,500. Ha! A measly $3,000. The board of directors. This is just, this is just… Who do you think you are? And to include this about my wife?" He tightened his jaw as his face turned red.

"Roger, you know who I am, and you know what I know. I think you'll have to agree that this is fair. And I want you to call off the hoodlums who drive by my house." I had mixed feelings—pride in a victory over a nasty opponent and optimism about my future—but deep inside, I pitied this man in front of me. He had reached a new low. I did have him over a barrel, but I was also affording him the means to start getting back on his feet.

Roger continued to mutter as he picked up a pen and scribbled his signature.

I walked out of Tom's office and breathed in a deep dose of fresh, Midwest country air. As I headed home to share the news with Ma, I held my head high and enjoyed a sense of contentment I had waited for all my life. It was a new day, a new day, all right... for *The Times*, for Hawthorne, for me, and even for Roger Ferguson.

Ma was sitting in the living room with a cup of Earl Grey. I poured two glasses of brandy and set one on the table next to her.

"I think this might be more appropriate this evening," I said.

She peered up at me and furrowed her brow. "What's this about?"

"You're looking at your new partner, Ma. Roger signed over his half of *The Times* to me this afternoon."

She glanced at me but spoke no words.

"I hope you will be happy with our future together, Ma."

My mother's eyes became teary as she stood up. At first, she stared at the floor. Then she raised her head and looked me in the eye. "Kate, I realize that I haven't been as supportive as I should have been these last few months, nor have I shown my appreciation, but I am so grateful for all you've done. I haven't looked at it through your eyes, and for that, I'm sorry. You have done so much for me, for *The Times*, and for our little Billy."

She paused and then continued, "Kate, I'm sorry I didn't acknowledge this last week. I have been watching you, and it's been hard for me to admit, but I think you can do as good a job, maybe even better, than your brother." She raised her glass. "Yes, this calls for a celebration, Partner. To our future! I am truly proud of you, and I know now that our newspaper, Liam's dream, is in good hands."

"Thanks, Ma," I started.

My shoulders relaxed and I couldn't help but smile. This truly was a new day. As much as I wanted to call Kevin, I decided to savor the moment and treasure this evening with Ma.

The following Monday, I went to my office—yes, *my* office—and wrote a column for the next edition:

Once again, there is a change for The Hawthorne Times. *Katherine Hurley has purchased one-half interest in our local paper and is now co-owner with Eleanor Hurley. It is a new day for all of us. We will continue to bring our residents the latest local and national news. We promise to bring the news with honesty, fairness, and objectivity. For years, this was the goal of Liam Hurley—Eleanor's son and Katherine's brother. We are committed to seeing his dream to fruition.*

Kevin came for supper that evening. We celebrated this milestone in my life and started planning for another.

CHAPTER 42

On a crisp, clear Saturday in September, with bagpipes playing in the background, Uncle Joe walked me down the aisle. Lisa was my maid of honor, while Doctor Leary stood up for Kevin. Billy carried the ring, only because Ma accompanied him, and she was thrilled to be part of the ceremony.

Father Declan greeted us and the crowd who assembled to witness our union. His words touched my heart as he recalled the events of my years here in the parish, all of which he had been an integral part. I had never heard some of the thoughts he shared from conversations with Ma. After all we'd been through the past two years, the tears this day were tears of joy.

A gentle breeze blew as we left the church and walked through gold and red leaves gathering on the church grounds. The celebration continued at The Grange, with old friends and new, old family and new. I am sure Da and Liam were sending their love down upon us, wishing us well as we followed the dreams they had for me, for Ma, and for Hawthorne.

When the evening came to an end, we raised our glasses and shared a toast from the heart of my da… "Sláinte!"

ACKNOWLEDGMENTS

This story could not have been written without the support of friends who told me I could really do it.

Sincere thanks go to my book club friends who read my first draft and gave me honest feedback: Ann Andersen, Barbara Burrell, Dina Gerber and Pat West. To my sister-in-law, Barbara Sylvester, who always told me to write a book. To my sister, Mary Kulawik, who traipsed around the Midwest with me as I researched small towns and local newspapers. To my friends and authors, Gail Murray and Barbara Botch, whose parallel journeys kept me on track. To my *special ghouls*—Mary Tompsett, Mary Lynch, and Joyce Cherek, who nudged me along to completion.

Special thanks also to Joyce Mochrie, my copy editor and proofreader, for her meticulous professional review of this manuscript.

Thank you to my children, Jim and Julie, whose own diligent lifestyles gave me inspiration. And most of all, I thank my husband, Ed Morken. He cheered me on and allowed me to hide, work in my room, hour after hour, day after day, and never let me give up.

DISCUSSION QUESTIONS FOR *THE WEEKLY EDITION*

1. Dissemination of the news has changed greatly since 1945. What do you see as the improvements? Drawbacks?
2. Do you think the role of journalism, in general, has changed? Has its place in society changed? How might this story have evolved in the twenty-first century?
3. Did the involvement of women in the newspaper business affect how news was reported in 1945? How has the role of women in the news changed since then?
4. How would you describe the working relationship between Ellie and Kate? What influenced their relationship?
5. Liam was highly esteemed in his community. Did Ellie receive that same respect? Was Kate's talent recognized and valued? Why or why not?
6. How did family dynamics impact the roles of men and women in this story? Were the family dynamics unique to the Hurley family? The Irish? Catholics? Midwest?

7. Did you like Father Declan? What role did he play in the story? How would you describe the relationship he shared with Ellie? The Hurley family?
8. Revealing secrets can ruin lives, but sometimes people have a right to know. How do you feel about the secrets kept within this story?
9. Were the progression and the ending of the story predictable?
10. If Liam had returned from the war and gone back into the newspaper business, do you think he and Roger would have been successful together?
11. Who was your favorite character in the story? Why? Who was your least favorite? Why? Did the author succeed at creating sympathy for the characters? If you could establish a friendship with one of the characters, which one would it be?

www.ingramcontent.com/pod-product-compliance
Lightning Source LLC
Chambersburg PA
CBHW070045080526
44586CB00013B/924